IN MY FATHER'S COUNTRY

IN MY FATHER'S COUNTRY

AN AFGHAN WOMAN DEFIES HER FATE

SAIMA WAHAB

CROWN PUBLISHERS
NEW YORK

Published in the United States by Crown Publishers, an imprint of the Crown Publishing Group,
a division of Random House, Inc., New York.

www.crownpublishing.com

CROWN and the Crown colophon are registered trademarks of Random House, Inc.

Library of Congress Cataloging-in-Publication Data is available upon request.

ISBN 978-0-307-88494-7
eISBN 978-0-307-88496-1

Printed in the United States of America

Book design by Christine Welch
Jacket photography by Vanessa Roberts

3 5 7 9 10 8 6 4 2

First Edition

TO MY FATHER
AND HIS FATHER

I SHOULD HAVE DIED when I was five.

We had just come from Kabul to my grandfather's village, having left behind everything, including any hopes that our father would walk through the door and end the nightmare of his disappearance. As a child of five, I didn't understand what was happening in Afghanistan; I just knew that my world had been turned upside down. One day I was in the city, waiting for my father to come home from work so I could climb onto his shoulders while he walked around the house or listened to the radio. The next day, it seemed, I was in a village where all the houses were made out of mud, where going outside meant having an adult open the gate because it weighed at least a ton, and, even if I had been brave enough to venture out, I couldn't have pushed it open by myself. The shock of what had happened was too shattering, so I slept a lot, sometimes through the whole day, hoping that when I woke up I would be back in the house my father had built with marble from Italy.

Our grandfather's qalat, as houses in the villages were called, was big, with a mud wall at least twelve feet high surrounding the rooms and the courtyard that we shared with the chickens and the cows. It had three bedrooms, one kitchen, two living rooms, two guest rooms—one for men, one for women—and one big underground room for storage. My sister, Najiba, my mother, and I shared one of the rooms, which was all the way in the back, past one of the living rooms and the kitchen.

On the day I should have died, I had gone into the bedroom unnoticed, while my mom was busy doing what Afghan women do all day: cooking, cleaning, sweeping constantly. My grandmother was taking care of the animals outside. In the frantic daily routine of village life it was easy to go unseen.

The Russian jets had no fixed time of the day when they bombed our village. They just did it randomly, and a lot later I would find out that our village was considered a stronghold of the mujahideen, which meant that we got targeted more than the other villages. I remember the constant fear of the sounds of the bombs dropping, whistling so loudly, permanently destroying most people's eardrums. So that even today, I don't hear well in my left ear.

I don't know how long I had been sleeping before the jets flew over the village, dropping the usual five or six bombs and leaving all of us in the dust before they flew off to the next target. I remember being shaken out of my sleep by what I thought was the roof falling on my head. I was so disoriented and overwhelmed by shock and terror that for a few seconds I couldn't even stand up to find the door. It was the sound of the walls, made of clay and mud, cracking and crumbling that shook me out of the daze.

Amid the commotion that always followed the bombardments, Mamai and my grandmother were frantically looking for me. Seeing me come out of the room, dusty and crying, must have given my mother the fright of her life. Villagers and family soon surrounded me, and Mamai grabbed me and checked me all over, as if to make sure that I was really alive. I looked behind me and saw that the room where I had been sleeping had collapsed. A bomb had dropped on the roof, hitting the corner farthest away from where I had been sleeping, and even though it had not detonated, the weight of it had completely demolished the walls and the roof. Everyone seemed amazed that I was alive—to have walked away from certain death, they exclaimed, I had to be the luckiest child in Afghanistan. One of the old ladies told Mamai to make sure she made a sacrifice to God for saving me.

Years later it dawned on me that that was the first of many moments when I would be protected by some unseen hand, as if there was a destiny I had to fulfill—one that weapons and explosions couldn't obstruct.

ONE

I was welcomed into this world with gunshots.

In Afghanistan, when a son is born, tradition dictates that the father rushes into the street with his pistol and fires a few rounds into the air to celebrate. My father did this for Khalid, my older brother, his firstborn, as was the Pashtun custom. A little over a year later, minutes after I was born, my father rushed outside with his weapon and did the same. His friends appeared and congratulated him on the birth of another son. My father laughed and said, "Oh no, my beautiful daughter was born today." But nobody celebrates the birth of a daughter with gunshots. His friends shook their heads at such eccentric behavior. "You will see!" he told them. "I promise that my daughter will prove that she is better than many Pashtun sons, and will do more for her people than one hundred sons combined."

I CARRY ONE of my father's pictures with me always. It is a photograph of him with the three of us—my brother, my sister, and me. It is small, black and white, and bears a collection of tiny holes, puncture marks from the pins and small nails that, over the years, have fixed it to my walls in Kabul, Ghazni Province, Peshawar, and, finally, Portland, Oregon. In his pictures he is a young man with sideburns and big, black-framed eyeglasses, wearing a diamond-patterend crewneck sweater and listening to the radio, while my brother, sister, and I are draped all over him. My brother, Khalid, who is now roughly the same age our father was when he disappeared, has a collection of sweaters with this same motif, most of them given to him by my sister, Najiba, and me.

In the background you can see our bunk beds pushed against the wall. It is not uncommon for Afghan families to sleep in the same room, and despite my father's Western tastes, despite his forward-thinking education—he was an attorney—and his radio program that explored Pashtun music and culture, our family was no different, and we all slept in the same room.

Even though I don't remember when the picture was taken, I cherish that moment. It brings me great comfort when I am faced with self-doubt, and reminds me of what he had predicted at the time of my birth, declaring my destiny to the world.

My father became one of the first prisoners of war during the Soviet occupation, taken from his home by KGB agents when most of the world didn't even know they were in Afghanistan. I became one of the millions of Afghan refugees of that war at age five, when I still had most of my baby teeth. I have flashes of memories from that nightmare, like taking my pet cat to a settlement of mud houses outside Kabul, leaving her in the center, hoping someone would take care of her because we had to flee the city and couldn't take her with us. I remember turning around in the car, trying to get one more glimpse of her before saying good-bye to her forever. Even today the sight of people with their pets fills me with sadness.

I remember getting on a donkey to cross the border into Pakistan, and being afraid that it would take off and I would lose the caravan of other refugees, leaving Mamai and Najiba behind with them. The journey to Pakistan took almost ten days. During that time we were at the mercy of kind strangers for food, shelter, and safety. I vividly remember one house where, in the true spirit of *Pashtunwali,* the ways of the Pashtun, they gave us their only two eggs, cooked in real butter. So delicious, I can close my eyes and instantly taste that butter. But after a while, what I return to most is not so much each individual painful memory but an ever-present feeling of certainty that I would not survive my childhood. I see effects of that overwhelming presence of terror in my childhood in me today, and I know I will feel it for the rest of my life. What is devastating is that there are thousands of us Afghan children, young and old, who suffered through the same journey, and who will forever bear the scars of those years of constant fear.

I DO HAVE some happy memories from my childhood. One of the very few cherished ones is of my brother, my sister, and me standing at the window on the second floor of our house in Kabul, waiting for my father to drive up in the Soap Dish—what we called his white Volkswagen Beetle—and running down to open the door so he could park, step out, and gather all three of us in a group embrace. He would then place Khalid on his shoulders, and Najiba and I would drape ourselves over his arms as he walked into the house, greeting Mamai with a smile.

On Fridays my father liked to cook big lunches for his family and friends. His lunches were legendary. He had many friends, and they would gather around our huge marble table, which sat thirty-eight people comfortably. Here they enjoyed his excellent cooking and shared many laughs at his expense. Even in Kabul, during the progressive mid-seventies, when women walked around the city in miniskirts and the latest European fashions, men never even entered a kitchen, unless they were searching for their wives to ask them what was for dinner. But my father not only loved to cook, he designed our kitchen to suit his strange methods. Traditionally, Afghan women squat on their heels while cooking because everything—the burners, the food—is on the ground level, but my father realized how much easier it was to cook while standing. So in the late seventies, we were the only family we knew in all of Kabul who had kitchen counters, and Mamai cooked standing up.

On one hot Friday afternoon in 1979, according to my mother, my father was in the kitchen putting the finishing touches on the meal when there was a knock on the door. It was one of our relatives, who'd arrived with a "friend." The relative asked my father to step outside for a moment. My father paused. He was wearing his slippers. Still, he did not want to insult his relative, so he stepped outside, closing the door behind him. The KGB had just begun secretly kidnapping and imprisoning people who spoke out against the Soviet Union's covert involvement in the Afghan government. My father was among the first to openly talk about the danger the Soviet presence in Kabul presented to Afghanistan. On his radio show, he announced to his listeners that the Soviets had arrived in Afghanistan with no good intentions. He let everyone know: They wanted to destroy the country of the proud Pashtun nation.

The food got cold while his friends sat around the big marble table, awaiting the return of their host. He never came back. Not that day or ever. I was too young to know what was going on, but Mamai and my uncles were crazy with worry—how could a grown man disappear in the middle of the day, out of his front door? No one seemed to know anything about it, and several family friends distanced themselves to the point of shutting doors in my uncles' faces, and telling them there was nothing they could do to help us. My father had been sold out by his countrymen, who were collaborating with the KGB. Several days later word arrived from one of my father's friends that my father had been taken to Pul-i-charkhi, the infamous prison on the outskirts of Kabul, for questioning.

What questions? Mamai wanted to know. She was frantic. But even in that more modern part of Afghanistan, a woman would never be allowed to visit a prison with her small children. Instead, every week my uncle would take my father a change of clothes and his favorite food. This went on for many weeks. Then one day my uncle showed up at the prison, at what had become his regular time, and the guard told him that there was no one there with my father's name, Taher. Mamai's nightmare recurred: My father had vanished again.

For a while, we remained in our large house in Kabul, hoping my father would return or that at least someone would bring us news of him. Khalid and I took to standing all day at the second-floor window, in order to be the first ones to spot him coming home. Najiba was still a babe in arms. Perhaps because she felt Mamai's anguish, she cried a lot.

That December, in 1979, Russian tanks openly rolled into Kabul.

Every day jets tore the sky overhead. We would hear their sharp hissing, then an eerie moment of silence, then explosions that shook the walls of our house and hurt our ears. At the time, our house was one of only a few two-story houses in Kabul, and whenever we heard the piercing squeal of the jets I was sure that our house was the logical target for the bombs, and that it was going to collapse on our heads at any moment.

Amid the chaos of the Russian invasion, we held out hopes that our father would somehow return, restoring us to a complete family, ready to make plans to survive the Soviet invasion together. No word ever came. With each passing week, Kabul became more and more dangerous. My Baba, my father's father, wanted us to come to his village, just a few hours away from Kabul, but Mamai resisted. She tossed and turned at night, worrying that if we left the city, my father wouldn't know where to find us, which was a silly fear since we had nowhere else to go but Baba's village. Eventually, Baba, who was gentle but persistent, convinced Mamai that we had to go. In Kabul, children were starting to go missing. Baba said that if she didn't leave, she would lose her children. One day the front door would be unlocked and someone would snatch us.

It was rumored that the Russians had started kidnapping children my brother's age—Khalid was six—and sending them to the Soviet Union to train them to be spies for the KGB. After several little boys disappeared from our own neighborhood, Mamai had to accept that Baba was right. We packed up very few belongings and left.

Khalid was at the age when Afghan mothers begin to entertain the hope that their child might survive to adulthood, to marry and have children. Pashtuns believe that at this point a child is old enough to be separated from his mother, if necessary. Some uncles on my father's side were heading across the border to Pakistan and took Khalid with them. There he would begin his schooling. Later I would learn that schooling was actually not the deciding factor for sending Khalid off to another country without us. The Russian soldiers were especially ruthless in killing off male children because they didn't want these young boys to grow up and pick up weapons against the Soviet regime. Mamai, Najiba, and I went to live with Baba in Ghazni Province, where both my parents were born.

My grandfather was the mullah of his village, the religious authority and most esteemed elder. During the late seventies, mullahs were still respected and well liked by communities, and as such he was the true *speen gerai*—"white-bearded one"—that I would, almost twenty years later, seek out in each village I visited. He was an accomplished learner and teacher—he taught the male children in the village and at home taught my aunts how to write their names. He had traveled to Saudi Arabia to memorize the Koran. He would make us read it every evening and would translate into Pashtu the parts that he wanted to point out to us, since we could only read the Arabic. Because he was our elder, our Baba, I never knew his name when I was growing up, and it would have been disrespectful to ask. I never knew my own last name until I moved to America. People would ask what my last name was, and I would be confused, thinking they were asking me for a name I had had before. I would say, *But I've always been Saima; that is what I was called last, too!*

Baba was no taller than five feet six, but when I was a little girl, he seemed like a tower. He always wore *shalwar kameez*, a white cotton turban, and a light-brown *patu*, a shawl worn by men. Even now, as you pass through villages all over Afghanistan, you can see men squatting by the side of the road, their *patus* tossed casually over their shoulders. It's an unsettling sight for the American soldiers, as *patus* are often used by suicide bombers to hide explosives strapped to their chests. But when I was five, I used to go snuggle in Baba's *patu* and feel invincible, like nothing—not even the Russian bombs falling from the skies—could touch me.

We arrived in the village as winter was approaching. I remember a wonderful fur coat that Baba wore. Against the bitter, bone-chilling cold of Afghanistan, that fur coat was the only defense he had. He was the only man I had ever seen in a fur coat; he had inherited it from his father, who had inherited it from his father, and so on, so that no one remembered the original owner. It was gold and cream-colored, probably sheep shearling. I could pet his arm for hours, it was so wonderfully soft. In the evening, after he'd spent the day teaching the boys, he would call

Najiba and me, open his coat wide, and let us crawl into his warm embrace. He told us stories. He asked after our day. He teased us. Two little girls receiving the love and undivided attention of the most respected man in the village was unheard-of in Pashtun culture.

At best, Pashtun parenting can be described as benign neglect. Children are largely ignored until it's time for them to do something for their parents. A son is barely spoken to until he reaches the age of fifteen and is told to go to Saudi Arabia or some other Gulf country to get a job and make some money. A daughter receives less attention than the cow in the yard, which at least needs to be milked every morning; then one day, when she's thirteen or fourteen, she's told that she's going to marry somebody on Friday. Her opinion in the matter is irrelevant.

But Baba was different. In Afghanistan most people aren't too concerned with what kids eat, but Baba used to make us eat our vegetables because, he said, they were good for us. Carrots, he said, were good for our eyesight. When I complained, he reminded me how important it was to have good vision so I could see the Russians coming and hide before they found me.

Perhaps his attention was an outgrowth of the pity he felt for Najiba and me having lost our father, but he displayed the same generosity to the villagers who worked his land. Even though most of the village belonged to him, and he would have been within his rights to collect food and rent from the people who lived there, he allowed them to keep the food they grew for their own families. God likes us to work for ourselves, he would say, so out into the fields he would go, growing the food to feed us. If he was too busy with the school or something else to get out to the fields to pick vegetables for our meal, we simply went without.

His favorite dish was *kadu*, sweet pumpkin. Sauté some onion, add fresh chopped pumpkin, milk, and sugar, and you have the worst-tasting dish on planet Earth—well, that's how I felt about it at age five. Now I ask my mom to make it for me in the rainy Oregon winter because it makes me feel warm inside. One day Baba brought home a donkey loaded down with as many pumpkins as it could possibly carry. At the sight of it I started to cry. Were we going to have to eat all of those pumpkins? I asked Baba when he inquired what was wrong. He laughed and told me he would give some of them away if I would just stop crying. He gave a few armfuls to one of his friends, but there were still too many as far as I was concerned. I begged his friend to take more—the fewer pumpkins, the less *kadu* we had to eat. For weeks afterward whenever a guest came to the house hoping to be lucky enough to eat some of my grandmother's famous *kadu,* Baba would laughingly confess that I had made him give all of our pumpkins away.

At the end of every autumn Afghans butcher one or two of their animals and hang the meat to dry. With no refrigeration, drying ensures that meat doesn't go bad, and it gets the family through the long winter ahead. When Najiba and I first arrived from Kabul we were so miserable, so lost. We didn't know where our father had gone, or why our mother was so heartbroken, and we cried all the time. To comfort us, Baba gave us a lamb to play with. The lamb became our pet. He followed us everywhere, just like in the American nursery rhyme. When the day came to butcher him, Najiba and I were hysterical. Baba took our hands and tried to explain to us about meat, about the reality of our lives. He even tried to use my dislike of *kadu,* saying that since we wouldn't eat his sweet pumpkin, we *had* to eat lamb. Najiba begged him to take one of the donkeys instead. We would happily eat the donkey. He laughed and explained to us that donkey meat was *haram,* forbidden. In the end, he gave us a few days to say good-bye, and then the lamb disappeared.

We lived in Baba's village for a year. There were bombs being dropped on our village day and night, causing an ever-present layer of dust to settle on everything, no matter how often Mamai and Grandmother cleaned. As the days passed and my father failed to materialize, Mamai grew increasingly certain that she was going to live the rest of her life as a widow. When I tell my close American friends the story of what happened to my parents, how my mother became a widow with three children before she was even thirty years old, they feel sad for me. Sadder for me, however, is the reality that my mother was only one of thousands of Afghan women who were dealt the same fate as a result of the Russian invasion.

Mamai moved slowly, in a state of shock, unable to believe that her husband, who had carried their children on his shoulders around the house and who loved to cook with her, would never return. She looked at us, but I knew she didn't really see us, her mind off in happier times. Having our grandparents was a blessing, not just for us but for her, because it gave her time to adjust to the harsh reality of her new life. The only time she became alive was when we would hear the sounds of the jets, because we all knew that bombs would follow within seconds. She would grab my hand, throw Najiba on her hip, and run fast for shelter in the small caves that pocketed the surrounding hills as the bombs rained down from the sky.

Even with all of the bombs dropped and mines left by the Russians, I felt safer in the village than in Kabul. Baba protected us the best he could. I felt he was so divine that God would watch out for him and, by extension, us. But more than that, he gave us so much attention and love that for hours I could forget where I was and what had happened and simply enjoy the serenity of his company.

Then the day came when my grandfather realized that life in the village had gotten too dangerous. He made the painful decision that Pashtuns dread more than death: He would leave the land that had belonged to our family for as many generations as could be traced back. He did it, however, to keep his word to my father—that his daughters would be allowed to have a life different from the one we were destined for.

For our journey out of our forefathers' land, Baba secured camels for Najiba and me. But we were city girls. We rode in cars and electric buses. We had never seen a camel and were terrified of them. They were impatient, irritable. They pawed the dust with their giant feet. We rocked back and forth toward the mountain trail that would take us to the border. I remember looking back at Najibas, thinking her camel was trying to bite my back as it got close to mine, and I screamed, "It's trying to eat me!" Had we been boys, my grandfather would have yelled at us for shrieking and acting up, but we were fatherless daughters, homeless half-orphans.

So he found a couple of donkeys the next day, and we were hoisted onto their backs. They were much gentler, even bored with the task of taking us to join Khalid and our family in Peshawar, Pakistan.

We were part of a small caravan that consisted of our family, our two camels, our two donkeys, and several other donkeys that belonged to families from the village. There was safety in numbers, but too large a group trying to cross the mountains into Pakistan would draw the attention of the Russian jets, which were known to bomb whole caravans, killing every man, woman, and child in them. The danger was so great that we traveled during the night and slept in caves and holes in the ground during the day. The lucky ones were the refugees who would find hosts in the villages on the way to Pakistan, who would give them a bite to eat and a place to sleep for a few hours.

The trip from Ghazni to Peshawar now takes just hours by car, but it took us over ten days and was a consistently grueling journey, during which we didn't know if we would make it to the next day. Crossing the vast desert and mountains with Russian jets often flying overhead, we were terrified that our end was near. I remember hearing the jets far away, and shutting my eyes tightly, hoping that if I couldn't see them, the Russians couldn't see me either. Miraculously, we found our way to the rest of our family in Pakistan. But the journey that began my new life was spent with my eyes tightly shut, hanging on to the back of a donkey, fearing that if I opened my eyes, I would be bombed to pieces.

T W O

I was first proposed to when I was nine.

Well, actually it wasn't really to me that the proposal was made. I only found out because one day not too long afterward, my brother, who had heard about it from the adults, was pulling my hair and harassing me, so I went crying to Mamai. When Mamai got mad at him, he said something like, "Oh, yeah, well, hopefully Baba will say yes and soon we will be rid of you!" I started crying even harder, hoping Khalid was wrong, and that there was no way Baba would give me away so soon. But if he were to follow our centuries-old customs, he would do exactly that. Marriages were arranged by grandfathers and fathers, between tribes and families, to strengthen their ties. Neither the appropriate age nor the consent of the children was necessary. The tribe that had wanted to be linked with mine was well respected, very wealthy, and powerful, and my grandfather would not have been unjustified in agreeing to the marriage.

I knew all of that, even from a very early age, because I had grown up hearing about my obligations and responsibilities toward the family and had always had a sense that my childhood days were numbered. I don't think I thought that I would be spared the harsh life of a married Afghan woman forever. I just didn't want my married life to begin at age nine.

Astonishingly, Baba didn't disappoint me. He told the other family that his granddaughter was too young for that kind of silliness, and that he had hopes that I would be able to at least graduate from sixth grade before marriage. The first time he refused a marriage proposal, he was very respectful, knowing how quickly you can make a mortal enemy out of a Pashtun by insulting him. But over the next couple of years, I heard stories of him kicking out men who came into our *mehmaan khana,* guest house, asking for my hand in marriage for their sons, Baba yelling at them, "Are there no other girls left in the world? Leave my granddaughter alone!"

As I grew older and became more aware of what he was doing to protect me, I loved him all the more. But in a culture where you are not allowed to express your love by declaring it casually, I didn't know how to show him what he meant to me. I would make his tea and take it to him, a large scarf covering my four-foot height, tripping on the edges of it as I walked up to the *mehmaan khana* where he stayed. He would usually be reading, but whenever he saw me enter the room, he would put his book down, give me a brilliant smile, and pat the ground next to him. I would put the teapot down, pour him a cup, and sit beside him. I was too shy to say anything about what he was doing, but he knew exactly what I felt and would put his arm around me. "Don't worry," he would say. "Everything will work out. As long as I am alive, everything will be fine." I believed him completely, and with him on my side, I felt like I could conquer any obstacle in life.

I felt lucky. Life was good for me. I knew that I was different, and not just in the way that most of us feel during preadolescence. For one thing, I went to school, which none of my friends were allowed to do. Sometimes I would be resentful that they were at home, playing with dolls and learning how to be little women, while I was forced to go to school and learn about subjects that I knew I would never use as a Pashtun woman. And when my friends would ask me to play with them after school, I had to say no because I would have homework to do.

I was the only girl in my class, until sixth grade—my fellow students never forgot to remind me that I was an abnormality and not a real girl, because real girls didn't go to school. For their vicious words, like a true

Pashtun, I took revenge. I earned the best grades every year, and memorized poems and times tables for extra credit. Yes, I admit, I became the teacher's pet and was asked to lead the prayers during the assemblies. I was also selected as the class proctor whenever our teacher had to leave the classroom, and was given a ruler to use to keep the boys in line. I used it without mercy. None of the boys were allowed to say a word, and if they gave me so much as a wrong look, I would ask them to stretch out their arms and would hit them on the back of their hands with the ruler. I used the back of their hands because I knew it hurt more than their palms.

Back at home, my brother would complain to Baba and Mamai because a couple of his friends were in my class and I wouldn't allow them to talk in class or to be rough on the playground. Baba would laugh, the deep laugh I loved, and look at me with a twinkle in his eyes.

Like any little girl growing up, I had a best friend, Nafisa, who lived a few houses from mine. She had two older brothers and two younger sisters. I hardly ever saw her because she was not allowed to go to school, and in the evening she had to take care of all of her siblings, as her mother was always either pregnant or ill. At age twelve, Nafisa was the woman of the house, expected to not indulge in silliness like friendship and school and talking. Although she had beautiful almond-shaped eyes, dark hair, and light skin, I always remember her with scars and bruises, because her brothers beat her constantly. I would ask her, "What are they accusing you of now?" I remember her crying, saying, "I didn't do anything, but they always find something to slap me for." Sometimes they would hit her because she took too long laying out the laundry on the roof to dry and they thought that she was slacking off or—worse— looking at a boy on the street. Sometimes they would hit her when she didn't get them tea or food fast enough. For one reason or another, they would leave a mark on her pretty face, turning it blue and yellow.

At no other time was the difference between my life and the lives of other Pashtun girls more clear. I would come home and busy myself with homework, terrified that at any point my life might be changed to what Nafisa had. I would look in fear at my brother, who was such a kidder, even at that age, and I would wonder, Will he beat me one day? No, he would never, I would try to reassure myself. Still, I felt terribly guilty that my best friend was living in hell, and I wanted so badly to beat her brothers for putting her there. Unfortunately, her brothers didn't go to school either, were much bigger, and could have easily killed me had I insulted them by interfering in their family business.

I felt like I was living in a delicate bubble. All around me were my female cousins and friends enduring an existence that I couldn't imagine. They were no different from me—for all intents and purposes, I should have been leading the same life. But there I was in the courtyard, getting into a car in which all the windows were covered in sheets (so no one could see inside) and being driven to a private school, where I was the only girl in my class. What made me so special? Was I the chosen one, or the cursed one? It was hard to tell at that early age, but I did know that I did not want the life of a typical Pashtun female, and I lived in constant terror that I would be forced into living that life. I desperately wanted to believe that my Baba could save me from that fate, yet the fear that he might not be strong enough to defy the centuries-old traditions of our people created in me deep insecurities that took years to overcome.

$\mathcal{T}$ H R E E

In the 1980s, the Russian invasion and eventual withdrawal created a great deal of political instability in Afghanistan and sparked a civil war that wrecked Afghan society beyond recognition. It became apparent to Baba that he might not be able to keep his promise to me that everything would be fine. So he started talking to his son in America to see if he could sponsor me, my brother and sister, and three other cousins. Mamai and my aunt, whom we all called Babo, were okay with the boys going but were opposed to sending the girls. But Baba was firm; the boys would go only if the girls were allowed to go with them.

Like everyone else growing up in a poor and conflicted country, I dreamed about America before going there. I knew that there were freedoms there beyond my wildest imagination, and rights that would be mine, if I could get to that land of equality. America could rescue me from the cultural restrictions and ancient customs that threatened to define my fate—if I could only get there. But it all seemed like a fantasy. I never believed that my dreams could come true.

To prepare for our possible move to America, we were switched from the school where I was the only girl to a private school that specialized in English. Here the boys and the girls were taught in separate classes. For the first time, I was not the only girl in class, but these girls were all from Pakistani families and spoke Urdu, so I was still the only Pashtun girl. We also began taking the bus to school and back because my uncle, the only one who knew how to drive, had gotten a job. (My mother and aunt weren't allowed to drive.)

One Thursday (I remember the day because we were wearing our white uniform, as we did every Thursday) we were rushing out of the house, late for the bus. I got to the road and saw that the bus was about to pull out. In my haste to not be left behind, I ran, not noticing the speeding public bus going the other way. It slammed into my left side and lifted me—Khalid swore it was at least fifteen feet—into the air. After flipping many times I fell in the middle of the road, landing on my shoulder and head.

I don't remember any of this. I woke up in the hospital after a three-day coma, from which nobody thought I would awaken. In Pakistan at that time there were no doctors trained in comas and no hospitals that offered trauma care, or at least not at the hospital in Peshawar. Mamai was told that if I woke up, it would be a miracle—and if I didn't, no one should be surprised, and it wouldn't be the doctor's fault. In a country where hit-and-runs are the norm, and where there aren't any insurance companies to deal with, I was told that the driver who hit me came to the hospital every day, bringing food for the family members who kept vigil for me. Three days after the accident I woke up and casually asked for some of the kebabs that I smelled. One of my relatives had brought them for Mamai, who had never left my bedside.

This was the second time Mamai was told to give a *khairath,* a sacrifice to show thanks to God for allowing me to continue living. Once I was released from the hospital, relatives and friends came to ask about my recovery, amazed that I was still alive.

I felt again like I had been saved for something—I didn't know what, but I knew there was a reason I stepped away from events that I had no business surviving. It was as if an invisible hand was directing me toward a unique destiny. I could sense that there was something greater waiting for me. Finding out what that was, exactly, and seeking it out was a powerful motivation for me. I couldn't wait for my future to unfold. As I lay there hearing Khalid tell the story of the bus hitting me, flipping me several times in the air, landing me so hard that people around me swore they heard the sound of my body slamming into the road echoing for days, I finally believed that I was chosen, and blessed. The fear of living a life like my best friend Nafisa's was still not far from my heart, but I began to consider then that I couldn't have lived through two near-death experiences for nothing. After all, I was just a human, allowed only one life with which to leave my mark.

$\mathcal{F}$ OUR

E vents that would change my life forever had been set into motion. We all call him *Ustaz,* "the teacher" in Pashtu. He was my father's oldest brother, and he had emigrated to the United States in the late 1960s to attend college. I'm not sure why he decided to stay in the States, but he settled in Portland, Oregon, which was a quiet city in the seventies. He then went on to gain tenure as a professor at a small liberal arts college there. The talks between him and Baba started out in secrecy. Something as significant as sending the children to America was not the kind of thing one discussed in public. I heard whispers, but the adults made sure that we weren't around when they were discussing the plans to send us to America for a better future. Now that it was a real possibility, I couldn't decide how I felt about the idea of going to America. On the one hand, it would take me away from everything I knew was wrong with the lives of Afghan women. I wouldn't have to marry someone just to bear him many children and die. At the tender age of ten or eleven, this was the bleak view I had of what lay ahead. I knew Baba wanted to protect me for as long as he could, but he was just one man, up against thousands of Pashtun men who would kill anyone they thought was trying to defy *Pashtunwali.* I was very much aware of his mortality and could see that he was aging. He had become confusingly forgetful at times; I now know that he was exhibiting early signs of Alzheimer's.

The knowledge that there wasn't much other than Baba standing in the way of my Afghan fate scared me sleepless at night, filling me with dread that the next day would be the one when I would be told I couldn't go to school and that the next month would be the ceremony to hand me over to another family to control my destiny for the rest of my life. This was not unfounded fear. I knew of many girls my age, some younger, who were told just a couple of weeks before their wedding day that they were now promised to be wed to a man they had never met. When I heard that Nafisa was being promised to one of her distant cousins, I cried and cried. Mamai thought that it was because I would miss Nafisa, so she tried to reassure me that she would come and visit her parents and see me, too. I couldn't explain to her that I cried in part for myself, fearing that the same fate might be awaiting me. I felt so guilty for worrying more about myself than about my best friend, but I couldn't help it.

NEARLY TWO YEARS later my uncle Kaka told us that we had to have passport pictures taken, making the plan to go to America real. I should have been ecstatic beyond measure, but I knew the plan wasn't foolproof, that people were denied entry for one reason or another all the time. I was afraid of setting my hopes too high, knowing I wouldn't be able to handle the letdown if it didn't work out. At the age of twelve, I already knew that I would be dealt many disappointments in my life, but this would be like no other, and for me there would be no returning to living like Nafisa, married to a distant cousin. I had to decide what I would do with my life if this didn't work. Would I have the courage to end it all if I failed to fulfill my father's prophecy? Without my being conscious of it, emigrating had become a life-and-death issue for me. On the one hand, I wanted to rejoice in the possibility of pursuing my destiny, living like no other woman in my whole family, tribe, or even in the province had ever lived. On the other hand, I couldn't escape the terror of what I would have to do to myself if I was denied a visa.

$\mathcal{F}$ I V E

We landed at Seattle-Tacoma International Airport in the middle of a dark, gloomy, and wet Washington night. There were six of us—three boys and three girls. It had been a torturous journey, not just because the flights were hours long. I kept reminding myself of the journey I had taken at age five, and to be thankful I didn't have to worry about being bombed. It took us more than a week to go from Peshawar to Karachi to Cairo to London to Portland. First we were stuck in Karachi because the customs agents wouldn't let us travel with Pakistani passports unless we bought round-trip tickets. We had to have Pakistani passports because there was no Afghan government, therefore no Afghan passports. We stayed at a hotel for a week, just six children, while Kaka came to meet us with the money and arrange the tickets. This was the first time we had been without adult supervision, and for me it happened when I was paralyzed by uncertainty about the future. The week in Karachi is a blur; I remember mainly my fear that it was all going to be for nothing, and that I would be going back to what I had already started thinking of as my previous life.

Once we were able to satisfy the requirements of the Pakistani airline, we were allowed to leave the country and move on to the next leg of the journey. I remember people looking at us very strangely. There we were, six children, all under the age of seventeen, with no adults to guide us, not to mention that we spoke almost no English.

I wasn't sure what I expected. For Afghan refugees our family was affluent and educated; still, for me, the whole world consisted of just two places: where I had been, Pakistan, and where I wanted to end up, America. Anyplace that was not Afghanistan or Pakistan was where Madonna and Michael Jackson lived. I imagined my uncle the Professor's house to be like our big house in Kabul, except much grander, because everything was better and bigger in America. I was shocked when I arrived to find it small, dark, and cramped. The worst thing about it was there were no walls to protect us from outsiders.

Because the Professor was all alone, a younger uncle, Uncle A, who worked as a city engineer, was enlisted to help take care of us and moved in. On the night we arrived, Uncle A had been so worried about collecting us from the airport that he'd forgotten about dinner. Moments after we walked in the door he opened a package of hot dogs, put them in the oven to cook, then forgot about them. He was showing us around the house when the smoke alarm went off. It sounded just like the blaring sirens that filled the streets of Kabul when the Russians were bombing. I was terrified. Had the Russians followed us to America, too? My first meal in America was a burned and blackened hot dog, and even if I could force myself to look beyond the charred pink meat, my appetite was ruined by the flashback of fleeing Russian bombs.

The Professor's house was built on a hill surrounded by trees. Every window had the same view, tall fir trees that blocked out the sun. I was fifteen years old when we arrived in America, on May 3, 1991. Later we would call that day Liberty Day, and celebrated it each year. Much later, when Khalid and Najiba and I lived together in our own place, we celebrated it there. I don't celebrate it anymore—I guess I have truly become American now, and take my liberty for granted.

The first order of business, according to the Professor, was learning English. Although I had been enrolled in a private English school in Pakistan I had never paid attention in class, thinking that if I learned

English but never actually made it to America, I would be even more resentful of my fate. The Professor put an ad for a tutor up on the job board at the college where he taught, and one morning while we were still groggy with jet lag there was a knock at the front door. Before the Professor and Uncle A had left for work they told us a tutor was coming to teach us English and that we should open the door for her. Khalid was the oldest, so he answered. A girl in dark jeans and a gray T-shirt stood on the porch. She wore her curly hair in a high ponytail.

We invited her to sit down at our dining room table. She put her hand on her heart and said, "My name is Jessica." Aziz and Emal came out of the bedroom they shared with Khalid. They stared. How did this American girl get into our house? I sat down beside her and placed my hand on my heart. Outside I could hear crows arguing in the trees.

"Saima," I said.

"Hello, Say-ma," she said.

"Sigh-ma," I said. "Khalid, Najiba, Jamila, Aziz, Emal," I said slowly, pointing out each one.

"Okay," she said, laughing. I could tell she was confused, and indeed, the entire time she came to our house she struggled with our names.

When she left that day she shook our hands. Emal was seven months younger than me, and Aziz was thirteen, the same age as Najiba. They had never touched the hand of a female who was not a member of our family. Khalid closed the door behind her. We watched through the front window as Jessica got into her little blue Honda and adjusted the mirror. I thought I saw her smile at herself. I remember feeling that I could never in a million years be a girl who wore jeans and drove a car and smiled for no reason. It all seemed so overwhelmingly impossible that I felt my eyes tear up. I should have stayed in the village, where I'd never have met this bright, happy girl and ached with desire to be just like her.

WHEN WE WEREN'T sitting around the table trying to have a conversation with Jessica, the Professor wanted us to read. He took us to the local branch of the Multnomah County Library and got us each our own library card. Before handing them out the uncles made sure we understood the rules: educational books only, and no movies. Each day, to pass the hours, we walked down the hill to the local middle school, where we sat on the grass and read our library books and watched people play soccer.

One hot day around lunchtime we were sitting in our usual spot atop a green hill overlooking the track and playing fields. We watched some people running laps, and I remember thinking Americans were crazy; in Afghanistan the only time people ran was to escape falling bombs and rockets. I leaned back on my arms. A breeze ruffled the leaves of some nearby trees. I couldn't believe we were just sitting out in the open, without anybody bothering us. At home in Peshawar, on the rare occasions when we were allowed to leave the house, men stared at us. Once, when I was maybe ten years old, I put my grandmother's eyedrops in my eyes because I was bored, or maybe because no one was watching and I thought it couldn't hurt—after all, she was using them to get better eyesight. I went completely blind in both eyes for hours. I was terrified and cried and told Mamai I couldn't see, and she panicked and wanted to send me to the doctor, who was just up the street. But I knew that I would have to walk past several shops, where the men out front would stare intently at me. I refused to go and told Mamai that I was already blind, did she have to subject me to the men, too? Of course, she forced me to go, and I was able to see just fine a few days later.

After watching the joggers run around the track for a while, someone said it was time to go home for lunch. It was just another clear beautiful day in Oregon, and my arms and legs felt wonderful in the rare heat, unlike the oppressive heat of Peshawar. "I'm not ready to go home," I said in Pashtu, at the time the only language we spoke with each other.

"There's that restaurant up the street," said Khalid. "We could pool our money together and just get one thing and share."

I can't remember how it was that we had money. The uncles must have given it to us, but why? We weren't supposed to go anywhere except to the library and the playground of the middle school. I knew it would be dangerous—to disobey our uncles. My nerves banished my hunger, but I also felt I had to go with them. The Chinese restaurant was in a strip mall. Khalid opened the door and we all crowded inside. It was hot and smelled like grease—delicious. I stood inside the door and waited for something big to happen. This was the first time in my life I had ever seen the inside of a restaurant. In Afghanistan and Pakistan, respectable women didn't go to restaurants, and so we weren't even allowed to go out to eat when we were little. Khalid pointed to a picture on the menu above our heads—a noodle dish with sautéed vegetables. The man behind the counter wrote it on a slip of paper, then turned and threw a handful of vegetables onto the grill sizzling behind him. I couldn't shake the feeling that my mother would disapprove of what I was doing, and yet at the same time I felt alive in a way I had never felt before. To do something that was frowned upon, not just by my mother but also by my uncles, and to not only get away with it but to end up eating something delicious as a result, was exhilarating. This is what freedom must be, I thought.

By the time we took the food back to the middle school, extracted the six plastic forks from the take-out bag, and dug in, I was famished. The noodles were hot and greasy, the vegetables so bright and crisp; it was the first and best Chinese food I have ever eaten.

It didn't take long for us to expand the boundaries of our disobedience. One day we decided that after spending some time at the library we would take a walk and see what was on the other side of the road. A few doors down from the Chinese restaurant was a 7-Eleven, the likes of which I had never seen back home (although I hadn't seen the inside of many stores at all). I was transfixed by the offerings at the 7-Eleven, the dozens of kinds of candy, the wall of coolers, the countless bottles of things to drink. While we decided which bag of chips we wanted—I had already developed a preference for barbecued—the buzzer would bleat, announcing kids our age busting through the doors. They headed to the far side of the store, where they bought huge paper cups of bright-blue icy drinks.

We knew without talking about it that the uncles must never find out. The Professor and Uncle A had made it abundantly clear that they'd gone to the trouble and expense of bringing us to America so we could learn English, become educated, and then go back to Afghanistan. This seemed like the noblest of goals, maybe a little overwhelming for six teenage children, but I still felt honored and privileged to be part of it. We were told as soon as we got to America that we were not like other kids our age, and were not to behave like them. Anything that threatened to distract us from our mission, like selecting and buying potato chips, was absolutely forbidden. The first bag of chips I ate, therefore, came with a deep feeling of guilt, guilt that had nothing to do with their nutritional offenses.

However, being children who had freedom of movement for the first time in our lives, we did disobey, again. There was a video store in the strip mall next door to the 7-Eleven. One day we walked inside, just to see what was there and look at all the pretty boxes lined up on the shelves. It must have been August, just before school started. The loud pink blossoms that had adorned the shrubs in our neighborhood had come and gone. The lawn at our middle school was turning gold.

Inside the video store we walked up and down the aisles, trying to pronounce the names of the different movie genres: Family. Drama. Action. Classic. Even if we had wanted to rent a movie, we didn't know how to do it, and had no money anyway. We were just looking—what harm could it do?

We walked outside and saw a woman unlocking her car door who looked very familiar: the Professor's secretary. She wore a long skirt and sandals and was carrying a white paper bag from the Subway next to the video store. Her face broke into a smile when she saw us. We heard her say a few of our names, then a slur of excited English. She patted my shoulder, because I was within reach. Behind me I could feel the collective gasp of my siblings and cousins. This was a disaster. We had been working with Jessica every morning, but we hadn't learned any words even close to *please don't tell our uncle you saw us coming out of a video store!*

That night the Professor came home around six o'clock, his usual time. We were sitting in the living room reading our books. Soon it would be time to turn on *ABC World News Tonight with Peter Jennings.*

The Professor thought Peter Jennings's English was worth emulating, so he required us to watch his news show every evening. He set his briefcase by the front door.

"So, what did you guys do today?" he asked.

We looked at one another, trying to figure out if this was a trick question. No one answered. He shook his head.

"Juanita said she ran into you today. But it's almost time for the news, so we'll talk about this more on Sunday."

Sunday? I looked up and met Najiba's worried gaze.

An American parent or uncle might have marched into the house and started in, but the Professor and Uncle A preferred to deliver their lectures once a week, at a Sunday family meeting. We were Afghans. We didn't talk about our issues or our feelings. Thus began the very much dreaded weekly tradition of Sunday meetings. At this first Sunday meeting, he told us that his secretary had indeed reported that she had run into us at the video store.

"I'm not against movies," he said. "Nor am I against renting movies, but *you* will not rent movies. I will."

He nodded at each one of us. We sat with our heads lowered. I was fifteen and had only known the life of a Pashtun girl. Still, I couldn't help thinking that what he said wasn't true. He *was* against movies, and I knew he would never rent one for us. He issued our punishment: no TV. I snuck a look at my brother, since he was the oldest, to see his reaction. He was looking as terrified and guilty as I'm sure I did.

SCHOOL WAS GOING to begin in September. So far, we had been wearing *shalwar kameez* at home, even when we went out to the middle school to sit around. But apparently the uncles had discussed it and decided that we were going to be outfitted in Western clothes. Uncle A took us shopping. Back home, we had never gone shopping for ourselves. Kaka bought our clothes, and I remember how much I had wished that I had been allowed to pick out my own. I would tell him to get me a brown shirt, and he would come home with a green shirt. At the time I thought he was just being cruel and didn't even want to give me something as simple as a brown shirt. Years later, while taking him to an eye exam in Oregon, I would find out he was color-blind—only then did I forgive him for never getting me the right color all those years ago.

Now that I was finally allowed to go out and choose my own clothes, I was unbelievably excited. I'm sure there were plenty of children being dragged to the mall for before-school shopping who would rather have been out playing, but for me, it was my dream of making my own choices coming true. That feeling would not last. As we followed Uncle A through one of the department stores, we passed a display of folded sweaters. A red one caught my eye. I showed it to Uncle A.

"Red is not a color worn by good women," he said.

What was he talking about? I didn't know I was a woman yet. I certainly wasn't allowed to act like one, or dress like one. I was dressed just like the boys, in baggy, thigh-length T-shirts and khaki pants that were several sizes too big. I was forbidden to wear makeup or jewelry. In fact, anything that drew attention to me was forbidden. I trudged after him in confusion. I guess I was only a woman when it came to wearing a red sweater. Was this the beginning of them letting me get close enough to enjoying personal freedom, only to have it snatched away? For that reason alone, the more I thought about not being allowed to have that sweater, the more I wanted it. Over the years, it came to symbolize everything I would be denied. One of the first purchases I made when I left my uncles' house was a red wool sweater. Even so, for the longest time, I couldn't make myself wear it.

Having been denied the red sweater, I was surprised when the uncles allowed me to get a haircut. The ends of my black hair brushed the small of my back. In Afghanistan, and then in Peshawar, there was no question of my cutting it. Long hair is a Pashtun woman's pride and symbolizes her husband's pride once she is married. Every little girl grew her hair, knowing what it represented, and never cut it because it was deeply frowned upon. This was the reason Mamai wanted me to grow my hair, and the reason I wanted to chop it off. I didn't want to do anything just to avoid upsetting some Afghan man. I wanted to do the opposite, thinking that if I chopped it off, no man would want me, and instead would find some other girl, a nice one with long hair. And I would be left alone to do whatever I wanted.

The uncles were a different matter, since they had already suggested that I not wear the scarf to school. They thought that high school kids were unforgiving, and it would be better if I attracted the least amount of attention possible. If they allowed me to go without covering my head, could I ask them if I could cut my hair? They said yes! I realize now their reasoning for that, too: If I went without a scarf, my thick, shiny black hair would draw just as much attention. So a short, preferably unflattering haircut would solve that problem.

That summer at the public library, I had discovered Lady Di, and for me she epitomized a modern, liberated, free woman. In the library I read countless magazine articles about her and found a book about her that I could never borrow because it didn't fall into any categories we were allowed to check out, but I would look at a few pages every chance I got. It took me many trips to the library to finish it, because I read English very slowly. There was still a little girl inside of me who loved her fairy-tale life, her beautiful clothes and tall husband. But most of all, I loved her stylish short hair. If I could have that haircut, I would be on the road to becoming a true American (I didn't realize at the time that she was English).

So Uncle A took me to Supercuts and I told the lady I wanted to look like Lady Di. When I emerged from the barbershop, I felt giddy, liberated. I couldn't stop myself from running my fingers through my hair. When we got home Najiba looked at me and said, "I'm never getting my hair cut." I didn't care. I was modern and free. No one would ever mistake me for a village girl anymore, I thought, looking in the mirror.

S I X

The first week of school a girl named Kristen introduced herself to me in the hallway. I couldn't find my locker. A lady from the office had shown it to me once, and now I couldn't find my way back to it. There were hundreds of lockers lining identical-looking hallways. How did the other students find theirs? Was there a secret way of telling? I never considered that they would have numbers and letters on them, and that I should have memorized mine. We had nothing like that in our school in Peshawar. We carried everything in backpacks, which weighed a ton.

Kristen was a pretty, perky, green-eyed blonde, quick to smile and laugh. She was in a few of my classes and was one of the friendliest Americans I'd met. I remember thinking that her parents had done a wonderful job raising her; looking back, I find this an odd thought, given that I was a teenager myself.

One of the first things she said to me was that she was interested in meeting someone from India.

"India?"

"The dot on your forehead."

In my excitement over cutting my long hair, I had totally forgotten the tribal tattoo I had been given by my grandmother when I was five, during my stay in the village. Tattooing was a rite of passage for young girls, and it was usually done at the same time we got our ears and nose pierced. I had been given one tattoo on my forehead, a green dot, but it had hurt so much that I begged my grandmother to not do anymore on my face. I did allow her to tattoo my hands. She gave me a tattoo of four dots on my right thumb. (Years later, I found out it is very similar to a California gang tattoo. On several occasions I have had to explain to people that I do not belong to a gang, nor does it mean I have killed four people.)

I tried to explain all this to Kristen in my limited English. I tried to also tell her that Indian females put red dots on their foreheads after marriage, but the dot between my eyebrows was green, therefore not the same thing. "Not India, Afghanistan" was all I managed.

"Cool." She shrugged. Kristen wasn't the only one curious about the green tribal tattoo between my brows. Some of my fellow students stared; others asked me about being Indian. When I mentioned this one day to the Professor, he pressed his thin lips into a frown.

"We should get them removed," he said.

I looked up and met his gaze. This may have been the first time I looked my uncle in the eyes. They were small and dark, his thick brows a little unkempt. He had a fine, straight nose and a downturned mouth. I don't know what he saw when he looked into my eyes, perhaps hope, even gratitude. Was he really going to help me take yet another step away from being that girl from the village? Was he going to help me fit in with my peers? I felt the desire rise in my chest.

"Other students are apparently paying too much attention to this. It's a distraction from your studies."

Najiba also had a green tribal tattoo between her brows, and one day the Professor took us to a doctor to have them removed. I sat on the exam table, the thin paper rustling beneath my trembling legs, while the doctor injected what I was told was a painkiller into my forehead, and then he pinched the skin together, sliced the dot off, and stitched together the wound. The pain roared in my ears, and I became nauseous. It was one of the last physical symbols of my tribal identity, and the removal of it was a pain that even today I vividly remember, burning deep into my being. The pain was so excruciating that, once again, I begged my uncle to not remove the ones on my hand. He gave in, and just the one on my forehead was removed. For the next month Najiba—who for some reason suffered less than I did—and I wore white squares of gauze taped to our foreheads. The uncles weren't interested in the disfigurement forming beneath our bandages; they gave no thought to moisturizing lotion or vitamin E. When the bandages were finally removed I had—and still have—a noticeable three-quarter-inch-long scar between my eyebrows. People ask about it all the time. They wonder whether I was in a car accident or have some other interesting anecdote about how I got it. I find it hard to explain that this is the only physical scar I carry from a time that left me with so many emotional ones. Sometimes I wish I had kept my tattoo—not that the Professor gave me an option. Once he had decided that it interfered with his plans for me, it had to go.

KRISTEN SHOWED ME how the lockers were numbered. We walked to her locker, then to mine. She showed me how to turn the dial and work the combination, right-left-right.

But no matter how helpful she was, she could not help me with my endless embarrassment. In the years before the Professor had sent for us in Peshawar, when I was daydreaming about what it would be like to be free in America, I had never imagined this constant sense of awkward humiliation. I was good at school; in Peshawar I was the best in the class. But in Peshawar I had classes in Islamic studies, not PE—and certainly not sex education.

I had no idea it was a required class here in my new country. When I walked into the sex-ed classroom I was just thrilled to have arrived on time at the right place. The sun shone through the big windows. The other students were giggling, poking one another, throwing things. I remember thinking how squirmy Americans were, like kittens, constantly moving. I looked around at the walls. There were drawings of human torsos, with arrows on them pointing to places that I wasn't supposed to know about. The pictures in the book the teacher passed out were even worse. That night I asked the uncles to write me a note excusing me from sex ed. I told them I was ashamed of sitting in that class with the other students, and that I didn't understand 80 percent of what the teacher was talking about anyway. I'm sure they were happy for me to remain clueless about sex, as a typical Pashtun woman was meant to be, so they agreed. There were several times over the first few years when the uncles would write us notes to get out of classes and activities I found too shocking to take part in, including dissecting a pig.

I also asked to be excused from swimming in PE, which I now regret since I realize what a great workout swimming is. But at the time the thought of shimmying into a tight swimsuit in the girls' locker room, then striding out to the pool was impossible. My mind could not envision such a thing, nor did I want it to. Such an action would bring shame to me and my family. I couldn't believe that the families of the other girls in class would allow them to walk around in public in what amounted to their underwear.

"Why don't you want to take swimming?" Kristen asked. "It's the most fun part of PE."

I looked at her. I understood her but couldn't begin to explain. "I don't know how to swim," I managed in English. This was true.

"But I can teach you!"

I wanted to tell her that where I was from women didn't walk around in their underwear, but I just shook my head.

I wish I could give a better account of that first year, of how great the cultural shock of just being in America was—let alone of going directly to high school and dealing with the terrifying newness of that environment. I was amazed by everything around me. The way the girls dressed—the short skirts they wore, the plunging necklines and low-rise jeans—was so alien, but especially shocking was the way they behaved. It went against everything I had ever been told about how women should act. The first couple of years of my life in the United States, I truly believed that the parents of these girls must not know how they were carrying on. How could a father be okay allowing his daughter to talk to boys in the hallways, wearing these revealing clothes? Didn't they know that it was shameful? And where was the tribe? How could they allow the children of one family to embarrass the whole tribe?

The boys were even more shocking. They weren't harassing the girls like they should have been, considering how the girls were dressed. In Afghanistan, girls who covered only their head and not their faces were free game for boys to humiliate. Would I ever get used to the way people lived in this new country? It didn't seem possible, and on those days when it got to be too much, I would desperately wish to be back in Afghanistan, or even Pakistan, where I understood the rules of conduct and knew my place in society.

The culture shock was mitigated by the fact that I didn't understand a lot of what was being said around me. I looked at my carefree peers and saw them as alien beings, people with whom I would never have anything in common. I was an observer, watching in order to learn what I should never become. I would see girls in their red sweaters talking and laughing with boys in the hallway and think, My uncles are right. These are not good girls, wearing the color of bad women and talking to boys who are not related to them. I am never going to be so shameless. I vowed I would listen to and obey my uncles. The consequences of doing otherwise were too frightening. It wasn't that I didn't want to be in America, living such a liberated life. I just didn't want to be like the girls I saw. And the list of what not to be was growing longer every day I spent in high school.

Khalid, Aziz, Emal, and I took the bus home right after school. There was no question of participating in after-school sports or theater or even the math or chess club. I was expected to get As, even though at the beginning I had to translate every homework assignment into Urdu, the language of my schooling, then back into English. A worksheet that would take a regular student twenty minutes to complete took me three hours or more, and then I would go back over my work, double-checking and second-guessing myself until I was exhausted. I was terrified that I might get a bad grade, which meant anything less than an A. I was anxious for my uncles to praise me during Sunday meetings and not point to me as the bad example.

Our school bus stopped in front of the middle school, where we collected Najiba and Jamila. Then we trudged up the hill to our uncles' house. The leaves of the deciduous trees had turned blood red. The slightest breeze sent them spiraling to the ground. We kicked at the leaves and teased one another. The boys liked to brag about their exploits in the cafeteria.

"At lunch I got up to get a drink and some kid tried to take my seat and I told him to get lost!" one of them would say.

"Really," Khalid would reply. "You told him to get lost?"

"Yeah, dude. And then I said that if he didn't get lost soon, I was going to kick his ass."

"You were going to kick his ass?"

"You should have seen the look on his face!"

"Tell me what you said again," Khalid would say.

Aziz or Emal would open his mouth, but before he could utter a word Khalid would add, "How did you say that in English? Because I'm sure the kid who stole your seat doesn't speak Pashtu."

Ha! We'd stumble up the street laughing. We all knew the truth: None of us was able to carry on long conversations in English with anyone. Once we got to our uncles' house one of us would make peanut butter and jelly sandwiches and another one would get six glasses out of the cupboard. We had been told that all American children love peanut butter and jelly sandwiches and ate them with milk. From the beginning, I liked my PB&J with orange juice, which would make Najiba cross.

"Americans drink milk with their sandwiches. You have to drink *milk*," she would insist. But I preferred orange juice. I realized I would have to accept that I was not like the rest of them. Eventually, I gave up PB&Js altogether, in order to avoid that conversation.

We had figured out that no one was going to know if we watched a little TV; that there was no alarm at the Professor's office that would go off if we touched the set while he was at work. So we decided we would watch a single episode of *Saved by the Bell* every day after school. Emal was skinny, with a long, thin face; we said he looked like Screech Powers, the nerdy kid. Khalid was stocky, with dimples and white teeth. We said he looked like A.C., the jock. Najiba, Jamila, and I, with our dark hair, brown eyes, and baggy dark T-shirts and pants, didn't look like any teen-age American girl on TV.

We allowed ourselves one show. We didn't dare watch another, in case the Professor came home and discovered that the TV was still warm. By four-thirty we would be sitting at the dining room table or on the living room sofa doing our homework. When the Professor returned from work around six o'clock it was as if he'd entered a study hall.

S E V E N

A year passed, then two. By the second year we spoke English, although I was still too shy to speak up in class. Once, when I was asked a question in chemistry, without thinking I stood up beside my desk, as I had learned to do in Pakistan, and answered in Urdu. Did my classmates snicker? I don't remember. I do remember that Mr. Ping, the teacher, encouraged me to answer in English next time. I sank back into my seat, turning pink.

The most difficult part of my life those first few years was that, much as I tried to obey my uncles, I always seemed to be doing something that would cause a stir. My senior year, in AP English, I decided to write my thesis comparing *Romeo and Juliet* to *Laila Majnu*, a much older Pashtun folktale of young lovers who are doomed never to be together.

In Afghanistan the tale is passed down from mother to daughter. Afghan women very rarely read or write, so the story is memorized, and has become part of Pashtun oral history. My aunt Babo used to tell it to us when we lived in Pakistan. We would sit on the veranda and drink tea. I would sit closest to her; I didn't want to miss a single word. As the eldest daughter in my family, I had the responsibility to learn the tale so that I could pass it on to my daughters, continuing the tradition of my great-great-grandmothers. It could take three or four days to tell one of these tales. She would tell us half an hour's worth before she would need to stop and prepare tea for the men or make a meal or sweep the floors. The next day she would sit us down and resume right where she'd left off.

When we read *Romeo and Juliet* in high school, I was shocked by how similar this story was to *Laila Majnu*—the young lovers, the family disapproval, the desperation to be together, the tragic ending. One day after class I approached Mrs. Johnson, who was sitting at her desk marking papers.

"I think Shakespeare stole the story of *Romeo and Juliet* from my people, and I would like to write my senior thesis on this."

"Wow! That is some claim! What makes you think that?" She put her pen down and leaned toward me. She was a tiny, middle-aged lady, kind and enthusiastic.

I briefly told her the tale, and how it had been around for centuries, and how Babo used to tell it to us between chores. Her eyes brightened as I spoke. When I finished she clapped her hands together. "This is wonderful," she said. "Work out an outline and let's have another chat once I look at that. I'd like you to present this to the class."

"You mean . . . stand up in front of the whole class?" Impossible, I thought. Only a few theses were chosen for presentations. It was considered a great honor. It also meant standing in front of the class speaking English for the entire period, fifty minutes.

"But you must. This is such a unique angle. I know you can do it."

"I wish I had the same faith in myself," I replied.

That day on the bus I leaned my head against the window and fretted. Khalid had graduated and was now in college. Najiba and Jamila were in high school now, along with Aziz, Emal, and me. They chattered with one another in Pashtu. They should be speaking English, I thought. We passed a video store and suddenly I had an idea. Indians had made a Bollywood movie of this folklore, called *Laila Majnu*. I would ask Uncle A to rent it for me, and then I could show clips to the class. The clips would take up most of the fifty minutes. I would only have to talk for twenty minutes, thirty max. The fewer minutes I imagined myself talking in front of the class, the happier I felt. The next day after class I told Ms. Johnson about my movie-rental idea. She thought it was brilliant.

That night, when he came home from work, I told Uncle A about *Romeo and Juliet* and how I was convinced Shakespeare had stolen the idea from the Afghans and how Ms. Johnson thought my idea was genius and how I was only one of a few students who'd been asked to present my thesis to the class, and how I wanted to round out my speech with clips from the Indian movie of *Laila Majnu* and could he please rent the movie for me so that I could start writing?

Uncle A nodded as he listened, then said he would discuss it with the Professor. Uncle A was a master at the inscrutable Pashtun expression. I couldn't tell what he was thinking, but I assumed he would say yes, because this was for an important school paper. Hadn't he told us eight thousand times since the day we arrived that he and the Professor expected us to excel at school? Wasn't that the entire reason we left our mothers and home in Afghanistan and came to America?

A few days passed, and neither the Professor nor Uncle A said anything to me. I thought perhaps they had forgotten about it, and so I tried to work up the courage to ask them again. Then it was Sunday, and we sat down for our usual, much dreaded Sunday meeting. Before I'd fully settled into my chair, the Professor demanded, "Why are you obsessed with this love story?"

He looked directly at me. Usually the Professor addressed all of us.

"It's part of my presentation for English class. My thesis," I explained. "Ms. Johnson asked me, and I—"

"Why did you choose a love story?"

"We are reading *Romeo and Juliet* in class," I said. Najiba and the others looked at me, wide-eyed. What had I done to be singled out this way again?

"Is there a boy in your class that you like? Is that what this is about?"

"It was a class assignment."

"Who is this boy that you love?"

"There is no boy. I just wanted to share my culture," I said quietly, mortified.

"You know I didn't bring you here so you could fall in love with a boy in your class and watch Indian movies together. I didn't bring you to America so you could hanky-panky." I felt hot shame burning my face. I had no idea what *hanky-panky* meant, but from the disgust on his face, I knew it was not anything a good Pashtun woman should ever be accused of.

There was nothing I could say. The Professor and Uncle A leaned forward on their forearms. They thought I was lying. Everything that came out of my mouth sounded feeble, ridiculous. Uncle A asked whether I was going to marry this boy. The Professor threatened to send me back to the village to get me married, to control my going wild, and told me how shameful it would be to waste the chance of a lifetime this way.

I returned to Ms. Johnson in tears. I told her I couldn't do the presentation because it was not going to be possible to rent the movie.

"What do you mean not possible? Did you try all the video stores? Maybe Movie Madness has it. They have a lot of older foreign films."

"No, no, it's not that." I started to cry. "It's just not possible."

"But why, Saima? What's happened?"

I felt the tears in my eyes. It would shame my family to tell her anything about what went on at home. I couldn't possibly share with her my uncles' disapproval, or try to describe the shame I felt at being singled out in the Sunday meeting. "My uncles forbid it," I said.

"Would you like me to talk to them about it?" asked Ms. Johnson.

"No!" I cried.

"Or I could write them a note and tell them that you're renting the movie for your thesis."

"That won't work either," I said. If they knew I was talking to an outsider about this, they would be even more furious.

In the end, Ms. Johnson rented *Laila Majnu* for me. English was the final period of the day, and I was the last one to present. I stood up in my loose T-shirt and pants, with my scar between my eyebrows, and told the class about the similarities between *Romeo and Juliet* and *Laila Majnu*, about Afghan women and the tales they memorize, about Babo and her gift for recitation. About how there were no libraries where I grew up, except the human ones, and how stories were passed to the next generation through memorization. The bell rang, but no one moved. They sat

and listened, and when it was over a boy whose name I can no longer recall, the smartest boy in the class and the one whom I always thought of
as my competition, came up to me as I was putting my papers back into
my notebook. He was tall, with glasses and long brown hair. "Saima," he
said, "that was one of the most interesting and arresting presentations
I've ever seen. You did an amazing job." I didn't understand his use of
"arresting presentation" at the time, but I understood his tone and was
very happy to hear it. Later I would realize that that was probably the
first time most of my classmates had heard about a culture and people
where it was still the norm to pass on cultural history and wisdom ver-
bally and through folklore songs.

IN THOSE FIRST years, I constantly forgave my uncles. It must have
been easier for them when we first arrived, when we must have seemed
like children. I had been fifteen—old enough to be married with a couple
of kids in Afghanistan—but I was small, quiet, and had an amazing ability to fold into myself physically, to become almost unnoticeable. After a
few years of eating healthy American food, we had grown a lot. We were
all true teenagers now, with pimples and bad moods. What were they to
do? I imagine they were afraid that we'd become too hard to control, and
that by being even stricter they would be preventing us from becoming
too Americanized and forgetting our life mission.

I might have continued making excuses for them, but then, at another
Sunday meeting, the Professor announced that the worst thing imagin-
able had happened, and that he was shamed beyond repair. He glared at
me. His fists were on the table. The others bent their heads reflexively.

"A boy called for you," he said.

For a split second I thought they had conspired against me by making up something so insane. I thought they wanted to teach the others a
lesson and to use me as an example. I honestly didn't believe anyone had
rung—we weren't even allowed to answer the phone.

"A boy called this house and asked for Saima. Who is he?"

"I don't know," I replied.

"I knew you could not be trusted with all the freedoms we gave you by bringing you here. You have become exactly what I was afraid you would become."

"I swear I don't know any boys," I pleaded.

"You can no longer be trusted. I don't see any reasons at all why I shouldn't send you back to the village. Let them handle you the way you are meant to be handled." The Professor had a way of saying exactly what would cut the deepest.

Shame and dread rose in me like a poisonous cloud, a familiar feeling. He had to know that I lived in constant terror of being sent back to what I perceived to be the cursed life of an Afghan woman. I had believed that once I came to America, that fear would leave me and I could relax enough to find my destiny in my new home—but it had not been that easy, especially with my uncles constantly threatening to take away my newfound liberties. I thought, I will never regain their trust. I should ask them just to send me back to Afghanistan immediately. I should just get it over with and leave here right now. But then another feeling rose in me, an alien one. I didn't know any boys who would have called me. But even if I had, why did my uncles insist on making such a harmless thing seem so dishonorable and dirty? Knowing how important virtue is for a Pashtun woman, why did they always attack mine for no reason? Having done nothing wrong, I let myself be furious at my uncles for the first time. The anger was liberating and scary at the same time.

While I sat through yet another Sunday meeting, something amazing and life-altering was happening inside of me. We Pashtuns are famous for our temper and destructive anger. When we feel slighted or insulted, we take revenge, even if it means our own death—if we think it is necessary, we will gladly give our lives in the name of avenging whatever or whoever offended us. My uncles had truly insulted me, and for the first time I saw their offensive mind-set clearly. For a second, I am sure, murder passed through my eyes. But then something miraculous occurred: The American in me rose up to the Pashtun in me and saw the challenge in my uncles' treatment of me. Instead of being angry at their implications that I was a woman of low morals who could not be trusted with freedoms, I decided that I would make it one of my life's goals to prove them wrong—to show them that I was capable of more than they had ever allowed me to envision for my future. The goal has fueled me time and time again. But little did I know then that I was embarking on a journey toward a destiny so far removed from the fate any Pashtun woman is born into.

At school the next day I told Kristen what had happened. I asked her if she knew who had called me.

"Probably Jason," she said. We were walking to the bus after class. "He told me he missed math and needed to get the homework assignment from you."

"But how did he get my number?"

"I gave it to him," she said.

"My uncles are so mad," I said. "They're totally . . . pissed off."

For a moment I thought she was going to comment on me saying "pissed off"—something I had never said before. She laughed and clapped her hands together. She was always on the lookout for evidence that I was becoming a real American teenager.

"Did you tell them Jason is a football player?" she said. "He's, like, the most popular guy in our class." I realized how confusing it must have been for the Americans around me to learn that what their parents might consider a good thing would send my uncles through the roof.

$\mathscr{E}$IGHT

I had decided to ask my uncles to send me back to the village.

The Professor and Uncle A had been more than generous in bringing us to Portland and arranging for our education, but after I enrolled at the Professor's college, I became increasingly aware of the hypocrisy in their behavior. When it came to our learning, they treated the boys and girls equally, but outside of the classroom they expected the girls to behave like traditional Pashtun females and the boys to behave, well, like boys. It is something I have realized over and over again throughout the years: Our uncles offered us a magnificent education, but they never counted on us applying what we learned to our own lives.

I'd made some friends of my own, other Muslim girls, but I wasn't allowed to go to their homes for dinner unless they ate really early. I had a 9:00 P.M. curfew—in college. But my brother and male cousins had no curfew. Uncle A had even bought another house into which he moved the boys. So now the girls lived in one house with the uncles and the boys lived in the other house by themselves. One of my girlfriends once told me that the boys were famous on campus for their parties. At family barbecues I would look at the American girls the boys invited, fuming inside that we weren't even allowed to have any guys call us, while their girlfriends were welcomed and fed at our family dinner table.

The injustice and inequality got under my skin. I was living in America, receiving an American education, and taking courses in human rights and women's studies, while the Professor and Uncle A treated me no differently than if I had stayed in the village in Afghanistan. Actually, it would have been easier to live with this hypocrisy in the village, where I wouldn't have known any better. I expected to be treated like a second-class citizen in Afghanistan, but it was hard to stomach it in Portland. So we fought, loudly. I cried and screamed at them. Every word out of my mouth would have earned me a stoning in Afghanistan; I'm sure my uncles would have been happy to do the honors. Conflicts were still handled at Sunday meetings. For years at those meetings I was the subject: my strong-willed nature, my refusal to be thankful to them for having given me the education to know the freedoms I had only dreamed of in Pakistan. Their plan had been simple: to educate us, make us citizens, and then send us back to marry some son of distant or not-so-distant cousins and bring him to America, where he could find a job, make money, and send it back home so that the whole tribe could benefit and prosper. I was expected to sacrifice my personal happiness for the good of the community—a true Pashtun sentiment. To this day, the memories of those Sunday nights make me feel sick to my stomach. Oh, how I envied the boys for being able to drive off to their home after those meetings!

I GRADUATED WITH a bachelor's degree in political science and was hired at a language agency. I was only allowed to take this job because the agency was run by an old lady who operated it out of her house. The Professor came to the interview with me to question the owner and made sure her answers were satisfactory before he allowed me to work there. I was expected to drive straight to her home in the morning, then straight home after work. I was the office manager, supervising a staff of four people who fielded calls for interpreters.

One Friday afternoon just as we were getting ready to leave for the day, one of our clients called for a Russian interpreter, whom they would need the very next morning at seven o'clock. Our usual Russian interpreter was Vasily, a textbook Russian. He was enormous, at six feet five and heavily muscled, a stern-faced, blue-eyed blond. He seemed to have made it a practice never to smile and was famous among the staff for being difficult. No one wanted to contact him so late for such an early appointment. They spent forty-five minutes trying to find alternatives and arguing over who should make the call, but I didn't have time for that nonsense and was anxious to get on the road. My uncles knew what time I got off work. More than once when the traffic had been bad and I'd return home late the Professor would be waiting, ready to pounce. "Where have you been? You get off at six o'clock and now it is six-thirty and it's a fifteen-minute drive home!"

I called and told Vasily we would need him at 7:00 A.M. and were sorry for the late notice. He laughed. Was I out of my mind? It was Friday night and he required a few days' notice before weekend appointments. But he said he'd take it, as long as I agreed to have dinner with him. Was *he* out of his mind? I told him not that night, but one day, when hell froze over, or when my uncles allowed me to date a Russian. The odds of hell freezing over were significantly better. Even though at first I didn't give in to his repeated invitations to dinner, he took the appointment.

Surprisingly, Vasily turned out to be charming and kind, and we began a strange relationship. I was almost twenty-three, but I had no concept of what it meant to have a boyfriend. He could only call me at work and we could only meet for lunch—and even then, he would bring me lunch and we would eat at my office. We watched one movie, Disney's *Tarzan*, during which I wept noisily. I tried to explain between hiccups that it was something about the music—Phil Collins singing about two worlds and one family. Vasily was baffled. Here he was, this menacing Slav, watching a matinee of an animated movie with a sobbing Afghan woman who wouldn't even let him try to comfort her by putting his arms around her.

Sex was out of the question, as was kissing and hugging. When I had known him for almost six months, I let him hold my hand once as we were leaving a restaurant, but I made him promise that he wouldn't take that to mean that it would go any further. Vasily believed it must be true love. "If any of my ex-girlfriends had ever said no to sex," he said, "my immediate question would have been 'Then why am I buying you dinner?'"

"You don't need to buy me dinner," I said, surprised. "I can buy my own dinner."

He was the first man to buy me jewelry: a necklace with a gold Red Wing charm, in honor of his favorite hockey team. He even told his mother, who lived in Ukraine, that he was going to marry me. He reported with some satisfaction that she was hysterical with fear that the men in my family were going to track him down and kill him.

I was never emotional about my relationship with Vasily, which I think is what made it so easy for me to draw boundaries. I was logical in my decision to see him, and never held what the Russian army had done to my people against him. For one thing, I knew that the Soviet government at the time of the invasion was not a democracy, elected by the people, and therefore did not represent a national consent to invade. For another thing, even if the public of the Soviet Union had been asked to vote on the matter, Vasily would have been too young to even remember the decision. How could I fault him for what he was never a part of? But my uncles indeed would have killed Vasily in a heartbeat, if they had been in a country that allowed honor killing. Luckily for me they were in America, not Afghanistan, when they eventually found out about him.

I think Vasily was the first person to whom I could express what I really wanted to say to my uncles. He would let me fume, and I knew he would never judge or tell anyone how ungrateful I was being toward my uncles. I did appreciate what they did for my life, but, ultimately, they asked me to give up the one thing I had wanted to have in America: a chance to find my destiny, uncontrolled.

So before they ended my dream of a life here, I decided, I was going to take control one last time, by asking them to send me back to the village. I could not handle living in America with the constant feeling that my days of freedom were numbered. I didn't want to be forced to return to marry. I was not going to let them win by getting me citizenship only to bring over a boy of their choice to replace them as the man meant to control me.

Before I could find the courage to ask them to send me back to Afghanistan, Uncle A found out about Vasily. The years-long Sunday-meeting tradition was broken, because on a Thursday night we were all told to meet in the dining room. That should have been my first clue that the gloves were about to come off. Even today, I think about that fateful day and I tremble.

They were enraged, and thought I was seeing Vasily only as a rebellion against them, and that I had chosen the most heinous country I could think of and picked the blue-eyed devil that they remembered from the Soviet invasion. All to get back at them. In retrospect, I can see why they thought that. But I was appalled by their closed-mindedness and their hypocrisy; although they talked with their American friends as if they were liberal, and expected American society to be tolerant of them, they were not tolerant of others. I knew that it was not going to be long before they took drastic measures to get me under control. If they had only tried to shame me for befriending a member of the opposite sex, something that is forbidden in Pashtun culture, I would have stopped seeing Vasily. Instead, they tried to shame me by casting him as responsible for my father's disappearance. The newly educated and worldly Saima knew this made no sense, whereas as a Pashtun, I knew the rules of *Pashtunwali*; I was a part of that society and was obliged to accept their rules.

I truly believe I would have ended up with a totally different life if the Professor had uttered any sentence other than the one he did: "Saima, your father would be ashamed of you." Those eight words changed the course of my life, by igniting the fierce Pashtun pride that had lain dormant in my heart since the day my father walked out of our house in his slippers. My ears started ringing when I heard the hatred in his tone and saw the disgust on Uncle A's face. He said other things, too, and gratefully I did not hear any of them, because my heart was beating so loudly, I couldn't hear anything over the roar of it in my head. I actually envisioned how easy it would have been for that to happen and kill me on the spot. I knew that what I had to do was going to require every ounce of the strength given to me by my father and grandfather. I knew I had not done what they were accusing me of. I knew that my father would *not* have been ashamed of me, but he would have been ashamed of how his brothers were treating me. I felt this to be the ultimate truth;

my father loved me and would have known that I was not a woman with loose or misguided morals. Had he been sitting there at the dining table, he would have protected me. My certainty of that fact gave me the courage I had been lacking all those years when I had lived in terror of being shoved into a life I didn't want; when I had been too much of a coward to stand up for myself. I would have loved to have been able to rise to my feet for what I said next, but I couldn't feel my legs. "Enough!" I said quietly, looking Uncle A squarely in the eyes.

"I will forgive you everything you have said to me until this day because you are my father's brothers, no matter how much that fact hurts me. But from this day forward, your words will never touch me or make me feel dirty and disgusting. I will not say any of the things I want to say because you are my Baba's children, and it would be disrespectful to him."

I didn't dare look at anybody else around the table, because I knew the horror on the faces of Najiba or any of the others would weaken my resolve, and if I lost that, I would have nothing to live for. I rose from the table, got my car keys, and started walking out. I didn't know where I was going; I just needed to leave my uncles' house.

Uncle A followed me to the door, trailed by a crying Najiba, who stopped at the doorstep.

"Where do you think you are going?" he asked icily.

"Out. I can't take this anymore," I answered with all my heart.

"If you walk out this door right now, you will never be allowed inside again, and you will never be allowed into the family either," he threatened calmly.

"I know," I said, just as calmly.

I looked up the steps again at Najiba standing there crying. Leaving her was one of the hardest things I've ever done, but I made a silent promise to her then; I would come back for her as soon as I could. Three years later, I did. But on that first night, I got into my car and drove away alone, leaving everything behind, just as I had done as a child more than a decade before. The difference was that I was in a Honda and not on a camel; I was a college graduate and not a child.

NINE

I was officially a disgrace to my family, in the United States and in Afghanistan and Pakistan. My uncles told everyone who would listen that I had moved out to live with my Russian boyfriend. For several years Mamai and I didn't speak.

I had not moved in with Vasily. He had wanted me to, but it had never been an option for me. The day I drove away from my uncles' house I broke up with him. I did not leave my family to move in with another man. My decision to be on my own had nothing to do with something as trivial as a boyfriend.

After staying a few days with a friend, I moved into the bottom floor of a house in Northeast Portland, an area that was at that time predominantly lower-class, the opposite of Southwest Portland, where I had lived until then. I decided to move into that area because I knew my uncles' prejudices; they would never wander off from Southwest Portland to look for me in Northeast. I had so much to learn about life. My landlord, Jimmy, had to show me where the grocery store was, where to buy gas, and how to get to my new job, since I had left the language agency and started working in an office downtown. I had to learn about utilities. Until I got my own place I never realized you had to pay for water—we never paid for it in Afghanistan.

Far from leading the raunchy American life my uncles gossiped about,

I was probably clinically depressed for a few years after being cast out from my family. In Pashtun culture, if you commit a crime or an offense against the community in which you live, the *shura,* a gathering of the residents, much like a jury of peers, decides to burn your house and, in some cases, kick you out of the village. I felt like I had been tried in the court of *Pashtunwali* and punished accordingly. I felt guilty for not following the ways of my loving Baba, who had protected me in his soft embrace. I slept long hours and lost weight. My days were dull and identical: I went to work, grabbed some takeout on the way home, ate it sitting in front of the TV, and went to bed. When I lived with my uncles and we battled over my 9:00 P.M. curfew I used to think, If I could just stay out until eleven, my life would be so much more fun. Suddenly I could stay out as late as I liked, but I didn't care. I was asleep by nine. I made a lot of tea, but I don't think I turned on the oven even once the whole time I lived there.

I'd fought for my freedom, achieved it, and then I withdrew from life. I didn't go on dates. I didn't travel. I didn't even go to the homes of my girlfriends. I didn't go to clubs, the very activity my uncles had claimed was the reason I had left their home, until nearly three years later—and even then it was only to spend time with my brother and his friends. I had no desire to enjoy my newly acquired liberties, because I felt the price I had paid for them was too great.

I slept a lot to try to avoid dwelling on my new reality and my choice to have walked away. In Afghanistan and Pakistan I'd grown up in a house with siblings, cousins, aunts, uncles, and grandparents. In the United States I'd spent every night eating dinner with seven people. Now I was completely alone, except for Jimmy, the landlord, who was rarely there and who certainly wasn't a replacement for a family. My father was long dead; my mother was all the way over in Pakistan, raging and ashamed at the trouble I was causing; my uncles had declared me the source of irreparable family embarrassment; my brother was busy living his own American life; and my sister, in her typical way, hid her feelings, but I know how I would have felt in her place—abandoned, forgotten.

Who is an Afghan woman without her family? I had no idea.

I had no real understanding of what an American woman was capable of doing, of what choices she had, but I wanted to find out. As a Pashtun female, from the age of about six I had been told how to behave, what it meant to be a Pashtun woman. Part of me was very secure and comfortable with this role, because I knew so much about it. Another, newer part of me wanted me to be an American woman—free, educated, resourceful, and most of all, independent. This was a role I didn't know half as much about, which made it difficult for me to balance the two parts. I wanted to take the good from the Pashtun in me and combine it with these new rights and choices I had been offered as an American—to blend the two to make a perfect woman, or at least a woman who would be perfectly me. To be honest with myself is to recognize that I also wanted to earn the envy of my friends back home, who believed I was enjoying an unimaginably carefree and happy life.

TO THIS DAY, my uncles have not forgiven me for walking out on their insanity in order to preserve my own sanity. I've realized that they inadvertently gave me the tools—education and anger—that I needed to become who I am. For that, I'm willing to spare them shame by dwelling no further on what they did to me.

I HAD STARTED working at a downtown import-export company that dealt mostly with soybeans and corn. Like hundreds of other carefree women all around me, I spent my lunch hour shopping. But freedom was not as sweet as I had imagined.

I met Greg on a setup date. I was twenty-four; he was twenty-one. He'd made some miscalculations in life that made him more mature than other guys his age. He had a three-year-old son, Riley, with an ex-girlfriend from high school with whom he shared custody, and was working his way through college as a car salesman. On our second date he asked me to marry him. I didn't want to hurt his feelings by laughing. Instead, I told him to ask me again in five years.

Greg's mother was English, and having lived in England until only a few years before, Greg retained enough of his British accent to grab my attention. He had seen me at the house of one of my coworkers when I was dropping her off one day. He was visiting her brother. That first meeting took less than two minutes; I was in a rush to get back on the road. He begged my coworker to set us up, so she in turn begged me to go out on one date, just one—and the rest, as they say, is history—an explosive but loving history.

Over the years we dated Greg was always there for me, holding me while I raged and sobbed over whatever hatred the uncles were circulating about me. My fury was like an emotional roadside bomb—it injured whoever came upon me. Often, it was Greg. I said the cruelest things to him. He understood that it was not about him and that I loved him for his unconditional support. Most nights, he'd come over after work and make me tea and my favorite chicken dish, draw me a warm bath and light some candles, then make sure I was in the tub before letting himself out. I took hundreds of baths during those first years, trying to soak away my stress and anger, hoping that it would disappear down the drain with the soapy water. But of course it didn't, and I felt restless and incomplete, even though I had the undying love of a wonderful man, in addition to a job where I was challenged daily to learn something new.

Greg was the most caring man I'd ever met. And yet, for reasons I couldn't articulate, even to myself, I couldn't imagine marrying him. I knew he deserved more than I could ever offer him. I had a jaded idea of the relationship between a man and a woman, and he was the first person with whom I had ever explored that. I couldn't seem to compromise on the littlest things, because I feared relinquishing any control, to Greg or anyone. Now, I understand that give-and-take is a necessary part of a healthy relationship. At that time, however, I was terrified that if I gave even a little of myself, I would be taken completely, again.

Our differences over money also got in the way. I had to be financially independent. I worked forty hours a week, lived frugally, and saved as much as I could. I needed to know that I could take care of myself. What kept me up at night was the fear that one day I would have to go crawling back to the uncles because I couldn't pay my rent and bills. Greg lived paycheck to paycheck. He would get a $500 bonus and want to splurge.

The only time I was aware of him making an effort to save was for an engagement ring for me. This should have made me feel better—look, he *is* capable of being careful with his money—but I felt extremely anxious whenever I thought about the moment when he would sink to one knee and produce the little velvet box, forcing me to make a choice between love and what I thought was my personal freedom.

So I lived in dread that he would propose to me and end a perfectly good relationship. When he would suggest we go to our favorite restaurant for dinner, I would worry that he was looking for a special occasion so I would make excuses about not being hungry. We would often go away for the weekend, but during the last few months of our relationship I would come up with reasons why I couldn't make it: "Greg, we can't go next weekend! Banana Republic is having a *huge* sale!" I knew that I couldn't keep this up for much longer and that I would have to deal with the issue one day. I was not looking forward to it.

In the meantime, I decided to do all I could to bring the two women who were most important to me back into my life: Najiba, whom I'd had to leave with our uncles almost three years earlier, and Mamai. My mother's life had been abysmal, in the typical Afghan way. After we'd left for America she'd lived with one of our uncles, his wife, and their two children—first in Peshawar, then in Abbottabad. She had had no rights, but that was not an unusual fate for a woman in Afghanistan. Mamai was required to ask permission to do everything, whether it was going shopping, visiting a friend, or seeing a doctor. No one cared that she'd lost her husband because of the war; there were tens of thousands of Afghan widows just like her, and she did not warrant any special considerations.

The uncles with whom she lived didn't believe in socializing, and at heart Mamai was a gregarious, fun-loving woman. They discouraged her from having friends over and wouldn't allow her to visit them. She was miserable, but didn't believe she had a right to happiness, or to be treated any differently. It drove me crazy to think of my own mother so oppressed and not believing that it was wrong. When I finally got in touch with her and encouraged her to press the uncles into at least allowing her some friendships, she refused. She said she didn't want to cause any trouble. There I was in Portland, able to question everything. Back in Pakistan, my mother questioned nothing. I knew she had turned on me and had no sympathy for what I had struggled to achieve, for my independence. Would she even appreciate the liberties I wanted to give her?

Getting Najiba from Southwest Portland to Northeast Portland turned out to be a lot easier: I told her our father's three children should live together, so Khalid, she, and I moved into a three-bedroom town house close to downtown where we all worked and started living a blissfully happy life; for the first time I didn't dread the thought of coming home. Uncle A had gotten married and wanted to enjoy married life with his wife without worrying about keeping an eye on Najiba, which is why he had let Najiba go so easily.

Bringing my mother to the United States was going to be a lot more difficult.

First I had to become a U.S. citizen. For years I had put off the decision. To become a citizen in America, I would have to give up the citizenship of Afghanistan. While I was a refugee in Pakistan, I never made fake papers, like hundreds of other refugees did in order to avoid harassment by the Pakistani police. I thought, If I hadn't denounced my Afghan citizenship then, why would I do so now? In my new adopted country no one was harassing me, and I could hold on to the Afghan in me and still be a good U.S. resident. I paid my taxes and obeyed all the laws of the land. The only thing I wasn't able to do was vote; like many U.S. citizens, I really didn't think much about it. But one thing I couldn't do as a resident was bring my mother to the land of the free. So I filed the papers and gave up the last physical symbol of being an Afghan—my green afghan passport; now I was an American, bearer of a much coveted blue passport.

After I had filed immigration papers to bring Mamai to Portland and her request for a visa to the United States was approved, Najiba flew to Peshawar to collect her.

The night she was due to arrive, Greg and I were sitting in the living room of the town house in Portland where I lived with Khalid and Najiba, finishing our tea. This was before my siblings and I bought a house, in which we hoped Mamai would feel more at home, as if that were possible. Greg's son, Riley, was playing an elaborate private game with his Transformers in front of the TV. I took my teacup to the sink and picked up my purse and keys. I said I had to go to the airport to pick up my mother and needed to say good night.

"Okay, let me get Riley. We'll all go," Greg said.

"I don't think that's a good idea," I said.

"You're not going to tell her about me, are you?"

"Not right away," I replied. I went up to where he was sitting next to Riley and gave him a hug to reassure him. "Don't jump to conclusions. I just don't think she's ready for the culture shock. This isn't the same as my meeting your mom. She doesn't even know what a boyfriend is and she doesn't know for sure that I have one."

"All right." I could hear the uncertainty in his voice. Greg was accommodating to a fault; it was his best and worst quality, the quality I both cherished and held against him. He told Riley they needed to go. I watched him place his hands on his small son's shoulders. I watched the way he carefully handled the toys. "I'll do what you ask of me," he said, looking away. "But I'm afraid things are going to change here. I wouldn't be able to handle not seeing you every day."

I bit my lip, said nothing, and tried not to be irritated. Like the drama with my uncles, this had nothing to do with Greg, with us. I was trying to give my mother—whom I hadn't seen or spoken to in years—time to get acclimated to this entirely new land and way of living. I remembered how it felt the first time I walked out of a U.S. airport, into, well, all that is America.

Mamai was fifty, old by Afghan standards. She had spent most of her life beneath the veil, and since our exodus from Afghanistan to Pakistan when she was just thirty had never exchanged words with a man to whom she was not related. If I showed up with Greg, Mamai would be horrified. She would see him as the greatest dishonor brought upon my father's name. She would believe, finally, that all the bad things the rest of my family had said about me were indeed true.

Khalid and I drove to the airport alone to pick up Najiba and Mamai. She followed Najiba as they pressed through the crowd of arriving passengers. I would not have recognized my mother had she not been dressed like a Pashtun woman in baggy black cotton pants, a long forest-green dress, and a big white scarf. I was surprised to see that on her feet she wore a pair of white tennis shoes. I was sure they'd come from Najiba, who'd likely lent them to her for the long trip. I poked Khalid and said, "Look! Our mother is already turning into an Oregonian. She doesn't care that she's wearing the wrong shoes with her outfit!"

Najiba carried both their carry-ons, leading Mamai out of the terminal. Mamai glimpsed Khalid and threw her arms around him, her handsome son, before hugging me nervously. I was stunned by how small she seemed, how shrunken. I was wearing my favorite shoes at the time, a pair of four-inch platform sandals. I loved how tall they made me, but I should never have worn them to pick up Mamai. In Pashtun culture, if a girl is taller than her mother, it is a sign of disrespect to stand beside her. I stood a good six inches above her.

We drove back to our town house in silence. When inside, she gave the place a quick once-over, then removed her jacket with resignation. In Pakistan her life was wretched, but she had lived in a large compound, with a big garden studded with mulberry and mango trees. Our town house was nice enough for three young adults, but it was less than a couple of miles from downtown, and on a busy street. Streetlights shone in the windows at night.

"Where is the yard?" she asked.

We told her there was no yard. But there was a swimming pool and a gym.

"Why is the kitchen inside the house?" she wanted to know.

We told her that Americans didn't have separate kitchen buildings. We directed her downstairs to the master bedroom, which she would share with Najiba, and she looked panic-stricken. There are no basements where we come from. The closest word in Pashtu—and it's a Farsi word actually—is *zarzaminee*, literally "under the earth." A lot of jail-houses are in *zarzaminee*. As she went down the stairs, I wondered if she viewed the master bedroom as her prison. That is not what I wanted her to feel about her new home in the United States.

On the third day Greg came over to meet her. Khalid sat on the sofa with Najiba, chatting and watching TV. Mamai perched on the edge of a chair, gazing at the Pres-to-Log in the fireplace, amazed that I was able to light it with a single match. "What will the Americans think of next?" she loved to say during those first few weeks.

I introduced Greg as a friend. He said hello and couldn't decide whether he should offer his hand to her. She wrapped her white scarf around the bottom of her face and gazed at the floor. She spoke no English, and he was not one of the men in her family. She wanted nothing to do with him.

Greg went into the kitchen and filled the teakettle with water. He returned with a tray bearing a silver pot of green tea and three white cups. He sat down next to me and poured me some tea. Mamai sensed what he was to me. I could feel her knowledge of our situation come on like a sudden fever. She abruptly stood up and scuttled downstairs.

Greg held the teapot in one hand, a cup and saucer in the other. He opened his mouth to say something. I sighed loudly and went after her. Downstairs Mamai was sobbing. I asked her what was going on. As if addressing the frayed ends of her scarf, she told me to send my brother down.

"There's no reason you can't talk to me," I said. "What's wrong?"

"Tell Alak to come here now." *Alak* is Pashtu for "boy." Just as I was always Angelee, Khalid was Alak.

Back upstairs, Najiba and Khalid were drinking tea with Greg. Someone had put out a bowl of pistachios. I didn't try to hide my irritation. Mamai would not be here if I had not had the resolve to rescue her from the tyranny of the Pashtun men in her life and to give her the better existence she deserved. I had puzzled out the paperwork, filed it, and kept after it.

"She wants to talk to her son!" I told Khalid.

After Khalid ambled downstairs I dropped onto the sofa beside Najiba. "Are you happy now, Greg?" I asked sarcastically.

"It's the jet lag," said Najiba, inspecting the ends of her long black hair. Najiba was the complacent daughter, the good daughter, the peacemaker, the angel. She offered around the bowl of pistachios.

"Not likely," I retorted.

Khalid was laughing as he came upstairs. "Mamai wants me to kick Greg out of the house and beat you up," he said.

"You should, according to your cultural duties," I replied.

"No, my cultural duty would be to kill both of you."

"This is ridiculous," I said. "She's going to have to get used to America, and to the fact that her children are grown and might have boyfriends and girlfriends."

"What did you tell her?" Greg asked Khalid.

"That I would go look for a nice bat to beat you two with."

But Greg wasn't discouraged. He went home but called later that evening to say good night, as though nothing had happened. I couldn't dismiss it so easily. What had I done, bringing this old Pashtun woman to America?

MAMAI, WHOSE NAME is Gul Pari—meaning "angel of the flower" in Pashtu—had been a pretty, vivacious, and spoiled child. She married my father at the relatively late age of seventeen, because her uncle didn't think anyone was good enough for her. So many potential suitors had been turned away that families had stopped asking for her hand. My father's people were from another village, far enough away to have missed the gossip about the girl, now nearly an old maid at seventeen, and the eccentric uncle who cherished her like a daughter. When my grandfather approached Gul Pari's uncle and father on behalf of my father, for some reason he said, Okay, bring your son here and I'll see if my niece and I like him. Seeking the prospective bride's opinion was unheard-of at the time. People thought Mamai's uncle was crazy to worry about her opinion, that he must be joking. He wasn't. My father met my mother before their marriage was finalized; I tease my mom that she must have been the first woman in Afghanistan to have gone on a "date" with her future husband, and how scandalous this must have been.

Although my parents' marriage was short, it was a happy one. My father had a sense of the world. He had studied abroad and traveled through the great capitals of Europe. He told Mamai that he wanted her to make her own choices. He wasn't going to bully her, wasn't going to beat her if she disagreed with him. He wanted her to be a modern woman.

They did their best to understand each other. My father occasionally visited friends in Beirut and Italy. When he returned from his travels he often brought my mother yards of expensive European fabric. It was the early 1970s. The fabrics were like nothing she had ever seen: swirls of hot pink, lime green, and chocolate-brown paisley polyester, or white voile with giant orange and red flowers. He thought she would be delighted. She found the bright European fabrics hideous. I wouldn't make drapes out of this! she thought, but thanked him with a gracious and loving smile.

The wives of his friends wore chic sleeveless A-line shifts and miniskirts. She wore dresses made of yards of heavy silk, royal blue, emerald green, or gold, encrusted with hundreds of tiny mirrors, thousands of pretty beads. Her ensembles were cumbersome and regal. They weighed many pounds. My father wanted my mother to be free to move her arms, to be able to stride through Kabul comfortably, on her way to anywhere she wanted to go. She, on the other hand, preferred her village clothes, weighed down by embellishments. Still, she wanted to please her husband, so she dutifully sewed new dresses and pants—she would never give up wearing pants beneath her dresses—using the hideous European fabric. She would wear her regular traditional clothes while my father was at work. When she heard his VW Bug roaring around the corner at the end of the day, she would quickly change into her new, more modern clothes.

Even though my mother had enjoyed a short marriage to a freethinker, by the time she moved to Portland she had spent many more years living a traditional Afghan life. Was being dragged to America at her relatively advanced age too much for her? Was she going to be able to cope with the freedoms I wished to give her? I had imagined her making friends and giving dinner parties, going to the park with a picnic on a nice day. I had thought that when she saw how free life could be, she would also appreciate my own struggles and desire to have this independence. I had believed that we could finally develop a modern mother-daughter relationship. Was that no less realistic than thinking she was capable of striding through Kabul in a miniskirt?

But within the first week she wanted my brother to fulfill his Pashtun duty and perform an honor killing, merely because I had Greg in my life. This was not a good sign.

Over the next few weeks things improved, but not much. It had taken only a week for her to recover her fierce opinions and compulsion to speak her mind. She never bothered Khalid—as a male, he could do what he wanted. And she never criticized Najiba, who was soft-spoken, slow to anger, and got her way simply by waiting people out.

But I had Greg, a car, a job, shopping dates with friends, dinners out. This life as an American woman was unspeakable to Mamai. She would badger me; demand answers to impossible questions. She would see me in my jeans and short-sleeved T-shirts and demand to know how I could possibly go out in public wearing that. What kind of message did I think I was sending? I understood why she was having issues with my baring my arms in public. In Pashtun culture, women are the protectors of family shame. A woman's behavior can ruin the status a family holds in the community. This strong link between women, pride, and shame is one of the primary reasons why women are so furiously protected and controlled. She disapproved of my going out after dark. No women did so in Afghanistan. It was not just shameful, it was dangerous. I would go to meet a friend for dessert after work, and she would demand, "Why are you going out so late? What are you doing out there?" I tried to be patient. I tried to explain that leaving the house at seven-thirty at night was completely safe and normal, but she wasn't having any of it.

I drew the line when she told me I needed to drop Greg. When she said that if he ever came to our house, she was leaving, I finally had a sit-down with her. I had no intentions of leaving Greg. He had been with me, unconditionally, during my depression follwing the horrible era of the uncles, when I hadn't been able to count on anyone else for support. She pointed out that he wasn't Afghan or Muslim. Yes, I hollered, the exact qualities I love in him. I challenged her to point out a single time he had disrespected me or her. She couldn't. He had never asked me to choose between him and my family, had never held my bad temper against me, and had always let me be who I was. Why would I kick someone like that out of my life? I hated saying this, but I ended my screaming match with Mamai by telling her that I would send her back to Afghanistan if she continued to do what my uncles had been doing before her. I couldn't believe that I was becoming just like my uncles, threatening my mother's rights, when I had only wanted to make her free. It made me doubt my own goodness, to be reminded of how selfish and inflexible I had become.

Later, at his apartment, I shared my doubts with Greg. "I'm just not sure this is going to work," I said.

"It'll just take her some time," he said.

"You don't know her. She says I get my stubborn streak from my dad, but I get it from her. She just covers it up better."

He put his arms around me. "Be patient. In a way, it's a little refreshing to have someone stand up to you. God knows I've fantasized about it many times, but I love you too much to actually do it." He laughed. I pretended to be upset but also found it funny.

Now I had two issues to deal with: my tense relationship with Mamai and the inevitable next step in my relationship with Greg. Although the link between the two was not lost on me, knowing they were connected did not make them any easier to reconcile.

T E N

Each of my father's three children dealt with his disappearance in his or her own way. For years we never discussed or talked much about what had happened or the experience of growing up fatherless in a culture in which you are identified only by who your father is. Khalid dealt with it by taking off for years after we emigrated to be alone and away from anything to do with the family. He avoided us all, and it was only years later that we would re-create the tight bond that the three of us share today. Being the youngest, Najiba doesn't have any memories of our father—what she remembers are the bits and pieces that she has collected through Mamai's stories of him.

I have always wished Najiba would face her feelings about growing up without her own memories of our father while hearing so much about him. She confessed that she hated Afghanistan for taking him, and never wanted to go back to try to reconnect with its people. It made my heart ache to hear her say that. I tried to make her see that our father had made a conscious choice to rebel against the Russians; that he saw something in his people worth giving up his life for.

Unlike Najiba, I wanted to know what that something was. Once I was secure in myself and in the freedoms that I enjoyed in the United States, once I was sure I could defend my rights by myself, I knew I would return to Afghanistan to find out for myself.

In late 2004, twelve years deep in the freedoms of America and perhaps not yet prepared for the return journey, an opportunity—and a choice—presented itself.

It was a gloomy wet day and I was sitting on my sofa in the living room. It was a blue-gray Pacific Northwest twilight, no different from most of the other days of the year. I sat with my feet curled beneath me, staring out the front window at an oak tree that was on the verge of losing its last golden leaves. Khalid and Najiba were still at work. Mamai was in her room, listening to BBC radio. I could hear the round tones of Pashtu burbling from her room. My cell phone rang. It was my friend Ahmed, who had just returned from Afghanistan, where he'd been working as a Farsi interpreter.

"They're desperate for Pashtu speakers over there," he said. "Especially females, especially female natives."

"I'm sure they have plenty of females who speak Pashtu in Afghanistan," I teased.

"Funny. I meant Pashtu-*English* speakers. As far as I know, they don't have even one."

"I knew what you meant," I said.

"You could have a job tomorrow."

Ahmed talked about the rush of working as a translator in a war zone, about the sense of doing work that meant something, about the good pay. I let him ramble on. I considered my less-than-thrilling nine-to-five job at a Japanese export firm downtown, and about the house we'd just bought in the drowsy Portland suburb of Beaverton so that my family could finally be all together.

"Thanks for thinking of me, Ahmed, but this is not a decision that I can make quickly."

I had been thinking about returning for a while—just not considering the *when* or the *how*. I'd never ever imagined I'd be doing anything connected with the U.S. military. Most Afghans, including my own extended family, considered the Americans to be no different from the Soviets. I was already the black sheep of the family; I couldn't imagine their response to my returning to Afghanistan as an employee of the invading infidels. I could hear the phone lines buzzing. What on earth is Saima doing now? She's run off to Afghanistan to revenge her father's death! She's going to use her Pashtu to target insurgents and tell the Americans who to kill! She's going to use her Pashtu to point out spies to the Americans and tell them who to torture!

It was out of the question. Or was it? What were my options? I could have visited my family in the village in Ghanzi Province for a week or two. While this sounded enticing, it also felt limited. I would spend time only with my relatives. The idea that by taking Ahmed up on his offer I could meet hundreds, if not thousands, of regular Afghans from all walks of life, stirred something inside me. It had been so long since I'd felt anything resembling excitement. My thoughts went round and round. I might be able to find out what inspired my father to give up his life to preserve the way of Pashtuns. Just that thought alone caused me to pick up my phone several times and put it back down.

Most of my work at the import-export firm was finished by 10:00 A.M., which gave me plenty of time to stare out the window at the Oregon sky and replay the conversation with Ahmed in my head. At lunch, as usual I walked to Banana Republic, where I looked at the same rack of cream-colored linen jackets every day. What would I be giving up as an adult—and what would I learn about what I had given up as a child?

A few days later I was sitting in a restaurant called Sweet Toma-toes with my friend Seema and her young son, Arsalan, eating a salad when my cell phone rang. I said hello, but the caller answered me in Pashtu. He asked how I was enjoying the weather. I didn't recognize the voice.

"Who is this?" I demanded.

"You don't know who this is?"

"Should I?" I could hear the hostility in my voice. Who was this man? The only male I spoke Pashtu with anymore was my brother. How did this random male Pashtu speaker get my number? I felt my inner Pash-tun female awaken. Why does this man think he can just address me in this way? It completely violated the code of the culture of the language being spoken.

He laughed. "Your friend Ahmed gave me your number."

"You should have introduced yourself in English and explained the reason for your call," I responded.

"I'm sorry; you are right. Ahmed gave me your number and said that I should convince you to come and work for us. There is a great need for female Pashtu speakers, and since you are female, you would be able to dictate the kind of assignment you want and they will do anything to make you happy so you will stay. This is your duty as a female and as an Afghan. We can't expect the American soldiers to know anything about our culture or language. We have to make sure they know, and you can do that like no one else can." I knew he was appealing to my sense of pride and also to the protectiveness I would feel for wanting to make sure my people's interests remained protected. "Now that I know you really do speak Pashtu I'd like to pass your number on to a recruiter who can set up an interview and testing," he continued.

The recruiter phoned a few hours later and volunteered to fill out all my paperwork, including the monstrous SF86 national security form. In three days it was done. I was officially a Category II interpreter, cleared to work for the U.S. Armed Forces in Afghanistan.

I WAS SCHEDULED to travel to Fairfax, Virginia, for a predeployment orientation before being sent to Afghanistan. The night before I left, Mamai and I had our worst argument yet. I can't remember how it started, but I remember telling her that I'd gone to the trouble of bringing her here to enjoy the freedoms that I knew America could give her.

"I wanted you to be able to see a doctor, or go visit your friends or call your sisters whenever you wanted to, without having to ask permission or feel guilty about it. I brought you here to enjoy a good life. I didn't bring you here to mother me. I've been without a mother for over a decade. I'm all grown up now. This isn't the village. It isn't Peshawar or Kabul. I need you to adjust to having me as a daughter." I hated to be so tough on her, but I needed the two of us to live together as two autonomous adults. I also wanted to push her to adjust faster because I knew that if I gave her too much time, if she thought too much about it, she wouldn't be able to deal with the cultural shock of being in America.

She looked at me sadly and said what she would say many times in her life: "I don't know what sins God is punishing me for by giving me a headstrong daughter like you."

The next morning, in the dark, Greg took me to the airport and I was gone.

THE NEW-EMPLOYEE ORIENTATION was held in a large chain hotel that tried to look fancier than it was. I had been hired as a Category II interpreter. CAT IIs, as they're called, are Afghans who are American citizens with security clearance. CAT I interpreters are either Afghan émigrés who possess a green card or work visa but no citizenship, or local Afghans who live in Afghanistan.

We spent the first two days filling out reams of paperwork to apply for security clearances. For reasons I didn't understand, we were also lectured on the basics of Afghan culture. In some of the sessions I was the only woman in a room full of Afghan men, good practice for what lay ahead of me in Afghanistan.

We took a written test in Pashtu. An older guy who before the week was over would ask me to be his second wife offered to lend me his dictionary. He was short and stocky, with tufts of white hair growing out of his ears.

"Dictionary!" I exclaimed. "There's a war going on. You're not going to have time to whip out your dictionary in the middle of a combat zone."

"It's just to pass the test. They don't care," he said.

"They should care. I care," I replied righteously.

On the third day I returned to my hotel room in the evening. I was standing in the middle of my room trying to figure out what to do for dinner, when the phone rang. Everyone I knew called me on my cell. I stared at the hotel phone. Its ring was loud to the point of aggression. I answered it rudely, just to stop it from ringing. It was Greg. Before I could ask why he was calling me on the hotel line he said, "Guess what?

I'm in the lobby. I wanted to surprise you, but they won't give me your room number."

"You are?" I was so happy to hear his voice. I had been afraid it was the dictionary lender with the hairy ears who had been calling.

"I got to thinking. If you go to Afghanistan, you'll miss our anniversary. So I came here to celebrate it early."

Greg was great with a map. That night he took me to an Afghan restaurant I'd heard about. The food wasn't very good, but it hardly mattered. The company was exactly what I needed. The next afternoon we went to the Smithsonian. We took the Metro into Washington, D.C., the first time in my life I'd ridden on a subway train. The clatter made it too loud to talk, but we had been together long enough for me to know he wasn't there just to celebrate. This wasn't any anniversary. When we had first met and he asked me to marry him, I had carelessly told him to come back and ask me in five years. It was nearly five years later.

While we were looking at the dinosaur skeletons he asked, casually, if I knew how many years we'd been together.

"These dinosaurs are amazing. I wish Riley could see this someday. Don't you think he would love this place?" I asked, hoping to distract him.

"We don't have to get married immediately. You can go do your Afghanistan thing, and we can just get engaged."

"I'm not sure I want to be engaged."

"We wouldn't have to tell anybody. It could just be our little secret."

"Now you sound like some old pervert," I said. Using humor as an escape was an Afghan trait I could always count on. "What's the purpose of that?" I continued. "Don't you think I would stay true to us?"

"I just want to be able to look forward to your return and starting a life with me. The rest is up to you; any way you want it, I want it."

"If it's up to me, I would prefer not to complicate our relationship."

I adored Greg. There was no one else in my life. I didn't want to end our relationship. I wanted to be with him, but I just didn't want to be married to him. I wasn't planning on walking away, I just needed to know that I would always have the freedom to do so. I had paid a great price for my independence and never wanted to give it up, ever.

I'm sure a psychologist would have a field day analyzing my aversion to marriage. When I was a child I once heard Mamai tell some friends a story about a thirteen-year-old girl in the village who'd been married to a man much older than she. One evening she cooked his dinner and either oversalted it or undersalted it, I can't remember which. She placed the food in front of him; he took one taste and was so displeased that he smacked her so hard he broke her neck and she died instantly. What amazed me when I heard them tell the story was not the horror of it happening but the casualness with which this story was shared and discussed. It wasn't shocking to them, nor was it a lesson not to marry young girls to old men—it was just told as general conversation, a piece of local gossip. When I thought about marriage I could never shake this story, couldn't file it under Beastly Things That Happen Only in Afghanistan. I couldn't dismiss from my mind the worry that one day I would get the salt wrong and Greg, who'd never even said an unkind word to me, would break my neck.

"Greg, you're not ready for life with me," I said. "You think you are, but you're not. You are so sweet, and so kind. I would just make you miserable. In thirty years you'd look back and realize how unhappy you were with me and your life would have been a waste."

"How can you even say that I would think that? You mean everything to me, and you know we belong together."

We'd found a bench in one of the galleries. I sat there and let him hold my hands. What could I say? That the thought of marriage made me feel like I was suffocating? That I would rather go to Afghanistan than get engaged to him? How could I protect the one person I cared the most about, while still keeping my own liberties, which I cared about even more?

AT THE END of the weeklong military training I was scheduled to board a military plane to Bishkek, Kyrgyzstan, where I would catch a plane to Bagram Airfield (BAF).

I called Najiba to say good-bye.

"This is ridiculous," she said. "Just come back."

"I'm going to try it for at least six months," I said. "That's the shortest contract they offer."

"Saima, you're talking about *Afghanistan.* Just because we were born there doesn't mean we belong there. You're too Americanized. Don't you like your life here? Plus, you can't even get along with the Afghans in your own family here in the States. What do you think is going to happen there? Those people aren't going to be welcoming you with open arms. Afghanistan is no place for an opinionated and pigheaded woman like you. They stone to death women like you."

ELEVEN

My recurring nightmares were coming true. I was on a plane back to Afghanistan.

The difference being, it wasn't my uncles making their threats a reality—I was returning of my own free will. As the flight crew read through the roll call for the manifest, I realized that the company I had chosen to go with knew exactly what they were doing when they decided to push me through all the paperwork and training within two weeks. If I had being given any more time to think about it, I would have backed out and decided to stay in sleepy Portland.

What was I thinking? For one thing, I have always thought that the only way to stop fearing something is to be immersed in it. Of course, I can't seem to make this work when it comes to swimming, but returning to Afghanistan I wanted and could do. So, I thought, I will sign up for the shortest contract—and if I needed to leave before that was over, I would do just that. Feeling in control of the situation and of the timing of my return made it a lot easier to get on that plane.

I had not been happy in America, not the way I knew I could be if I took care of what I considered unfinished business from my childhood. I had left Afghanistan under the worst possible conditions. All those years later, sitting in Oregon, trying to find satisfaction and happiness in freedom, I would randomly be reminded of one thing or another from my early years in Afghanistan, and it would instantly take me back to the despair of my childhood.

ATLANTA TO SHANNON to Bishkek to Bagram. On the outside, the plane looked like a commercial jetliner, but inside it had been stripped down to the basics. Wires dangled from the ceiling. There were no overhead bins, no inner shell, no disguising the fact that we were traveling in a tin can with wings. The back of the plane was reserved for cargo—mostly food and ammunition. As I crawled over duffel bags and stretched legs to find a seat, I vowed to never complain about flying coach again.

The engines were loud enough to warrant earplugs. The soldiers all had them, but no one came down the aisle, offering them. You were meant to have grabbed them from a tray as you boarded, but I hadn't known that. From this I learned one thing: It's impossible to doze off while trying to cover your ears with your hands.

The transport plane landed in the middle of the night at a U.S. Air Force base in Bishkek, in a blizzard. Almost twenty hours of flying to get there had given me plenty of time to doubt my decision to return to this war-ravaged country, where it seemed that there was a price for everything and everything was for sale. For a few dollars, people would sell you anything, even their grandmother—or at least that is what I had been told during orientation by a couple of the guys who had spent time in Afghanistan as interpreters. Would the country my father sacrificed his life for be a country where the very values—friendship, loyalty, family—he gave his life to were for sale? On that long flight to my motherland, I made two promises to myself: one, that if ever I saw that Afghanistan had become a country my father would be ashamed of, I would leave that same day. The second was inspired by my paranoia, a true American quality, that I would be stranded without my American passport, which guaranteed my rights and gave me freedom of movement: I would guard my American passport with my life. I feared that the men of Afghanistan would suck me back into a life with no rights, a life that I thought I had escaped—the shackles that so many Afghan women accept as their fate.

Did I expect to come out of it alive? Was this a rational decision? Or had I been guided by a greater force? Had it been my destiny from the beginning to be an Afghan woman in Afghanistan, one that I had only postponed by going to America? Is it foolish to try to run away from your fate?

I had not slept for hours, with these answerless questions racing through my head as I sat in that loud cabin, surrounded by very young American men in uniform who had the ability to fall asleep before the plane had even lifted off. Did they not worry about what lay ahead of them? How I envied their acceptance of whatever was coming their way. Later, I would find out that, in reality, most of them didn't know what was coming their way.

As the engines were turned off, I still had the buzzing in my ears that would persist for a couple of days. I lugged my duffel bags across the icy tarmac to a Kmart-sized tent where I joined the other soldiers and civilians waiting for a flight to Afghanistan. I sat in a cold metal chair. Three televisions broadcast the same football game. There was no sound. I thought the volume of the TVs was just turned down, then a soldier offered me a bottle of water and I was forced to read his lips. I was temporarily deaf from the roar of the engines. At least I hoped it was temporary.

I sat and waited. Morning came. The day passed. If there is one thing that Pashtuns excel at, it's waiting. All around me soldiers slouched in chairs, watching TV, listening to their iPods. Some slept with their heads thrown back, snoring as if they were in their own beds at home, and I'm sure in their dreams they were.

The tent was overheated to compensate for the frigid temperature outside, but a burst of cold air came in every time one of the soldiers entered or exited. I slept on one of the hard sofas in my turtleneck, my arms wrapped around myself. On the morning of the third day I wondered if I'd been forgotten. Was it possible? Would someone have noticed if I'd boarded the military transport in Atlanta and had never arrived at Bagram Airfield? I could have asked someone, but I was too intimidated. I'd spent all my time in the United States in Oregon, a state with no major military installations. The only experience I'd had with people in uniforms was signing for packages from the cute UPS man who'd come to my office every day. The young soldiers with their brush cuts, desert fatigues, and weapons made me nervous. Had they used those oiled black guns, which they strapped to themselves so casually, to kill an enemy? Could they tell I was an Afghan? Would they consider me an outsider? An enemy? Would they hate me because my people were the reason they were so far away from their families? I have always been too afraid to ask my soldier friends this question because I knew I would resent leaving my family if the boot was on the other foot, so to speak. How might I react to their resentment? Would I be insulted by their attitude? How would I avenge their insult? I was so busy with these incessant, one-way conversations in my head that it was three days before I even thought about going up to the window and asking if they had my name on any list.

Eventually, in the early afternoon of the fourth day, a guy with a clipboard called out the last four digits of my social security number. I boarded a plane that had a row of seats running along the cabin sides and two Land Cruisers strapped down in the center. They looked like beasts that had been captured and were being taken to a faraway zoo. Once more the engines were loud enough to make your joints hurt. But this time I had remembered to grab a pair of earplugs as I boarded.

"So, what are you?" the soldier sitting next to me yelled. He nodded at my civilian outfit, my gray down jacket, Express jeans, and the same turtleneck I'd been wearing now for half a week.

"An interpreter," I said. "A Pashtu *turjuman.*" It sounded strange to me to be introducing myself as an interpreter. It was an alien title.

"Awesome. Can you come with me and my soldiers?" His grin conveyed the easy charm that I would later see in almost every soldier I met out there.

I opened my mouth and laughter probably spilled out, but I couldn't hear it. "I think you'll have to ask my site manager!"

"I'm working on my Pashtu." He unzipped one of the many pockets on the arm of his uniform and showed me a small Pashtu dictionary with a tattered pale-blue cover.

"Ah! I know that dictionary! It's put out by Pakistani Pashtu speak-ers." I recognized it, having seen one in a bookstore in Portland when I was looking for a Pashtu dictionary.

"Is it good?" He flipped through it. I could see dog-eared pages and words underlined. "I want to be able to say a few things in Pashtu to Af-ghans I meet on patrols," he shouted.

"I'm not sure," I said. I couldn't possibly explain over the noise that, like everything else in Afghanistan, the language issue is maddeningly complicated. Ahmed had told me that the army routinely sent Farsiban interpreters who spoke only Dari, as Afghan Farsi is called, into Pashtun villages. While a lot of Pashtuns might understand Dari, they dislike speaking it because of the historical ethnic tensions between the two main groups of Afghans. The Pashtuns have their own language, Pashtu, which is the language they expected the U.S. Army to speak if the Ameri-cans wanted their support in the fight against terrorism. Otherwise, the army would be wasting the Pashtun men's time, and if the Afghans were to agree on anything, it would have been that the Pashtuns were running out of time.

THERE ARE 60 million Pashtu speakers worldwide (although hard data hasn't been collected to confirm this number), most of whom live in Afghanistan and Pakistan. According to *The CIA World Factbook,* Pash-tuns comprise over 40 percent of the population of Afghanistan, the other five or six major ethnic groups making up the rest. I have asked Pashtuns in remote villages about how many Pashtuns they think are in Afghanistan, and their response is millions. For as long as I can remem-ber, and long before then, Farsiban and Pashtuns have been throwing around percentages and numbers to claim majority, but due to the inse-curity and inability of anyone to go door-to-door, no one has solid data. In my experience, having worked all over remote Afghanistan, I find it safe to say that more people speak Pashtu than Dari, the other official language. For the last three hundred years, whenever Afghanistan has had a king, he's been Pashtun, and the national anthem of Afghanistan is sung in Pashtu; still, Dari has traditionally been the language of business and higher education, which accounts for the often arrogant and condescending attitude of Farsiban people toward Pashtuns. Dari was the lone official language until 1936, when Pashtu was added by royal decree.

Pashtu is complex. In general, there are two grammatical genders, as well as singular and plural. Verbs must agree in person, number, grammatical gender, and tense, and word order is usually subject-object-verb. However, there are so many exceptions to the rule that attempting to learn Pashtu by grammar and word order will drive almost anyone to just throw up his hands and seek out another language, any other language, to learn. I have mastered several languages, but I know that if Pashtu had not been my mother tongue, I would never have been able to learn it. I tell my soldier friends who wish to speak Pashtu fluently that they shouldn't bother. You can speak Pashtu if you are born with Pashtun genes—otherwise, it's impossible to keep track of the rules and countless exceptions.

There are major regional accents, even for words describing simple, everyday activities. A favorite pastime of Pashtuns all over Afghanistan is to try to convince one another that their form of Pashtu is the correct one. I can't count how many times I have sat in villages surrounded by young and old men, while they tell me my Pashtu is not the real one because I pronounced my "sh" sounds as "gha," for example. Of course, it was expected that I would make fun of their Pashtu, too, and I did, gladly.

Even before setting foot in Afghanistan I knew that we couldn't expect to build rapport with the locals or show that our soldiers were there to help them, not conquer them, if we didn't even understand the difference between the two official languages, not to mention the locally well-known historical ethnic tensions between their speakers.

So I was both surprised and relieved that this soldier at least knew the importance of learning Pashtu to speak to Pashtuns. I couldn't bring myself to tell him that his little dictionary was useless, that in some parts of Afghanistan the animosity toward Pakistan was so great that he shouldn't even try if he was going to make the mistake of speaking Pakistani Pashtu. The hostility most Afghans feel for their Pakistani neighbors is nothing like the good-hearted humor Americans employ when talking about Canadians.

I'm unlike your typical Pashtun in many ways, but even my blood pressure rises a tiny bit when someone mistakes me for a Pakistani. It is not hard to imagine how villagers who have lived under the conditions of war most of their lives, and who blame the conflicts on the involvement of Pakistan, feel when someone addresses them in Pakistani Pashtu. And, unfortunately, the accent is unmistakable.

Speaking the right language is a matter of respect and shows that you understand the history behind the language. You understand the tensions between the two groups and you are respecting the Pashtun history by bringing in a Pashtu speaker instead of a Farsi speaker, who might insult with his tone or attitude, which I have seen happen in meetings where I was asked to observe. Pashtuns expected American soldiers to bring competent interpreters who spoke the correct dialect and with the right accent. On that first meeting I felt bad for the soldier, who was obviously eager to do the right thing, but I was too new at my job to know that I should have told him what little I knew about Afghans at the time.

"You're the first soldier I've ever met!" I said.

We shouted a short conversation about his tour, which was lost in the roar of the aircraft. He nodded a lot and maintained his white-toothed American smile. I watched him tuck his useless dictionary inside the pocket of his duffel bag and was reminded of my biggest worry. If Afghans would be insulted by this well-meaning soldier's failure to address them in the proper language, what would they think of *me*, a female Pashtun working with the same American soldiers? Would they find me unworthy of speaking with them? Would they insult me in front of the soldiers of my adopted country? There I was thinking of myself as a bridge between the two cultures most dear to me, but would they burn down a bridge for what they perceived to be my unforgiving attempt at being American? I had left my father's country when I was six, the continent when I was fifteen. At twenty-four I became an American citizen.

Given all this, daring to show my face in some parts of Afghanistan might even be a stoning offense.

It was becoming impossible to ignore the cold. When I sighed I could see my breath. The soldier on the other side of me was curled up in his seat, shivering in his sleep. He didn't even look old enough to buy a beer. He didn't have a jacket. Feeling protective of him, I took my army-issue blanket out of my duffel bag and laid it over him.

When he awoke he thanked me so sincerely that I was humiliated. Here was a kid, who in an ideal world should only be worried about girls and sports, on his way to my country to try to improve my people's lives. And he was thanking me for this tiny gesture compared with what he was potentially sacrificing for my country.

The plane landed in the middle of a village that didn't appear on many maps. There are certain images that burn in our brains, that we can recall in their sharpest detail at a moment's notice. For some people, it is the birth of their firstborn. For others, it might be a beautiful day with a loved one in Hawaii. For me, it is my first look at the mountains of Afghanistan as I deplaned that day. I had packed my camera in a duffel bag—a mistake I will always regret, as I would have loved nothing more than to have captured my vision of those mountains. It had recently snowed. When I stepped down from the plane, they appeared to be the purest white, and were so close I felt as if I could reach out and touch their snowy crags. The sky was a bright, raw blue, and the snow sparkled in the sun. It looked as if humans had never set foot there. Even today, I can close my eyes and in a heartbeat be standing in front of those majestic mountains, shining like they were on fire, feeling so close yet so out of touch that I thought I was imagining them.

My limbs were heavy. My contact lenses felt as if they were made of sandpaper. It was below freezing, and the strong wind whipped my hair around my head. I stood there gazing at the mountains, dazed by their beauty. Finally, the soldier standing behind me gave my shoulder a little shove to get me moving.

$\mathcal{T}$ W E L V E

The news of the bus accident spread quickly. A group of local interpreters was traveling in a bus that a U.S. company had hired to transport them to Bagram Airfield from Kabul. Even the non-mountainous roads in Afghanistan are famously terrible, rutted with potholes, lined with improvised explosive devices (IEDs), and today, in 2011, openly patrolled by insurgents. The driver was speeding, the bus flipped over, and the few who didn't die were severely injured. Suddenly there was a shortage of interpreters, and everyone who could speak Dari or Pashtu—even those like me, waiting to be sent elsewhere—was called to help.

Bagram air base is the size of a small city. It appears to sit in the palm of a giant's claw, surrounded by the rocky crags of the Hindu Kush. Afghanistan is a landlocked country through which the Silk Road once ran, bordered by Pakistan to the south, China to the east, Iran to the west, and the -stans to the north: Turkmenistan, Uzbekistan, and Tajikistan, all part of the former Soviet Union. Every Afghan alive today knows of Maidan, as Bagram is known by the locals, and BAF, as it is called by the Americans who have either lived there or used it as a transit point for reaching the rest of the country. During the time of the Soviet occupation, from 1979 to 1988, it was known as Howa-i-Maidan, the Dari word for "airport," which is what it was used for by the Soviets. Wrecks of burned-out Soviet planes still sit rusting beside the main runway. Years ago, because of its strategic importance, the Taliban and the Northern Alliance forces slaughtered one another like animals while fighting for its control.

In January 2005, when I arrived at BAF, the few buildings left standing at the base were scarred from rocket-propelled grenades (RPGs) and bullets from these battles. A busy Burger King operated out of a blue CONEX (a military acronym for Container Express, basically a shipping container) with a giant burger painted on the side. There was also a movie theater, a beauty parlor, a library, and a paved main street called Disney Drive.

Afghan men in *shalwar kameez* and hard hats worked like ants upgrading buildings, digging, hammering, and kicking up the dust. They cleaned the bathrooms, replenished the gravel on the base's many walkways, and drove the water trucks every few hours to spray down the dust to settle it. Every clutch of local laborers had its minder, an American supervisor who worked for Halliburton and whose primary task was making sure the Afghans didn't steal anything or build bombs from smuggled pieces of explosives. Later, as the war entered its eighth year, those American supervisors were replaced by third world nationals, probably in order to cut back on costs, since they worked for a lot less than U.S. citizens.

When I first landed at BAF there were thousands of soldiers stationed there, working in one of the hundreds of offices, but there were also hundreds of soldiers trying to get flights out to wherever in the country they were permanently stationed. The soldiers who worked on the Forward Operating Base (FOB) did so from early morning to late at night. The soldiers in transit killed time playing video games in transient B-huts, watched movies, exercised at one of the enormous gyms, and shopped at the PX (the store operated by the military) or local shops on the FOB, just waiting for their flights to manifest.

I was only a few miles from my birthplace in Kabul, but arriving at Bagram was like no homecoming I had romanticized about. I kept wondering what I was doing there. I had left Afghanistan as a girl of six, and I hadn't been back. I'd expected it to be less foreign and more bittersweet, but there was nothing about BAF that matched what I had imagined Afghanistan to be while I had been away. The Afghans there did not speak Pashtu, the language I had come to interpret in. Instead, I was surrounded by non-Pashtu speakers and might as well have not have left Oregon. I didn't hear a word of Pashtu for several days after I arrived. These were not my father's people, I was reminded.

. Even the women who shared the living quarters with me were Farsiban. One of them was Suraya, a hairdresser from Southern California who was on her second contract as an interpreter for a private defense contractor. Her room was the room of someone who was there to stay. An ironing board was set up, draped with piles of clothes. A line of shoes was parked against one wall. I spied a curling iron and a flatiron.

Moments after I arrived she said to me, in Farsi, "You must be terribly jet-lagged. Go to sleep, and when you wake up we can talk."

I did as she instructed. I was new, and I *was* jet-lagged. I needed to sleep. Suraya was in her late fifties, older than Mamai. I thought that she might look after me as she would a daughter, and perhaps show me the ropes, even if she was Farsiban.

I slept through the evening and night, waking up at dawn. I lay in bed, trying to hear if any of the other ladies were up yet. We were staying in a B-hut—a square plywood structure that housed up to eight people, each in a narrow room, the rooms separated by flimsy walls, much like a beehive, thus the name. With only thin plywood between us, I could hear the quiet breathing of the other female interpreters as they slept. I had left a huge master bedroom with a vaulted ceiling and walk-in closet for a square box that was shared by at least three other women I didn't know. I'm crazy, I told myself, and sighed. What could I find out here that I couldn't have come to terms with in America? My mind went in circles, trying to figure out if I was already ready to call it quits. Well, I'm here, and I might as well take a shower, I thought to myself, trying to escape more incessant questions. So I got up, collected a change of clothes and my traveling kit in the dark, and walked outside, where the light was so bright it hurt my eyes.

BAF was spooky that early in the morning. Hardly anyone was moving around, and those who were were doing so very slowly, as if sleep-walking. The women's bathrooms were double-stacked CONEXes, with the shower on top. As I walked up the metal stairs, I froze. They say our sense of smell has a longer memory than any of our other senses, and I believed it then. I inhaled deeply, taking in the powerful scent of fresh fires from the village next to our base. Instantly, I was five again, in my Baba's village, standing next to Mamai as she made our bread on an open fire. With that vivid memory I was reminded of my resolve to discover more about what had made my father give the ultimate sacrifice. Standing on those stairs, clutching shampoo in one hand and trying to hold my jacket tight with the other, feeling miserably cold, I knew that I was where I belonged at that moment. I was exactly where I needed to be in order to find peace in myself, for myself.

I showered; the water was probably at least half chemicals, as there were too many things living in the local water for it to be safe for us to shower in it untreated. Therefore you came out of the shower smelling like you just took a dip in a highly chlorinated pool. It took a while to get used to that—and in the process, it stripped my skin and I lost most of my hair. During the first month of using the water, I watched my skin fall off in chunks, like snakeskin, and I was mesmerized by the process. I thought, I am stripping off my American skin to get in touch with the Afghan inside. It made perfect sense that I would have to go through this physically painful transformation to get to the person I wanted and needed to be.

I came back to the B-hut and saw that Suraya was awake, in full makeup, smoking by the door. I said "Salaam alaikum," the universal Muslim greeting. She replied the same, and then asked, in English, how my night was. After a bit of chitchatting she asked me what I would get asked a million times over the next five years: Where was I from?

I said, in Pashtu, "I am actually Pashtun."

In English, she said, "I was married to a Pashtun once."

In Pashtu, I replied, "So there will be no problem speaking Pashtu."

"Yes, but we should speak English."

I found it very strange that she claimed to speak Pashtu but wouldn't speak a word of it to me. Much later I would find out that the army required all its interpreters in Afghanistan to speak Pashtu, even the ones hired as Farsiban. Because of this requirement, a lot of Farsiban, who traditionally and historically had never liked to speak Pashtu, suddenly swore that they were fluent, just to keep their jobs as interpreters. When it came to translating, they always reverted to Farsi, and expected the Pashtun locals to understand and respond to their inquiries, which of course resulted in local resentment toward Americans for not understanding Pashtun history. It was a vicious, destructive circle.

When the call came to report to the site manager's office, I was lying on my bed in the B-hut, reading a book. Or maybe I was wandering around the PX pretending to shop, or checking my e-mail at the Morale, Welfare and Recreation (MWR) building, or reading a book at the library, which I found by following the signs (written only in English and Farsi). Wherever I was, whatever I was doing, I'm sure I was bored, frustrated, and cold.

For almost a month I'd been waiting to be deployed. I'd been stuck at BAF, trying to keep myself entertained. In my memory those early days were like *Groundhog Day*, each day just like the one that came before, blending together so that I couldn't distinguish what date it was. The only day I could identify for sure was Friday because there were fewer local laborers on the FOB, since it was a holy day and most locals didn't work.

My personal disappointment at having wasted over a month was so great that I wasn't even ready to address it at that point. Every day felt like a failure. I had given myself six months to get to know my roots, to learn secrets about myself and my people that would make it possible for me to achieve inner peace and happiness no matter where I was. Instead, I had spent every day for the past month walking around the FOB, receiving hostile, glaring stares from Farsiban, feeling like I had wasted any chance of pursuing my destiny.

I talked to Greg twice, sometimes three times a day. I called Mamai and e-mailed Naj and Khalid constantly because I was so homesick. Still, when Greg started asking me to come back home, I stopped complaining to him. Returning would mean failing in my mission, which was not an option. This was my chance at eternal happiness. It sounded cheesy, even to me, and so I never uttered those words out loud, but I could not deny that I felt them.

Every afternoon I checked with the site manager, who oversaw which interpreter was shipped out to which base, and every afternoon he said the army language manager was still trying to figure out where to send me. He confided that it was rare to find a female who was fluent in both English and Pashtu, so rare, apparently, that in 2005 I was the only Pashtun female who spoke fluent English and who had a security clearance in the country. While they sorted it out, I waited, and wasted my time, time that could have been spent doing what I was there for. I was frustrated to be in my father's country but not actually interacting with any of his people.

THE DAY AFTER the bus accident the site manager told me to go to the hospital on the FOB. On Wednesdays and Saturdays the medics opened a clinic for the local community. The locals who were brave enough, or desperate enough, to be seen walking into an American military installation for medical assistance were there to be seen by the army doctors, and they needed interpreters. I could feel my heart thumping as I hurried along the gravel path leading to the hospital. BAF is nearly a mile high, and just a few miles from the foothills of the Hindu Kush. The mountains, postcard beautiful, loomed over the valley like disapproving parents. The dry, freezing weather was merciless. The shiny gravel crunching beneath my feet was mixed with beads of ice, glinting with flecks of silvery ore, hiding all evidence of warmth in the soil. It was like walking on icy diamonds. Now that I was about to do what I'd been hired to do, I was nervous. I spoke English and Pashtu, but I did not speak sick and desperate.

My family joked that I would have made the world's worst doctor. I'm susceptible to sympathy pains. When my mom complained about her joints aching, mine ached too. When my sister reported that she had a stomachache, I felt nauseous. As a result, I refused to listen to anyone tell me what ailed them because I knew I would feel the symptoms shortly thereafter.

It didn't help matters that from the moment I arrived in Afghanistan every Afghan I met complained of having a headache. At first I thought this was just an aspect of general conversation: *How are you doing today? My body aches. I have a headache.* Later I would realize that the entire nation lived in a perpetual state of dehydration. When asked, most villagers confessed to not having had a drink of water in two or three days. They had had tea, of course. Arguing that this wasn't the same as water was futile. I thought they were insane, going for days without it, as I swigged regularly from my Aquafina spring water, provided by the U.S. government. Then I remembered living in the village when I was five years old, and walking with my mom to the *kareez*, the ancient irrigation system consisting of channels that run both above and below ground, to fetch our daily *mungai*, the water pot made of clay. The *kareez* was our only source of fresh water; the *mungai* held no more than three gallons and had to last the day. Mamai washed our faces with it, used it for our meals, and made our tea with it. If there were guests, she used it for their food and tea. Like all Afghan women, my mother had constant chores. If we ran out of water early in the day, sometimes she wouldn't have time until the next morning to walk to the stream to fetch some more, and we would have to do without it.

I worried that the hospital would not be the best place to start my new job. But I was desperate to meet and interact with real Afghans and maybe even some Afghan women. I agonized over what to wear. This would be my first meeting with my father's people in my father's country, and I was determined not to wear anything that would take away from the importance of this solemn day. On my narrow bed in the interpreters' transient B-hut, I'd laid out jeans and a long-sleeved T-shirt. Then I put them away. If there were women for whom I would be asked to translate, they might think I was being disrespectful by dressing like a man. I'd sewn a handful of long, colorful tunics and MC Hammer–style pants, as my American friends called them, before I'd left Portland. This outfit was more constricting and would provide no protection against the chilly wind, but I didn't feel that I had a choice. I wanted to dress as much like the local women as possible.

I folded my arms against the cold as I turned onto Disney Drive, BAF's main road and the only paved one at the time. The hospital was a huge structure with canvas walls, equipped with exhaust fans that sounded like the exhalations of a huge asthmatic monster. Once inside I told the first female medic I saw that I was the Pashtu interpreter, there to translate.

"Yes!" she said. "Doc is going to be so excited that we've got a female Pashtu speaker." She pulled out her radio to let everyone know.

Then I felt someone touching my elbow. I turned to see another medic, a stethoscope slung over one shoulder. She was small, with short, dark blond hair tucked behind her ears. "You're a *turjuman*? I was waiting for our regular 'terp, but you know what happened. I've got a little girl in here who really needs to be treated, but I can't talk to her mother without you," she said. All soldiers knew how to say two things in Afghanistan: the traditional Muslim greeting, *Salaam alaikum,* or "Peace be unto you," and *Turjuman,* which could mean "Are you the interpreter?" or "Help, I need an interpreter" or "Get me an interpreter, now!" depending on the tone of the speaker.

She was a fast walker; a woman with too many patients. I followed her to the ICU. Every room I passed held several beds containing people swathed in bandages and hooked up to blinking, beeping machines. I couldn't help wondering, as I peeked into one room and saw both American soldiers and local villagers lying there, whether the Americans despised their Afghan roommates, whether they blamed them for the terrible situation in which they found themselves. At the time, I was not as aware of the dynamics of the relationship between the Afghan patients and the injured American soldiers. Years later, I would ask soldiers what they were thinking as they lay in beds next to local Afghans, some of whom might have been the ones shooting at them through the fire of combat. But that day in BAF, I was too stressed about my own first interaction with local Afghans to pay attention to the tensions between them and the U.S. soldiers.

The air was circulated by the roaring ceiling vents, but they couldn't dispel the rusty smell of blood and bleach. I felt myself perspiring inside my tunic, beneath my hair.

"Her mother brought her in," the medic explained. "We're not sure what happened. Might have been a fire or explosion. I don't think it was an IED." Afghan men refused to allow their wives to come to the clinic, regardless of how sick they were. An injury from a land mine or an IED seemed to be the exception, overriding their old fear of the airfield, where the Soviets raped their women or sold them to other Soviet soldiers.

The medic showed me to a bed in which lay a tiny girl, no more than three years old. I bit my lip to keep from gasping. The girl's enormous eyes and pug nose reminded me of my own three-year-old cousin, Mariana, back home in Oregon.

I would have been surprised to learn that she weighed more than thirty pounds. One side of her face was shiny with burns dressed with a thick yellow lotion. One eyelid was charred and swollen shut. Her other eye, fringed with thick black lashes, followed me as I sat on the side of her bed. An IV needle was injected into her hand. A thin white tube disappeared into one small nostril. She reached up to touch my hand, to grab my attention, as if I could look anywhere else.

"*Durdh*," she whimpered.

Durdh is the Pashtu word for "pain." I thought again of Mariana. One day not long before I came to Afghanistan, I bought her a cup of strawberry ice cream. She was just beginning to form sentences. I asked her if the ice cream was yummy, and I could have sworn she almost rolled her eyes. "No, it's not yummy. It's delicious," she replied. I couldn't help comparing her with this little girl, who already knew the word for "pain." I wondered if this girl had ever eaten ice cream.

I told the medic that the little girl was still in pain. She injected some liquid—probably morphine—into her IV.

The girl's mother stood beside her bed, her face covered completely beneath her red scarf. The scarf was beautiful, its edges embroidered with beads and tiny mirrors, in the traditional Pashtun way. I could see

she, too, had suffered burns; her hands, the only visible parts of her
body, were also dressed with the thick yellow lotion.

"Why are you trying to save my daughter? Why won't you show her
some mercy and let her die?" the mother asked me in an angry and
pained voice. I must have looked stunned. How could a mother say this
about her beautiful little daughter? The astonishment must have shown
on my face because she made an impatient huffing sound. Her fingers
trembled as she tried to hold her scarf around her face. "Can you imagine what life is going to be like for her? She's going to be scarred. No one
will marry her. Her brothers are all dead. She will have more of a chance
at happiness if she dies and goes to heaven. She will grow up to curse
you for saving her. Is that what you people want?" The strong belief in
the afterlife is what holds the faith of many Muslims in Afghanistan. It's
like they have given up on ever finding happiness on earth, and so they
grasp on to the promise of eternal happiness, living in misery but counting down the days until they can be welcomed to a heaven filled with all
the joys they were denied in this life.

The air from the vents roared in my ears. Of course—how could I
have forgotten what it would mean to be a scarred Pashtun woman with
no men to take care of you? I had introduced myself to her as a Pashtun,
and she was looking at me with scorn, as if I didn't understand the first
thing about her or her life.

"What's she saying?" the medic asked.

"She wants to know why we're trying to save her daughter," I told her.
Would the medic understand that in Afghan culture it's better for a female with no male relatives to be dead than disfigured? Telling her such
a thing might make her throw up her hands—why help a child when her
own mother could cast her aside this way? I was so new at this, I couldn't
think of a way to communicate the mother's cultural logic, or her love for
her child, or her concern, or the hopelessness she must have been feeling, looking at her young daughter in pain, believing that things would
only get worse if she survived. I realized at that moment how distant I
had become from my own people, and how difficult my role as a *turjuman* was going to be.

"Can you ask her what happened?" the medic requested.

Bit by bit, the story came out. The mother had been in her kitchen cooking when their brand-new heater ran out of kerosene. Heater? I asked. What heater? The one that had been handed out in her village by a *modisa,* an NGO, just days before. Her children had been playing inside and trying to keep warm. She asked one of the older boys—he was nine—to fill the heater with kerosene. She had had no idea how the heater worked. When the NGO had brought the heaters to the village, they had passed them out with the cans of kerosene. Her son started to refill the heater without first turning it off. The explosion killed the boy and his two brothers on the spot. The parents survived, the little girl just barely.

I recounted the tragedy to the medic. Well-meaning but inept NGOs are legion—this one had donated some kerosene heaters to a local village without telling the locals how to use them or how dangerous they could be. I couldn't help but remember how the actions of another NGO had caused the death of one of my distant young cousins. Inspired by *The Kite Runner,* this NGO had decided that it would bring some joy into the lives of some Afghan children by giving them new kites. The organization purchased the kites in the United States and shipped them to Kabul, where local representatives traveled to a few villages and passed them out to the kids. Then the kids did what kids the world over would do—they went crazy with excitement. They launched the kites into the air and ran into the surrounding fields. The NGO didn't think to check with the village elders before they passed out the kites to the kids, who in the process of flying the kites ran over old mines left there from Soviet times. My cousin, a seven-year-old boy, was killed instantly, and several others were injured. The elders went around collecting the kites from the kids and burned them to save any other children from dying. Villagers recount this story to show that, no matter how well meaning, Americans often don't take the time to understand other people or their past.

The medics took the mother to another room to attend to her burns. After she left, I sat holding the little girl late into the afternoon. Looking down at her ruined cheek, her cracked lips, I was again reminded of my cousin. I understood this Afghan mother's concern—she wasn't being cruel, she was being realistic—but I couldn't imagine the desperation of a mother in that position, or how hard it must have been for her to verbalize it. The little girl hung on to a handful of my hair as if it were a cherished security blanket, something I'm sure she'd never had. Sometime later I noticed that my tunic was smeared with the dark yellow lotion dressing of her burns. No matter what happened to her, if her parents didn't want her, much as I couldn't imagine that, I would take care of her, I silently promised her.

AT FIVE O'CLOCK the clinic closed, and the locals who weren't patients had to leave. The mother pressed her hand into mine and thanked me. Her anger was spent, and she had remembered to be thankful that at least I understood the source of her anguish. Like most women all over Afghanistan, she had nothing to give but her prayers. She said she would ask God to grant me heaven.

"Before you go," I said to her in Pashtu, "what is your daughter's name?"

She furrowed her brow as if she didn't understand what I was asking. "Angelee," she replied, using the Pashtu word for "girl." Since so many Afghan children die in infancy, many of them are not called by their proper names until they are much older, and this angelee was no different. Of course this is a protective mechanism mothers have come up with, knowing that when you name a child, only to lose him or her to one of several diseases that claim thousands of young lives in Afghanistan, it is harder to get over the grief. In fact, it's not unusual for mothers to wait to start using the names of their children until after they're old enough to marry. My own mother calls me Angelee to this day.

That angelee's mother scurried off. Later, the medic would tell me she should have been admitted; her burns were more severe than they appeared.

I dragged myself back to my hut, over the gravel that reminded me of diamonds. My head ached, as if someone had jammed a crown of steel into my brow. An icy wind swept down from the mountains, making my ears and eyes burn. Back at my B-hut, I changed my clothes, but my hair and skin still reeked of the hospital.

I hated the hospital: the smell of blood and chlorine, the loud drone of the huge exhaust fans, the doctors pulling me in different directions, the burned and bandaged bodies, the mewling sounds of people in pain. I vowed to talk to my site manager about being reassigned. I'd go anywhere, do anything. This wasn't what I signed up for. Then I berated myself: I knew I'd accepted the interpreter position hastily. The company had been so eager to hire me, a college-educated Pashtu-speaking female, and I had caught their enthusiasm. My job in Portland had become so routine. I had known that this would be exciting, meaningful work, helping the people of my native and adopted country learn to understand one another. It had all sounded so airy and romantic then. I had never imagined it would include sitting and holding the cool, trembling hand of a severely burned three-year-old. Just because I was the only female Pashtu interpreter on base, that didn't mean I didn't have a choice. I was a civilian contractor. I had a say in the matter, didn't I?

I took a shower. I had never thought I was the type of person who would yearn for better plumbing, but I missed my bathroom back in Portland as if it were a person. I hated the smell of the chemicals on my skin after I showered. I had e-mailed my sister and asked her to go to Bath & Body Works and buy an assortment of the smelliest shower gels and lotions she could get her hands on and send them to me the fastest way possible. At first I was embarrassed to take tubes of fragrant shower gels and lotion into the shower, but then I was relieved to learn that every woman on base, whether army or civilian, depended on scented shampoos, conditioners, shower gels, and lotions to conceal the awful smell. When a soldier ended her rotation, or a civilian's contract was up, she donated her cache to those of us left behind.

But that day I didn't even bother trying to smell good. Instead, I stood zombielike under the water until it turned cold.

No matter how I attempted to shuffle my thoughts, no matter how I tried to convince myself that I would be just as useful somewhere less horrible, I couldn't escape the fact that I'd promised the little girl that I would check in on her tomorrow, so the next day I returned.

The weather had turned frigid. It had snowed in the mountains. I entered the hospital to find the exact same scene as the day before, nurses paging their doctors when they saw me coming, doctors sidling up to me wanting me to duck into a room for just a minute to interpret for them.

I knew I should have stopped and helped every one of them, but my mission was to keep my promise to Angelee.

As I rounded the corner into the ICU she heard my voice and began to cry. Her bed was the last one in the row. In Pashtu she named everything that hurt. I had thought I would go for a few minutes to say hello, but I wound up staying for six hours.

I asked Angelee whether she might like to go outside and sit in the sun, and she looked at me with what I took to be interest. So I put her in a wheelchair and rolled her to the back door. But outside, the diamond-like gravel was bumpy beneath the wheels. I pushed her over it; and with every bounce she cried out. I called for the nurse, who gave her a shot of morphine. After a few minutes, I picked up Angelee in my arms and the nurse took away the wheelchair.

I sat her on my lap. I could smell her burnt hair and the oily medicinal odor of the dark yellow lotion. I had hoped for a view of the snowcapped mountains, but all we saw were a collection of sand-colored CONEXes. Still, Angelee was more responsive sitting on my lap than she'd been inside, where she would shut her eyes and sigh every few minutes.

Suddenly I felt shy. I had no idea what to talk about. What is wrong with me? I wondered. I had never had any trouble talking to my three-year-old cousin, Mariana. I started having doubts about my ability to do what I was hired to do. If I couldn't talk to a little girl, how was I going to speak with adult Afghans, who would be much harsher judges of what I was saying and doing? I was relieved when a medic appeared with some biscuits and a small stuffed bear and gave me a break from my thoughts.

"What's the word for 'bear?'" he asked me, wanting to tell Angelee himself what it was.

I blinked and shifted Angelee on my lap. She was so light. What *was* the word for bear in Pashtu? I swallowed, felt another twinge of panic. Here I was, failing on my first mission. But it wasn't like I had cause to use the word *bear* much, in English or Pashtu. Angelee took the bear and held it on her knee. She didn't seem to notice or care that I was unable to come up with the right word.

Her mother didn't come to visit her that day, or the next. Both days the medic who had given Angelee the stuffed bear asked me whether the mother had stopped by. I knew what he was thinking, but I had to say no; the mother was gone.

If the doctor was not going to allow Angelee to die, then the mother's next best hope was to abandon her, hoping one of the American soldiers or doctors would take pity and adopt her. In America she could get skin grafts and plastic surgery. In America there was hope for her. In the end, the mother believed that the mercy of the American people was greater than the mercy of her own people.

As I sat beside Angelee's bed I tested out the idea of adoption. Even though I knew that she would be only the first of many children I would want to adopt, I imagined bringing her home with me to Portland, thinking of the playdates she would have with Mariana, the strawberry ice cream I would give her as a treat. It was pure fantasy, of course. As a military contractor I was forbidden to adopt any locals, and in any case, there is no official system in Afghanistan for adoption. Hamid Karzai, Afghanistan's president, had passed legislation making Western-style adoption of Afghan children by other nationalities illegal.

I went to the hospital to see Angelee every day for almost a week, but one morning I arrived to find her bed empty. I asked around, thinking maybe her mother had come back for her after all, but the medic told me that a day earlier a man had shown up saying he was the girl's uncle.

He said the girl's mother and father had both died of infection from their burns.

"Are you sure he was her uncle?" I asked.

The medic shrugged. "He said he was. We didn't have any choice but to release her. We couldn't just keep her here forever."

I hurried back to my B-hut, avoiding the clusters of Farsiban interpreters who stood around smoking and chatting. I stared at the ground as I rushed by them, hoping they wouldn't stop me to chat. I wanted to be alone with my thoughts. I tried to feel optimistic. I, too, had had caring uncles as a child. Eventually they turned on me, but when I was Angelee's age, they had taken me in. I chose to hope that, since Angelee's uncle had come all the way to an American installation to pick her up, he would be good to her, or at least try to protect her for as long as he could from the cruelties of an Afghan world.

THIRTEEN

One late afternoon I was packing up a box of gravel to send to Najiba when the site manager knocked on the door of the B-hut. I opened the door for him to come into the little space that was serving as a living room. I could tell by the look on his face that he had no clue why I was sending home a box full of rocks. I explained how I talked to my mother and sister every night, and how I told them that the ground beneath my feet was covered with rocks that looked like diamonds. "I'm sending them some," I said, "so they can have a piece of Afghanistan in Portland, Oregon."

I was transfixed by this gravel. When the sun was at a certain angle the reflection was blinding. I couldn't look away. Outside the base there was a huge pile of the stuff, used for surfacing the walkways and paths of every base, the expedient—and politically practical—alternative to paving. To pave a road in one of the American bases in Afghanistan means you are here to stay. In the Afghan mind, pavement equals permanence, and that was not a message the United States wanted to convey. Over the years the gravel would grow dirty, but in the winter of 2005 it was still fresh, clean, and promising.

The site manager looked at me blankly. He'd advised me several times to "keep myself busy and entertained" while I was waiting at BAF, but from the look on his face I could tell that sending rocks home to my family was not what he had had in mind.

"You're going to Farah," he said.

"They do know that I'm here to speak Pashtu, and that Farah is a Farsiban province?" I admit my tone might have been that of a know-it-all.

"I don't know," he said. "All I know is that you're approved to go to Farah as soon as you can get there."

I took my package of gravel to the post office on base and hurried back. I wasn't 100 percent sure where Farah was, just that it was on the border with Iran. I had to consult a map. Seeing how far west it was, all I could imagine was the wide-open space, the glorious heat. I love heat. I stuffed all my clothes into my duffel bag and rushed to the terminal, hoping to catch the next flight out. I sat for six hours, waiting to be called, but there was no flight that day.

I wasn't sure why I was being sent to Farah. During the orientation in Virginia I was given no real information about what I would be doing—no handbook, no packet, no FAQ brochure. As contractors, we were simply supposed to allow ourselves to be herded along.

Much later I would learn that asking questions like *Do you know what I'm going to be translating?* Or, *Where am I going to end up?* Or, *If I'm in the middle of a meeting and there's a firefight, what am I supposed to do?* will get you labeled as a difficult interpreter. Asking questions as I did, questions like *You do know we're Afghans, right? Why are you wasting our time and yours teaching us about Afghan* culture? will brand you as a troublemaker. And troublemakers were sent to far-flung outposts, where it was assumed no one of sound mind would want to work, and where they couldn't ask too many questions or raise too many red flags.

I called Greg and told him I was shipping out. Since our meeting in Fairfax he'd decided to apply for a job in Afghanistan, working as a contract manager for Kellogg Brown & Root (KBR). He was adamant, saying he didn't care if the country was at war, he was willing to leave everything behind to be with me. He'd been processing out in Houston for a month, and now he was on his way to BAF. Even though he didn't lose his temper—he never did—I could hear the disbelief in his voice.

"I'm coming all the way to Bagram to be with you and you're *leaving* Bagram?"

"I don't have any say in it, Greg. I signed up to go anywhere they send me."

"Are you doing this just to get away from me? Is that what's going on?"

"Even if I didn't go to Farah, they'd send me somewhere else. I'm here to work, not sit around BAF. That's the whole point, to go where I'm needed."

Our relationship had become just another casualty of war. In the beginning, I had used the satellite phone several times a day to call him, but the more he asked me to come back home, the less I called. It was easier to e-mail, so I did, knowing well that e-mailing was not Greg's strong point. So we started to drift apart, prompting him—I believe—to apply for a job at BAF.

I called Mamai and told her I was headed to Farah. She was relieved. She listened to *World News* every day, just as my father had. I told her Farah was the safest place in the country, and in February 2005 it really was.

I returned to the terminal the next day and the next. Finally, a Chinook helicopter was scheduled to depart early the following day. After dragging my suitcases back and forth to the PAX terminal for three days, in disgust, I decided to leave them behind. In the end, I was told that the plane could not carry too much cargo because it was already transporting mail, ammunition, and other containers, and that I could bring only essentials—my backpack with my toothbrush, toothpaste, and a change of clothes. I had the shoes on my feet. My site manager promised to put the rest of my stuff on the next plane to Farah. I would get the rest of my stuff almost three months later.

We took off after midnight. Flying by night wouldn't save us from being hit by a heat-seeking RPG, but it would lessen our chances of being clipped by an insurgent crouched on a hillside with a Kalashnikov. I only understood this later. At the time I thought it was just another case of the army's inexplicable way of doing things. I wore my heaviest coat, but it wasn't heavy enough for a winter Afghan night in a Chinook. We flew all night, ascending and descending, zigzagging across the country, dropping off food and ammunition, refueling, picking up and dropping off soldiers at bases in Jalalabad, Khost, Gardez, and Kandahar before we finally made it to Farah.

From the air, the Farah Provincial Reconstruction Team (PRT) looked like a piece of circuitry—a gray rectangle studded with flecks of beige and green. It sat in the middle of a wide valley amid outcroppings of rust-colored rocks. The soldiers called it "Fort Apache," which I understood as having something to do with the Wild West. It was a no-man's-land in the blasted desert of a desert nation, with scorpions, venomous snakes, and swirling sandstorms that obscured the tall, craggy mountains looming on the horizon. The only things that grew here were a few saplings and the candy-colored poppies that provide most of the world's opium.

We deplaned into a dust cloud. I pulled the collar of my jacket over my nose to keep from inhaling the dust. A female army specialist picked me up in a little truck and took me to my room, a cement structure I would share with her and two other female soldiers. I dropped my backpack by the only unoccupied bed and rushed back outside. I stood in the dusty haze and stared at the distant mountains. They were every shade of orange in the morning light. It was just past dawn, but already I could tell it was going to be much warmer than BAF, which cheered and energized me after the long night of freezing travel. The desert climate was extreme, but I felt comforted by the presence of the bare orange mountains looking down on me.

Farah was a tiny PRT in the middle of a vast plain. The first unit ever in the area was still there when I arrived. When a PRT or an FOB opens, the first order of business is to establish the perimeter around the area by assembling the HESCOs, as the steel-mesh containers filled with rocks, gravel, and dirt that create a thick wall of protection are called. When I arrived at Farah, the HESCOs were all in place, and there were five guard towers, so brand-new that the paint was still wet; the foundations for a few buildings were still being poured. Farah PRT was so small and cozy that everyone knew one another. It felt to me like one big extended family, much like an Afghan family. I could tell they all belonged to the same tribe by the way they dressed, behaved, and spoke. The U.S. Army tribe. I was not sure, as a civilian, that I would be welcomed.

When I arrived at BAF I knew I was going to work with a PRT, but I had no idea what a PRT did.

After routing the Taliban in 2001 the United States realized that, in order to stabilize the country and begin to rebuild the remote regions (90 percent of the country qualifies as remote), operating bases would need to be established across the country. The PRT employs a mix of U.S. military personnel and civilians to oversee the reconstruction of schools, clinics, roads, and water-supply systems; now the PRT has evolved to mentor the Afghan governmental officials at the provincial level and to some degree do the same for the Afghan National Security Forces (ANSF), the collective title for the Afghan National Army, the Afghan National Police, and any other national security forces. Most important, the PRT is supposed to link up the Afghan public with the central government in Kabul. And, of course, an unofficial function of U.S. PRTs is acting as a friendly link between the coalition forces and the Afghan people. Another unofficial function that the locals had assigned to the PRT, and one that hasn't changed to this day, is to provide Afghans with a place to come and complain about the corruption and ineptness of the Government of the Islamic Republic of Afghanistan (GIRoA).

During the years I spent in Afghanistan the mandate of the PRT changed. In 2005 the focus was on reconstruction and, on a smaller scale, development. PRTs used their tiny budgets to build and rebuild structures for the local government. As time passed, the locals grew to rely on the PRT to provide not only the buildings but also the services that should have been provided by the Afghan government. We were expected to fund and train the teachers for the schools and the medical personnel for the clinics and hospitals we built in the middle of the villages too remote for the central government to even know they existed.

The balance between offering assistance and supporting the country is precarious. To avoid any appearance of trying to replace the GIRoA, the PRT mission evolved. Our focus shifted to mentoring Afghan government officials and helping them serve the public's need for reconstruction and development. The transition wasn't easy. Prior to the new mandate, Afghans had been taught to put in a request at the PRT for a new school or clinic; within days a Civil Affairs Team (CAT) would show up for an assessment. Under the new system, they were told to submit the request at the office of the governor or subgovernor. It would take months to get a response, if they received one at all. The Afghans would then return to the PRT, complaining that their own government had been unresponsive and expecting the PRT to step in on their behalf.

The system had other flaws, as well. Simply put, the job of the PRT commander was to mentor the local governor, and the job of the company commander, who answered to the PRT commander, was to mentor the subgovernors. The mission sounded reasonable, in theory. In practice, it was another story. It might work with the right PRT commander because he is older and has more experience. But how could the military expect a twenty-six-year-old officer whose primary responsibility was to ensure the safety of the two dozen soldiers in his company, making sure they returned home to their families as unscathed as possible, to "mentor" an Afghan subgovernor?

A typical relationship between the U.S. Army and an Afghan official plays out something like this: Most likely, the subgovernor was appointed because he was the governor's crony. He knows little, if anything, about how to govern. He might not even know what's going on in his own district. The company commander who's supposed to teach him his job has had little, if any, training in governance in the United States, let alone governance in a foreign culture such as Afghanistan. He doesn't know the first thing about running an Afghan province and probably knows even less about Islam, which is heavily intertwined with the Afghan constitution as far as the villagers are concerned.

Still, the company commander tries to set up a meeting. It's the first step. The subgovernor hems and haws, makes excuses. He tells the company commander that he has to go to the doctor in Kabul. He says one of his relatives has died. Most often, it is a female relative, because how would an American company commander be able to confirm this? How would the commander know how many female relatives the subgovernor has? How would *anyone* know?

He's full of excuses for why it will be difficult to meet. He knows the Americans are supposed to help, but he doesn't want a meeting. It's not safe. Most of the people in his province don't know who their subgovernor is. They don't care. If he hosts a meeting with the Americans, word will get out. Gossip will spread. Within hours the insurgents will know his name. Anyone connected with the Afghan government, anyone connected with promoting their cause, will become a target. If and when he finally agrees to meet, he knows he is putting a bull's-eye on his own back. The subgovernor, while he might be uneducated, is not stupid. Even though he is a marked man, he knows that the more ineffectual he is, the longer he will live. His goal becomes not governance but doing as little as possible for as long as possible to avoid assassination while continuing to receive a nice paycheck, plus all the potential bribes—an unadvertised bonus of most official positions in Afghanistan.

The subgovernor's refusing to be seen out connecting with the constituents of his district but still fighting opponents for the seat might land this subgovernor on a satirical news program like *The Daily Show* back in the States, but in Afghanistan it is the root of all that has gone wrong the last decade. Enter into this mess a U.S. PRT, whose purpose is to connect the Afghans to this ineffectual and corrupt subgovernor. In the mind of the average Afghan, this has created a fundamental, deep-seated distrust of Americans. However simple they may seem to people of the first world, the villagers know what's going on in their own country. Why wouldn't they doubt the United States' good intentions when the United States is encouraging the Afghans to connect with a government that's stupendously incompetent and equally corrupt?

• • •

AFTER A FEW weeks, when it became clear that my suitcase wasn't going to be catching up with me anytime soon, I asked the PRT acting commander whether I could go outside the wire to the local bazaar and buy some things I needed. This was a normal enough request in March 2005. The country, newly purged of Taliban, was safer than ever.

Major Carrillo, the tall and handsome Hispanic deputy commanding officer (DCO), flashed me a white-toothed grin and said, "Sounds like you're feeling adventurous, Saima. We should make it a mission, to get out there and meet some of the locals, too."

The next morning I set out for the Farah bazaar with a dozen soldiers and two CAT I interpreters, named Omar and Johnny Cash. For personal security reasons, most CAT I and II interpreters don't use their real names. A code name does double duty: It prevents anyone from tracking their names back to their family, which would make them a target for insurgents, and it makes it easier for American soldiers (who often have a hard time with foreign names) to remember them. Later, I, too, would have a code name, but in those early weeks back in Afghanistan I used my real name.

The soldiers all wore desert camouflage (a shade of beige that matched the endless sand and every hut and wall constructed of it), interceptor body armor (IBA), heavy boots, helmets, sunglasses, and several radios for communicating with the PRT and one another. I wore a green, vaguely Afghan-looking tunic I had designed and sewn at home and a pair of jeans. I was thrilled to emerge and have the opportunity to engage with Afghans. By midmorning it was warm, verging on hot. Winter was on its way out. I felt the sun on my scalp as we stood by the convoy for the brief before leaving the wire.

As we drove out of the Entry Control Point (ECP) and into the bazaar a couple of miles away, I noticed little kids running alongside the HMMWV (Humvee) screaming something. It was hard for me to understand them at first, but as more voices joined in, I was able to hear what they were saying, and it warmed my heart. "I love you! I love you!" they screamed. I felt as if all my fears about being judged by Afghans were silly. See? They loved me, and loved all of us. I can do this, I thought. I will be very good at what I am here to do, because how could I let these children down?

The Farah bazaar was a sleepy huddle of narrow shops selling more or less the same items: groceries, shampoo, shoes, and fabric. The stalls were crowded beneath an overhang of corrugated metal, protecting the goods from the sun. A few shopkeepers wandered over, and a group of adorable little kids chased us, calling out, "Pen, mister! Pen, mister!" I felt a swell of pride that these Afghan children were begging us for pens and not chewing gum or candy, like my little cousins did back in the States. They were just so interested in educating themselves, I naïvely thought.

I don't know what the shopkeepers were thinking, but I could see the stunned looks on their faces when I asked them in Pashtu if they had shampoo. Over the years I had picked up little accents from Jalalabad, Peshawar, Kandahar, and of course my own Ghazni Pashtu, and I was using all four of those to make sure no one could pinpoint where I was from. This was a trick I had decided to use to make sure that no one harassed my family in Afghanistan because of what I was doing. Just as I spoke to the Afghans around me, I turned and spoke to the soldiers in English. The locals had seen female soldiers, but I wasn't in uniform. Was I some sort of special guest? An ambassador, perhaps? The shopkeepers ducked their heads and grinned. One wondered aloud, in Pashtu, for the enjoyment of the growing crowd, "Is she Afghan? No, I think she is American. Listen to her speaking English to those American guys. She is not shy at all, and they are all listening to her and laughing with her like she is one of them."

I picked up a dusty bottle of hot pink shampoo and asked the price. The shopkeeper blinked at me from beneath his gray turban.

"I think ten dollars," he said.

"Ten dollars? That can't be right." The inborn bargainer in me was waking up. In the States, I had missed being able to bargain for shampoo.

"But it's rose shampoo," he said.

"Sure, it's pink, but that doesn't mean it's rose. It could be bubble gum. Or it could just be pink, because I can't smell any rose or bubble gum."

"But you are a rich American. You are supposed to help Afghans. Just do your part, daughter, and buy the shampoo."

A tall, thin boy stepped forward from the crowd. He wore a long, dusty green shirt and the traditional loose pants. He placed his hand on my arm.

"What are you doing?" I asked in Pashtu.

"Where did you learn Pashtu?"

"Where did *you* learn Pashtu?" I countered.

"I learned it from my mother," he said.

"That's funny; I learned it from my mother, too!" I said.

The boy groaned and rolled his eyes, unimpressed. Another boy asked whether I'd taken a class, and if so, could he take a class and speak English, too? I felt so relaxed and at home with these kids. They were too young to judge me on how many Pashtun gender customs I was breaking, too young to try to ascertain exactly why I was there. Their eyes were bright with curiosity. They were beautiful and silly. I felt a bit sad knowing how different they would be in just a few years, as sullen, angry Afghan teenagers, old enough to know how impossible and miserable their lives were.

The soldiers providing security weren't too comfortable standing around in the middle of the bazaar. They seemed to grow anxious if we stayed in one place for too long. I could tell by the way they scanned the hardpan dirt street that fronted the shops. They suggested we get going. As our Humvees rolled back to the PRT, I felt good about the day. I was in Afghanistan, connecting with real Afghans; no one gazed at me with murder in his eyes. And I had done my expected American duty by buying the expensive shampoo (even at the agreed-upon $3), and helping the local shopkeeper.

The next morning as I headed to the chow hall for breakfast, Major

Carrillo caught up with me. He'd spoken to the governor about me, and it had been decided that I would be the perfect person to represent Farah PRT at the upcoming celebration in honor of International Women's Day.

"It's a party?" I asked. I had never heard of International Women's Day.

"Yes, a party," he said. "But first you'll give a little speech."

"I don't think I can do that. How about you give the speech and I'll interpret?"

It turned out I didn't have much say in the matter. I wasn't army, so they couldn't order me to stand up and tell them what it was like to be an Afghan American woman, but they did impress upon me how thrilled and honored they were to be able to send to the celebration a genuine Pashtun, *and* a female, a native speaker who could address the local people in their own language.

Major Carrillo assured me it would be a small gathering of local women and that I would only have to say a few words. I thought that if I could just imagine I was chatting to Mamai and a few cousins, it wouldn't be so bad. It might even be fun. I could talk about how I had learned English by watching Peter Jennings on the nightly news, and what it had been like to go to college. And how many women could they get together for this party, anyway? Couldn't be more than a dozen, I assumed.

The next day I went to the center for the Department of Women's Affairs at the appointed time. The weather had turned cold, even though the sun shone, and the celebration was held in the courtyard outside. There was a small wooden podium in front of a row of plastic chairs, where I was told to sit once the event started, beside the director of the department. Mrs. Sadiqqi was a kind Farsiban woman who'd just returned from Iran, where she had been a refugee for many years. Several principals and teachers from the local schools sat nearby.

Directly in front of the podium were a few rows of chairs for the token women. It was, after all, International Women's Day. They wore big black burqas that made them look like birds of prey. On either side of the women were rows and rows of men, sitting there looking dull-eyed and resentful beneath their turbans. I had not seen this coming; the men would also be listening to my speech. I asked the member of Civil Affairs who'd accompanied me what the men were doing there, and she said she thought they were guests of the governor.

I laughed. Of course. In the same way I was pressed to be here against my will, these men were forced to be there by the governor, who wanted to show the Americans, who had paid for the party, that he was interested in promoting gender equality.

Here was my fear, realized. Now I would be put on display to be judged and despised by my father's people. I could see their judgments in their eyes. "The most heinous thing that could ever happen to a Pashtun woman has happened, and there it is in front of us." I was a living nightmare. I was corrupt, a Pashtun woman gone bad, and here I was about to speak to their women in public. If a woman from a respected family even speaks to a woman of loose morals, she will bring shame to her family. In a few minutes, I would be talking to all these respected women from respected families, and I knew that the men were not happy about it. I felt in danger and was glad that the soldiers were there in case any of the men took it upon themselves to perform an honor killing. It was a strange feeling, to be afraid of the Afghan men but comforted by the presence of the American men. I felt so conflicted. I was wearing a tunic and jeans but no scarf. I hoped they would see a new kind of Afghan woman, one who could be modest and respect tradition without having to wear a scarf, one who could also speak English without causing dishonor.

I kept my distance from the men. They likely thought that since my head was uncovered, they could approach me. As I stood around trying to mingle before the speeches, some of the younger men started coming my way, so I turned away and walked toward the other women, not wanting the men to think they could approach me just because I wasn't covered head to toe. Many of the women glared at me. They were hostile, embarrassed both for themselves and for me. But I was determined. I wanted to show that just because my head was bare, that didn't mean

I was a woman without morals. I wanted to convey to them that in my adopted culture modesty was communicated by how we behaved, and by how we allowed others to treat us, not just by the thickness of the fabric of our *hijabs,* head coverings.

When it was my turn to speak, I stood up, legs shaking. As a young girl in Afghanistan and then Pakistan, I used to stutter when I was in front of people I didn't know. My stammer eventually disappeared, but I still fear it will suddenly return when I am about to address a large group. It doesn't help that my mother still reminds me of how I used to be tongue-tied, except she says it in a wishful way, like she wishes I would stop arguing with her. On that occasion I wasn't sure if I was going to be able to say what everyone was waiting to hear. I have no idea what came out—I just remember thinking, What am I doing up here? I'm just an interpreter. I didn't stutter. At the end I was given a bouquet of gaudy plastic flowers, sprinkled with glitter and scented with sickly sweet perfume, and a scarf.

I joked about the scarf. I said, "I guess you're trying to tell me something."

"No, no, it's just our tradition," said Mrs. Sadiqqi. "Women get scarves and men get turbans."

"I know about our traditions, but I would have liked a turban better."

Later, when I visited the governor, he gave me a beautiful turban, gray raw silk woven with gold threads.

ℱOURTEEN

When I first arrived at Farah PRT, I avoided the chow hall as much as possible. It seemed as if everything contained some form of pork. Hot dogs, pepperoni pizza, chicken Cordon Bleu, bacon and eggs. As a Muslim I don't eat pork, so I would ask one of the local CAT I interpreters to buy me some chicken kebabs and *doughdi* (flat bread) from outside the wire, which they were happy to do because I would make sure I paid them more than the food cost, to thank them for their trouble. Or I made do with vegetables, cereal, and bread. I loved salads, but, like all food items, the lettuce was flown by the U.S. Army from Europe to BAF, then loaded into a refrigerated CONEX to be trucked all over Afghanistan. It always happened that the refrigerator would break down somewhere on the slow roads, and by the time the lettuce reached us, it would be beyond wilted.

I planned to tackle the issue of what to eat at the PRT at some point, but initially, I wanted to take some time to observe how the soldiers interacted on this small (compared with BAF) FOB and find myself a niche. In my time at BAF, waiting to be sent here, and then working at the hospital, I had naïvely romanticized my coming back to Afghanistan, imagining that I'd instantly connect with the people and be welcomed without any hardships. I should have realized that if leaving Afghanistan at the age of six had been such a trauma, coming back nearly twenty-five years later was going to be just as traumatizing, if not more so.

The soldiers in the unit had been there long enough to develop routines that seemed second nature at this point. There was a set time for every daily activity, down to calling their families back home. Most of the time was spent on responsibilities to do with their army chores, and so there was very little time left for me to interact with them. However, there was one thing we all did three times a day: eat at the chow hall. So I resolved that, no matter how horrifying and culturally insensitive I found the food to be, I would be there, eating dry cereal at every meal if I had to, just so I could be sitting with the U.S. soldiers, speaking with them about Afghanistan, America, family, or whatever they wanted to talk about.

THE HUB OF our base was a U-shaped structure that housed the medics' office, the laundry rooms, bathrooms, and barracks for both male and female soldiers. The chow hall, the Civil-Military Operations Center (CMOC), and the Tactical Operations Center (TOC) were housed in separate buildings on one side of the U; a small gym was on the other.

At the bend in the U was a huge porch with a view of the mountains where the soldiers liked to congregate. Every evening after the soldiers had completed their chores, one of them would sit on the porch and play his guitar; several others would surround him, smoking or chewing tobacco, most with their eyes closed, leaning against the building. Every morning Arif, a local who worked as an administrator at the CMOC, would bring me homemade milk tea—made with cardamom pods, milk, and black tea boiled together in a pan. I had told him I liked drinking chai in the morning, and he decided to make it every day. Yes, I realized, he wasn't doing that just to be a nice guy, but I didn't know how to tell him not to bother. In those early days, I was so afraid of offending the local Afghans that I thought it was better to just drink the tea and hope that he would stop on his own. No way was I going to willingly make my childhood nightmare come true by marrying anyone from my culture, even if he was sweet enough to make me chai every morning.

One morning, almost three weeks after I arrived at the PRT, on my way to the CMOC, which was my workplace while I waited for the PRT commander to get back from his R & R, I glimpsed a soldier I hadn't seen before. He stood with his back to me talking to Major Carrillo on the porch. It was already hot. He wore his desert camouflage pants and a beige T-shirt. Had he been wearing his regular army shirt, which advertised his rank and name, I might have acted differently. Maybe.

As I passed him he called out, "You must be the new interpreter they've finally sent me."

I turned and gave him a withering look. He had dark hair cut close to his scalp in the army way, big, dark eyes, and lines in his forehead that revealed that he wasn't a kid. He smiled a lot, I would soon find out. He could easily have been an Afghan man, which didn't endear him to me. He struck me as being full of himself.

I'd been told that Lieutenant Colonel Eric Peerman, the PRT commander, was going to be my boss. Who was this guy?

"Last time I checked I wasn't anyone's anything," I said, "but I'd be happy to work with you if you need an interpreter."

"You really know how to make a first impression," he said.

"No more than you," I said. "You act as if you own the PRT and everyone in it."

"Well, as a matter of fact, as the commander of the PRT I do own everything here."

I suddenly realized I'd been talking to Lieutenant Colonel Peerman. I still didn't like the possessive way he was talking to me, and as a civilian I knew I didn't have to take it. "Well, not me." Men who are too strong and cocky have always made me uncomfortable; my response is to want to get as far away as I can, as fast as I can.

I turned around and walked away from the two of them on the porch, hastily making my way to the CMOC. I'm not going to lie; I was a little nervous about how I had behaved. My curse in life was my attitude, it seemed, and I really did not want him to send me back for having too much of it.

Half an hour later Lieutenant Colonel Peerman found me at CMOC.

"I think we got off on the wrong foot," he offered. He asked me if I would take a walk with him. We strolled around the base. He wanted to show me the sights, even though I protested that I'd been there for nearly a month and knew where everything was. He was annoyed that no one had given me a proper tour. "When I'm not here no one can do anything," he huffed. "Have you seen the shop and met Muhammad?"

"I've been sitting on the bench near his shop since I got here," I said. "It's my favorite place on the base."

"You've already met Major Carrillo, then?"

"Sure. The only one I had not met was you."

So he took me on a tour of the whole PRT. I could hear the pride in his voice as he talked about everything he and his soldiers had built from scratch. Watching him interact with those under his command, I could see that he loved them. I forgave and forgot his earlier arrogance.

LIFE AT THE Farah PRT was surreal, like life always is on a military installation, especially for the civilians, and even more so for the female civilians. It didn't take me long to notice that I was one of just five women on a base of more than a hundred male soldiers and the only female civilian. This female-to-male ratio was about the same on every base I would work at over the next five years. The soldiers used terms such as "deployment nine" or "deployment queen" to talk about the female soldiers on the base or ones they knew in Iraq. Once they explained what these terms meant, I would get mad at them for using them, so at least in front of me they refrained from using them. When I arrived at Farah, some of the soldiers had been there for almost eight months. Being a single Pashtun female, that elusive creature they had all heard about but had hardly seen, apparently made me harder to resist. Soldiers would declare their love to me within days of meeting me, without knowing what they were saying. I was not a psychologist, but it was clear to me what they were going through. Not knowing whether or not they would make it out of Afghanistan alive they wanted one last chance at love, happiness, and most coveted of all, companionship.

As soon as a soldier would say that he loved me and was always think-ing about me, I would try to talk sense into him by explaining why he was feeling that way. My purpose was not to embarrass him or make light of his feelings. I have always been very protective of our young soldiers in uniform, deployed to a land few of them barely knew existed until just a few years earlier.

It was a thorny role I had to adjust to. I didn't want to stop talking to the soldiers, because I wanted them to come to me when they had ques-tions about anything Afghan. I just didn't want to mislead them. The constant adrenaline rush that comes from living with the stress of daily combat intensifies all emotions, and love was no exception. That atten-tion could easily have gone to my head had I not been very comfortable in my own skin. I remember sending an e-mail to Najiba from Farah, jokingly saying, "I had no idea I was so hot! All these guys love me!" And, my sister being the wiser one, and maybe being a little worried, said, "Just remember those feelings might only be good in Afghanistan, and most likely will expire once you leave the country." That Greg and I were having real issues around this time might have made me suscep-tible to the soldiers' romantic overtures, but there were underlying issues for me that did not allow the male attention to go beyond flattery. My fear of being controlled by men made it hard for me to relax around most of them because they threatened my sense of independence. I had been accused by several casual dates, who were trying to take our relationship further, that I built walls around my heart. One of them who was famil-iar with Afghan architecture said that those walls resembled the tall, huge walls called *char dewal* (Farsi for "four walls") you see around *qalats*. How accurate he was! It had taken a long time for me to lower my guard around Greg. He was my first real relationship and the man who I could see myself potentially growing old with, if he wasn't so stuck on the idea of marriage in the traditional sense.

The soldiers' casual use of those three precious words—I love you—scared me to the point where I started having doubts about Greg's use of the same words at the end of every phone conversation. Perhaps his feelings weren't genuine either. Did he have any more clue than they did about who I was? This doubt only widened the chasm between Greg and me. I couldn't handle the distance or the disconnect. Greg and I broke up, and even though I was devastated to lose that unconditional love and support, I knew that in the long run he would be better off with a nice girl who didn't bear my childhood scars, and who wasn't cursed with a past like mine.

FIFTEEN

J ust outside the chow hall was a row of small troughs where you
could wash your hands. I ran my hands back and forth beneath the
little plastic faucet, but it didn't work. I tried the next one, which
was also broken. As I moved on to the third one, a voice behind me said,
"What, you think you're at Nordstrom? Use the pedal!"

I turned and saw Lieutenant Colonel Peerman. He wore a big grin.

"Hello, *Eric,*" I said, ignoring his comment. In Afghanistan people
rarely call one another by their last names, so I called everyone, even
high-ranking officers, by their first.

When I took this job I knew so little about the military, I hadn't realized they insisted on using only last names. Later, I would give briefs
and refer to a colonel as Mike, which would make the entire room gasp
in disbelief, thinking, "No one calls him Mike but his mom!" I worried
that I was being disrespectful, but the officers assured me that they preferred it that way. To address them by their first names showed their
soldiers that I was outside the chain of command, reinforcing that I was
at the PRT in an advisory capacity.

Eric and I walked into the chow hall and got our food. Because it was
a small room with very few available chairs, we sat next to some soldiers
who gave big smiles and a "Hello, Saima" and a timid "Sir" to Eric, ate
quickly, and got up. Eric gave me a strange look and said, "You need to

be careful how friendly you are with my guys. They are young and they are at war; their emotions are running high, and you are a beautiful female, and being a Pashtun makes you even more exotic and appealing. But I would hate for your reputation to get ruined at my PRT." I thought this was a very strange thing to say, and asked him if he said this to all the female newcomers. He said he knew the female soldiers could take care of themselves, but he felt more protective of a female civilian. I reassured him that I wasn't interested in any relationship with anyone, and the soldiers knew it. Eric said something then that I have heard many times over the years; "In the army, perception is reality." Also very true in Pashtun culture.

The next afternoon the rain began. In the far west of Afghanistan there are a few weeks of blood-warming sun between winter and the monsoon spring. The day would dawn bright, the sun beating hard on the PRT, the mountains their usual rosy orange. By late afternoon a hard rain would come, as if someone was tipping a giant pitcher over the desert. After ten minutes, it would stop as suddenly as it had begun. The first time it happened, I thought the entire PRT would be washed away. Arif noticed I'd grown shaky and pale. He laughed when I told him that every time there was some epic act of nature or natural disaster I was sure it was God's wrath, directed at me. It is the Pashtun ego in me; my sins had to be the greatest and therefore the only cause of God's wrath.

Most of my interpretation duties involved accompanying Eric to meetings with the governor twice a week. Each province in Afghanistan has a governor appointed by President Karzai, but each one conducts his business in his own way. This particular governor, Izzatullah Wasifi, enjoyed socializing with Americans. He called for biweekly meetings and also threw huge barbecues on Friday nights. Wasifi didn't really need my services; his family had fled to New York during the Soviet invasion, and he was completely Americanized. He'd owned a pizza franchise in New York before being convicted of selling heroin in Las Vegas. He was scrawny, with dark hair, dark skin, and a quick smile—but behind his smile you could see that he would be just as quick to anger. This made him only more Afghan in my eyes, because most Afghans hold their anger very closely behind their smiles. It can be scary, because you never know what might cause the thin veil to lift, making you the recipient of the famous Afghan temper. Being the PRT commander's interpreter, I knew I was protected from Wasifi's temper because he was always on his best behavior with Eric. Most governors try their best to nurture cordial relationships with the PRT commanders because they view them as allies who can deflect any negative attention from the U.S. forces away from them, and provide them with monetary assistance. Unless a commander is tuned in to Afghans' thoughts, and also has a skilled interpreter who translates more than just words, he might not have a good sense of the agenda of the people he is dealing with when interacting with Afghans.

Eric immediately saw my potential value for the PRT. In 2005 there was no talk of counterinsurgency and building relationships with Afghans. COIN was not yet a sexy term thrown around at meetings, the way it is now, but some commanders, especially those with military backgrounds like Eric's, were realizing the impact of building genuine relationships with the locals.

Eric figured that Omar, the CAT I interpreter, was well qualified to do the basic translation; the most important thing I could do was to help him understand what Wasifi was *really* saying to him, as well as to the other Afghans in the room. I could read and assess their body language and tell him what they were communicating to one another in Pashtu. Being Afghan gave me a greater capacity for deciphering Afghan behavior. Over time it became clear that on paper I may have been an interpreter, but in reality I was doing something else. I was an observer first. I observed the relationship dynamics between the Afghans and their government, between the PRT and the locals, and between the PRT and officials from the central government.

It became clear over the years to those at the forefront of development efforts in Afghanistan, that if the PRT focused on building relationships with the governmental officials, while neglecting the locals, the United States would eventually lose the fight for the hearts and minds of the Afghans. The governors were temporary; as soon as there were any rumors of corruption on the part of a governor, Karzai would pull him and place him in another province. It was a kind of musical-chairs game, except everyone got a chair. They just didn't know which chair they would be sitting in when the music stopped. Things only got worse as time went on, and rumors of corruption started before the governor even got to a province. Later, in 2009 when I was in eastern Afghanistan, locals would start lobbying against corrupt subgovernors before they were sent there by Kabul.

When I wasn't at meetings with the governor I sometimes went out with the deputy commanding officer or one of the Civil Affairs Teams, just so I didn't have to sit idle. One day, the Civil Affairs Team was going to the local hospital to make an assessment, and I asked if I could go along, in case there were females and they needed me to translate for them. When we got to the hospital in Farah City I met a local girl who had tried to end her life by burning herself alive a couple of days before. In talking with her mother, I learned her horror story, one that is disturbingly common all over Afghanistan. Shaista, "beautiful" in Pashtu, was indeed a remarkably beautiful girl of about sixteen (judging by what was left of her face) who had been sold by her mother to a forty-five-year-old man as a second wife. The first wife and the husband both beat her and made her work like a slave. She complained to her mother, but having used up the dowry to feed her other children, her mother sent her back to the abusive couple. Finding no help, Shaista took matters into her own hands: She poured gasoline on herself and set herself on fire. Her husband's first wife caught her in time and put out the fire; the husband brought her to the hospital to try to save her life.

When I met Shaista she was surrounded by her family, including her mother and her husband. Half of her face was covered with gauze, with the now familiar yellow ointment at the edges. She stared up at me beseechingly with one lashless brown eye. The conditions at the public hospital were dirty; the doctors had hung filthy sheets around the bed to create a little tent to keep flies away, but she was still covered with them.

If Angelee, the tiny girl I'd tried to help care for in BAF, reminded me of my cousin Mariana, this young bride was a stark reminder of what I myself could very easily have become. This young burned Afghan woman was about the same age I was when I was sent away to the land of freedom and opportunities. If my uncles had delayed even a few months, could this have been my fate? Suddenly, I felt truly blessed from above and lucky to have the men in my life be the hands of God in reshaping my fate. This was the day I started to forgive my uncles, because no matter how they had ended up making me feel, it was the Professor's sponsorship that had me standing over the bed in that hospital right then, instead of being the one in the bed.

The girl wouldn't talk to me; she only cried. But I could feel her desperation. I wondered how it must have been for her, uncorking the plastic container and splashing the gasoline on her dress and her long shiny hair. Did the smell make her swoon? The second before she lit the match, was she afraid or relieved? When she lit the match, did her hands shake? Did she worry about God, and whether or not He would judge her harshly? Did she judge Him to be unjust? Did she hold her mother responsible? Did she want to be saved?

I thought of how trapped, angry, and depressed I'd felt during the last days under my uncles' roof, how much I despised them, how sometimes, after having one of my arguments with them, I would sit in my room and feel so desperate that I couldn't breathe. I would have to stand and walk up and down the length of the room just to stop myself from screaming out loud. But even in my darkest moments, I could never imagine killing myself. Looking at the burned girl, I tried to imagine the degree of hopelessness she must have felt, but—blessedly—I couldn't. My inability to put myself in her place made me feel horrible about what I had been doing with my life. All I had wanted was the freedom to stay out past 9:00 P.M. Now that I had my freedom, was I using it in a way that would make my father and grandfather proud of me? It had been slowly sneaking up on me until that moment, when it was screaming loud in my face: I was not proud of how little I had done since that night when I drove off from my uncles' house.

The husband stood guard by her bedside. His anger felt like a toxic cloud in the room. Of course I knew and the wife knew that he had tried to save her not out of love but because he had paid money for her and wanted to get good use out of her before allowing her to move on to the next world. I got rid of him by inventing an urgent question that could only be answered by the doctor. Having soldiers standing next to me made it hard for him to refuse my request. After the husband left the girl told me she hated him, and she hated her mother for what she had done to her. The girl's mother sat there listening, no emotion on her face. She said she'd had no choice, that her other children were starving and the only commodity she had was her beautiful daughter. I was distraught. I didn't know what I was supposed to do for the girl.

I returned to the PRT and asked Eric whether we couldn't fly her to BAF, or anywhere where they could so something, anything, for her. He said no, it was impossible. Eric had been trained as a medic and knew from experience that most likely this girl would die before we could transport her to BAF. Her family had waited too long before bringing her to the hospital. Infections had already invaded her burns. It was awful and unfortunate, but the hard truth was that if she died in a U.S. military installation, we'd be held responsible for the death of a civilian. The fact that she was female would make it even worse. The United States simply could not afford the bad PR. I understood his point, even admired his appreciation of the difficulty of the situation, and yet I argued with him. Even though I viewed myself as being in the unique position of belonging and having a total understanding of both the girl and army regulations, I thought the least I could do for her was to fight for her. Five days later I sent Omar to check on the girl at the hospital. She had died feverishly of infections three days after I saw her. It was one of the very few times in my life I prayed to God for something. I prayed for peace and comfort and a better chance at happiness in the afterlife for Shaista.

I THOUGHT ABOUT Eric when he wasn't around, a lot. I couldn't help but be dazzled by his charisma. Bit by bit I learned about his background. He had inherited his dark good looks from his Argentinean father, who lived in Florida with his Italian mother. He had two ex-wives and two children, also in Florida. Before Afghanistan he'd lived all over Latin America, performing secret missions—he could never talk about them, and I never asked. The less I knew, the better it was for our relationship. His bravery and dedication to the army had earned him many medals and commendations. Then, in 2001, after the invasion, he was posted to Jalalabad as part of a special-forces operation, where his mission involved interacting with the locals. He lived in a safe house within the community, spent time drinking tea with the shopkeepers. He knew what made Pashtuns tick and was good at figuring them out. I had to wonder if this was why he knew so well how to push my buttons and get reactions out of me that so far had been reserved for family members and very close friends. He also felt great respect for the way Pashtuns protected their females. He found Afghan men's treatment of women to be less admirable. More than once he got upset if one of his soldiers became too familiar toward me, which to Eric meant looking at me and smiling for no specific reason! I liked and appreciated that he understood the predicament I was in—wanting to be there for everyone at the PRT to answer their questions but wanting to maintain the strict gender roles of my Pashtun culture.

While eating at the chow hall, I spied him talking to his soldiers. He knew their names, seemed to know what was going on with them and their families. I could see that they liked him. I may have been a civilian, but I'd figured out quickly that if the soldiers liked and respected their commanding officer, it said a lot about his character. Before every meal he would say grace, and after every meal he thanked Agha, the local cook, for the fine meal. I was impressed by this. I thought it was so polite and sweet. It had been years since I'd prayed, and I was envious of anyone who had that kind of relationship with God.

One day we were preparing to visit the governor. I was hauling on my IBA—the fifty-pound body armor with removable plates that could easily pull double duty in Mr. Universe's training routine—when I noticed one of the back plates wasn't sitting right in the vest. I removed it and as I was fumbling with the vest and trying to shove it back in, I dropped it on my foot. The nail on my big toe cracked in half. For days I was forced to walk around in open-toed shoes, which then led to an infection. I went to the clinic, and the medic told me he'd have to remove the nail.

"You tell me when you have a couple of days off, and we'll take care of it," he said.

Eric teased me when I told him. "Wow, your big toe. We wouldn't want the best interpreter at PRT Farah to lose her big toe. You should take time off to get that surgery done ASAP."

"Do you realize I'm supposed to get Sundays off and I haven't asked for a single Sunday off since I got here? How about you give me all the Sundays I've accrued? That's the least you could do."

"All right, settle down," he said. "You need to take care of this."

"Okay, then," I said.

"It's surgery on a big toe," he couldn't resist adding.

I snorted and walked away.

I'd since been moved to my own room, closer to Eric's, so if there was an emergency off-hours and he needed an interpreter, he would be able to grab me as quickly as possible. Several times, in the middle of the night, I would hear a knock on my door and find Eric standing there, holding his phone because the chief of police or an ANA commander was trying to give him updates of ongoing missions or insurgent activities. Since Omar was a CAT I interpreter and couldn't live in the barracks with U.S. soldiers, it was decided that I would take those late-night calls, no matter how hard it was for me to wake up and speak coherently in the middle of the night, in any language.

ONE DAY AFTER my surgery I was recuperating in my room, my foot propped up on my backpack. In the mornings, when soldiers were out on patrols, at the CAT meeting with the governor, or just with villagers, it was so quiet and boring. I would wait for someone to knock on my half-open door and talk to me for a few minutes. I hated being immobilized this way, so I welcomed any interaction. Over the couple of months since I had been there, I'd become friends with the lieutenant of the FORCE-PRO named Peter, who often stopped by to see how I was doing and ask me if I needed anything. On this Friday, since Fridays were down days, he brought me green tea and a handful of DVDs. We were going to watch a movie.

This was before I realized that "watch a movie" was army code for hooking up. I thought when a soldier asked you to watch a movie he was really asking you to do so, which made me marvel at how many movies these guys watched. Personally I am not big on watching movies. I love to read. I used to encourage whoever was asking me to watch a movie to read instead, and offer him several books from which to choose, and then invite him to come sit on my favorite bench and read with me. In any case, as a Pashtun female I'd been taught never to be alone in a room with a man who wasn't related to me by blood. It was easier to ignore that upbringing in the States. But I was back in Afghanistan, even though on an American base. No matter who was in the room with me, I always had the door open.

But Pete and I were friends, and other soldiers were dropping in to see how I was doing and if I needed anything. My door was wide open. It was the middle of a bright afternoon, and I was fully expecting other soldiers to join us.

Pete had brought his collection of DVDs and had spread them out on the other twin bed. He was sorting through them when, through the open door, I glimpsed Eric looking dashing in his uniform, standing in the hallway. He grinned and strode in, ready for some serious fun at my expense. He hadn't seen Pete sitting on the opposite side of the room, going through his movies.

"Oh! I didn't realize you had company. I just wanted to check on you. Make sure you had everything you needed. See if everything went okay." His smile had vanished.

"It went fine," I said. "I'm not even on any painkillers."

He turned away, mumbling. I knew he despised surprises. "Okay, if you need anything, well, you certainly don't need my help, if you need anything, I'm sure the LT here can get you anything you need, or someone else can."

I spent most of the next week sitting around with my foot elevated. It wasn't that it had been a big surgery; it was just that there was gravel everywhere, and walking on the little rocks with open-toed sandals was unsanitary and painful. So I had to wrap my foot in gauze and cloth and walk on one foot. Eric never checked on me again. After a few days, I hopped on one foot from my bed to my bench, my favorite place to sit and think. Farah PRT was a little over an acre, so flat and barren it felt as if you were in the middle of a sand ocean. My bench was set off from the barracks, the CMOC, and the chow hall, beside the door of the single shop. On the other side was the only sapling on base—it looked as if it had a future as a provider of shade, maybe in another twenty years. Muhammad, the shopkeeper, watered it in the mornings. The bench faced the orange wall of faraway mountains. I sat there many mornings. But still no Eric. I was furious at him, then furious at myself for being furious. He was the PRT commander, my boss. This was the army. This was Afghanistan. I was *not* a teenager. This was silly. And I hated being silly.

The day I was finally able to return to work, I ran into him at the CMOC. He pretended to be busy with a folder. He said he didn't realize I was fully recovered. I wanted to say, *You didn't know because you never came to see me!* But I held my tongue.

It was Friday, the day of the governor's weekly barbecue. Business was rarely discussed at these gatherings; mostly our goal was simply to eat Afghan food and drink tea and mingle with the community, building relationships.

In 2005 it was still safe to leave the wire in an armored Land Cruiser, accompanied by the FORCEPRO in three or four Humvees. Later, it would be impossible to travel anywhere in the country without a convoy of nine or more Humvees or mine-resistant, ambush-protected vehicles (MRAPs), equipped with "birdcages" on the exterior doors to catch the rocket-propelled grenades favored by insurgents. Back then we could tool around in a simple, bulletproof Land Cruiser.

Eric had had his own driver, but once the rains came in late March he decided he preferred to drive himself. Omar and I would sit in the back, while Eric roared along the road, making sure to hit every rain-filled pothole. He said it eased his mind, took the pressure off.

Today he'd given Omar a break. So Eric and I left the PRT in the Land Cruiser by ourselves, with the FORCEPRO (force protection) following closely, and started up the ten-minute ride to the governor's compound in Farah City. I stared out the window, trying to interest myself in the scenery. It was strangely tense in the car; I felt like there was something we both wanted to say, but each of us was waiting for the other to take the lead. White clouds skipped along overhead. It hadn't rained for several days, and the potholes were dry.

"Are you angry with me?" he asked.

"Why would you think that? What have you done that might have pissed me off?"

"I have no idea. But I'm sure you'll tell me when you're ready."

"How come you didn't even check on me to see how I was doing?" I hated that I had to know.

"I can't really tell you anything," he replied.

"Well, you're going to have to say something because we are going to be stuck with each other for the rest of the evening."

"I wish I could," he said.

"How come you didn't even check to see how I was doing?" I asked again.

"You didn't have any shortage of people checking on you every minute, and I really didn't want to be just one more soldier hanging around your doorway, wanting to be noticed by you," Eric replied, staring straight ahead at the road.

"You stayed away because you think something is going on between me and Pete? The door was open! Nothing happened! I'm the only Pashtun female your soldiers will probably ever come into contact with, and I'm not going to allow you to cheapen my professional interaction with them."

"This has nothing to do with you, and everything to do with how I feel about you," he muttered.

The seats squeaked on their springs as we bounced along. Two boys walked along the shoulder of the road, wearing baggy white trousers, sandals, and oversized down jackets. I raised my hand to wave at them, and when they saw I was a woman their mouths fell open in unison. I could have easily changed the subject to the reaction of these boys.

"So now we're going to talk about feelings. Do you talk to Omar about your feelings, too?"

"When I'm done here I don't plan to make Omar part of my life, so no, the answer would be no."

"You're pretty cocky if you think I'm going to let you be part of my life, just like that," I said. "Especially when you didn't come and visit me after my surgery." I was teasing, but only just.

"Are you serious? You don't want me in your life?" He twisted around and looked at me; I tried to look the other way so he wouldn't see my smile.

And then we were at the governor's house.

Eric was so attentive at the barbecue that it was hard not to laugh. He peeled my oranges and cracked my pistachios, as I sat there talking to other Afghans. Usually I was the only female at these gatherings. As we were walking in, I saw an old woman, all covered in traditional scarves, sitting next to a mud wall, which I later found out was the kitchen of the governor's compound. One of the things that I initially had the hardest time getting used to at my uncles' house in America was that the kitchen was inside. In Afghan homes, kitchens are always outside the house, in the courtyard. Therefore, we walked by the kitchen in the courtyard of the governor's compound as we made our way to the living rooms. Usually the governors hired male cooks because in most of Afghanistan women were not allowed to work outside their homes. In the bigger cities, like Kabul and maybe Herat, you might see women cooking or cleaning in a government building, but not in remote provinces like Farah. As I walked by, following Eric and the soldiers who were going to be pulling security for us, I saw the old lady sitting next to the wall, trying to cover herself even more so we wouldn't see any of her. She reminded me of Mamai, who tried to cover every inch of her body, even if my male friends were the only ones around. I told Eric I wanted to go talk to her and asked him if they could stay behind so that she would be more comfortable. In those days, in the relative safety of Farah, I was allowed to approach a totally covered lady, but later on, as we stayed longer in Afghanistan and came upon the phenomenon of suicide bombers, I wouldn't need to be told that approaching a stranger like that would be, well, suicide! I talked to her for a while, and she said she wanted a job at the governor's. So when I saw the governor I asked him if he could please hire her as a cook. "I do have a cook, Miriam, but I will hire her, too, just to make you Americans happy," the governor said, laughing. After that I saw her many times in his kitchen. It made me happy, knowing I had gotten that done—silly, I know, but it was a very good feeling, one I could easily get addicted to.

We arrived back at the base around ten o'clock, parked the Land Cruiser, and after a short debrief, Eric and I walked to my favorite bench on the far side of the base. The sky was black and messy with stars. There was no question of going back to his room or mine. Even though so much of me was American, the Pashtun in me was always there, and my traditional upbringing popped up in the most annoying and inconvenient ways. I was still terrified that people would talk, that my reputation would be ruined, and with it that of my whole family.

"I will let you come to my favorite bench," I said, "even though you're not my favorite person today." I was still upset with his insinuation that I was too friendly with the soldiers.

"Well, that's okay. I'll just stand beside it, then," he said.

"No, it's fine. You can sit on it," I replied grandly.

We talked until three in the morning. Eric told me about his long, successful army career, his failed marriages, his children, who lived with their mothers in Florida, his concerns for his oldest boy, who was eager to join the army, and his father's heart troubles. We gazed up at the Milky Way. Afghanistan is the only place on earth where I have seen the magnificent way that it lights up the night sky. I remember looking at the Milky Way and feeling so insignificant compared with what was above me and, at the same time, awesome to be part of this breathtaking galaxy in the country where I was born, sitting here with the man I thought I could easily find eternal happiness with.

Eric was also a great listener. I confessed to him my personal doubts about what I had done in my life, and how I saw the role of an unofficial ambassador to be the only way I could bridge the two cultures that were so dear to me that I couldn't pick one over the other. I talked about my struggle to move between cultures, and how it was impossible to embrace my American side without becoming painfully aware of my Pashtun side, and vice versa. I talked about missing Najiba and Khalid, and Mamai, whom I hadn't seen in months. I neglected to tell him about the uncles. As I like to say to Najiba, some history is just too much information—TMI.

From the moment I had laid eyes on him, I knew Eric was going to be a big chapter in the book of my life. Although I deflected the attention from soldiers without much effort or thought, I saw their confusion about my true identity, and how that could be alluring to them. Standing there in my jeans and polo shirt, no scarf, admonishing them for telling me how they felt about me, and telling them how that behavior outside the wire could easily get them killed by insulted male relatives, even I was confused as to my true identity.

But Eric was different. There was a twinkle in his eye that I felt was there just for me and that I knew was sincere. He had a deep under-standing of where I came from and an appreciation for what it could mean to be involved with me. He went into our relationship with his eyes wide open, and that told me a lot about what kind of person he was. I trusted his feelings because he seemed realistic about the future. He was not an eighteen-year-old boy who didn't know the ramifications of an Afghan Muslim woman's entertaining the idea of a marriage with a non-Afghan—and even worse, a non-Muslim.

At first I fought myself long and hard, trying to talk myself out of the ideas he was planting in my head, the feelings that I knew were growing stronger every minute we spent together. I still wasn't comfortable about giving up control of my life to a man, which was how I viewed marriage. But after the heartache of the breakup with Greg, I had decided there was going to be no casual dating for me. I didn't want to get close to someone only to have him not be part of my life again. As confused as I was about my emotions, one thing I did know was that I had always looked for an ambitious and strong man like Eric to stand next to me in a true partnership. I wanted my marriage to be one of equals in every sense, and I thought that in Eric I had potentially found a man who was not going to be threatened by my refusal to let him control me, with whom I could share a mutually supportive, enriching life.

Even thinking about the possibility that Eric might be the right person for me made me feel horrible about what I had done to Greg, the kindest and most giving man I had ever known. I had needed to be with someone like Greg while I was going through my anger at my uncles, and if I had stayed in Portland, fuming, for many more years, instead of coming to Afghanistan to come to terms with the anger, I would have remained committed to Greg, maybe even forever. But after spending just a few months in Afghanistan, I realized that my anger was only getting in the way of my own happiness, and I was ready to let the famous Pashtun anger cool off. I knew that at this new stage of my life, I was better suited for the more aggressive and realistic type of relationship that Eric offered, a relationship that would endure any relapse to the old angry me without falling apart.

Our romance was like something out of the Victorian novels I was forced to read in my high school English-literature class. It was a love affair conducted with complete decorum. I hung out at the CMOC, where the locals came to request meetings. Because Farah was a brand-new PRT, small and far-flung, we encouraged people to show up at our gate without an appointment, any time they wanted to talk to us. Eric made excuses to drop in at the CMOC three or four times a day, and I would make excuses to go to the TOC and chat with Nick, an older enlisted soldier whose office was next door to Eric's. It felt like the old days with Vasily—the last time I had had a courtship in secret. Even though years had passed, I still couldn't express my feelings for a man freely in public.

It was not any easier for Eric. There was always a strange tension in the room during our meetings with the governor. Wasifi would have with him various assistants and clerks, young and sometimes handsome Afghan men who worked for him in some capacity. I would be the only woman in the room, and probably the only Afghan female they'd ever spent any time with, aside from their relatives. They had many questions for me, some personal, all of them about my family.

It made Eric anxious on several levels. He was worried about my security.

In Afghanistan, the only thing that travels faster than gossip is bullets. Who knew what would happen to me if the insurgents found out that a Pashtun female was working for the Americans? Such knowledge could also put my family still living in Afghanistan in danger. Any one of them might be kidnapped and held for ransom, or simply murdered, in revenge for my presumed treason.

Eric rechristened me Miriam, a common Afghan name. To every new person I met, that was the name I gave. It was for my safety, he insisted. It also didn't escape my notice that by becoming Miriam I was preventing the handsome young Afghan men from knowing who I really was and tracking me down after I left.

Even though we were supposed to be fostering relationships with the locals, Eric found it unbearable when I would strike up a conversation in Pashtu with an eligible-looking Afghan. Usually, when we returned from a meeting he would compliment me on the good job I'd done and thank me for some insight or observation. On the days he'd suffered a bout of jealousy he'd be gruff and uncommunicative. I'd ask him how the meeting went and he'd give me the silent treatment. Fine. Good. Great.

"What's going on here?" I would finally ask.

"I hate seeing you talking to all those men."

"Right, because at any minute I might run off with one of them to the village and become their baby machine."

"If you were to marry a good-looking Afghan, you could take him home and everyone would approve . . ."

He didn't finish his thought. I was sympathetic. Eric was handsome, accomplished, decorated for his service in the special forces, where he was a respected commander of brave American men. He was a star. Still, he knew Afghans. He knew that those things would never matter to my family and that an illiterate, unemployed Pashtun would be their preference for me.

"But I don't like Afghan men like that. It's not something I'm just saying to you. I have been saying that since I was ten years old in Peshawar.

Afghan men are controlling. I've said repeatedly that I'll never marry one. I want to marry someone like you, who's ambitious and romantic and adventurous. Frankly, you need to be more worried about your soldiers than about any Afghan."

"Which soldier? Who's hitting on you?"

"No one!" I said. "I was just trying to make a point."

Still, he took every opportunity to show that I was taken, without ever saying anything outright. Sometimes, in the chow hall, when I couldn't bear to eat another bowl of cereal, another apple or peanut butter and jelly sandwich, Eric would march into the kitchen and scramble some eggs for the two of us. He loved to do this during mealtime rush hour, when he could reappear with the plate of eggs and place them in front of me with a flourish saying, "I want you to have energy for our meeting."

No one missed the message. In private I would beg him to please make it clear that we were meeting with the governor, but the very next time he would load his announcement with even more innuendo: "Miriam, eat this. You're going to need your energy for later."

I loved being Eric's interpreter, but when he was off taking care of army business, I was happy to join any outgoing team in their Humvees to get a chance to interact with regular Afghans. The Afghans I met at the governor's were not the villagers, who I have always believed represent the true spirit of what it means to be an Afghan. If my mission was to get reconnected with my past and learn about my father's people, I needed to be in the villages.

It was another Friday, but Eric was in BAF for some PRT Commanders' Conference and so I was going out on a mission with the CAT. We were going through a village, and as we passed one compound an old woman in dusty clothes ran to the edge of the road, waving her arms and talking loudly. The tank commander (TC) told the soldiers to be alert, that there might be some trouble ahead. I twisted around in my seat to get a look through the front of the Humvee to see what the commotion was all about. I got a very quick and distorted look at her face, but her agony was clear. She was probably only forty years old, but with her deep wrinkles and bony eye sockets she could have easily passed for sixty.

I could see that she wasn't any threat to us, that she wasn't part of an ambush, and her suffering was genuine. She really needed our help. In today's Afghanistan, I would never ask the TC to stop the convoy, but in 2005, Farah was a mostly green province, one that was relatively calm and safe, and I saw a chance to actually impact the life of at least one more Afghan.

"Stop!" I touched the shoulder of the TC who was sitting in front of me. "Please! Just stop for a moment. It's okay. Let me talk to her."

I struggled to open the heavy door of the Humvee, and before I could step out she scuttled over to me, already crying.

"Please, tell me what is wrong," I said in Pashtu.

She gasped. Her eyes filled with fresh tears. "You are Pashtun? How can this be?"

"Don't worry about that," I said. "Tell me why you are crying."

She began thanking and praising God for bringing me to her, a Pashtun and a female, someone she could communicate with, someone who could really understand her and help her. Even in all that excitement, her confidence in my ability to relate to her was touching, and boosted my confidence in myself. She was a poor woman, one of thousands in Afghanistan. She lived in a tent with her six children, in the front yard of the compound we'd just passed. A kind man, a complete stranger, and his wife had offered her living space in his yard and given her the tent. Sometimes he brought food out to her and her children, but he was not a rich man himself, and when one of her daughters had fallen ill, he didn't have enough money to give her to take her daughter to the doctor.

I asked what was wrong with her daughter. The woman didn't know. She wrung her hands. She was so hot, her head ached, she hadn't eaten or drunk anything in many days, and now she was dying.

Our medic happened to be in the convoy, and I asked the woman if she would let him look at her daughter. She hesitated only a moment before giving her consent. When you are dying, you don't have the luxury of worrying about the gender of your savior.

The medic and I followed the woman to her tent. Inside, her daughter, who was perhaps eleven, lay curled on a rug. The sharp, yeasty smell of infection made my eyes water. The girl was listless. Her eyes glittered with fever. She'd been this way almost two days, the woman said.

The medic asked the girl to lift her head, but she couldn't. Instead, she turned it slightly, and in the dim light we could see frothy yellow pus running from her ear. The medic thought she had an ear infection that had gone septic. Her mother was right: She would die in days if she didn't get treated soon.

The medic and I went back to the convoy. I asked him if we could take her to the PRT, but he said he didn't have any resources to treat her there. He could call the BAF hospital and make sure she was admitted without having to wait for the normal screening at the ECP there, but there wasn't anything to be done for her in Farah. There was no hope for the girl unless she was admitted to the hospital at BAF within the next forty-eight hours. But BAF was on the other side of the country. How would she get there in time? There were few roads in Farah in 2005, and the rough and unpaved journey would be torturous for her. I remembered how long it had taken me to get to Farah on a plane. And, anyway, the medic said she couldn't be airlifted because of the ear infection. I asked the mother if she could get a taxi and get her daughter to BAF. She said she didn't even have money to buy her Iranian medicine in the local bazaar, much less to get a taxi.

When soldiers are posted on PRTs far from BAF, they don't have ready access to their money. The finance department tries to fly out to these sites, bringing cash, but because of the flight restrictions and difficulties, that money source is not regular and can't be counted on. The soldiers are allowed to take out only a couple of hundred dollars a month from their accounts for incidentals—sodas, cigarettes, and chew. They tend to be very careful with how they spend money because no one knows how long it will be until the finance people are able to come back to their installations. I can't remember whose idea it was, but when the soldiers in the convoy heard the story, every one of them emptied his pockets, donating whatever was on him, to get this girl to BAF as soon as possible. I pressed the cash—almost two hundred dollars—into the old woman's hands and told her to get a taxi to drive her daughter to BAF immediately.

This selfless act of the American soldiers, most of whom were young adults, touched me even more than it could have touched that woman. She was of course grateful but probably believed that the soldiers had endless bags of money at their disposal. I had always felt bad about loving being an American more than being an Afghan, but seeing the goodness of these soldiers made me feel better about being more American than Afghan. Over the years I would see how cruel many Afghans are to one another, calling it ethnic politics, or religious preference, or just plain fighting for survival. I remembered all the nasty, hurtful things my uncles in Oregon had said about me. I had experienced Afghan cruelty firsthand, from my own blood, and that had made me fear what other Afghans would be capable of doing to me, if given a chance. The spontaneous generosity of these American soldiers on behalf of an Afghan woman and her daughter began to restore my faith in the choices I had made over the years.

There was a chance, of course, that the woman would have allowed her daughter to die and fed herself and the rest of her children with the soldiers' money, but a few weeks later she showed up at the PRT to tell me that her daughter had been treated in BAF and had recovered, and that every day she prayed for a safe return to America for every American soldier in Afghanistan.

SIXTEEN

The winter of 2005 had been one of the snowiest in a decade. March 2005 brought record rainfall. By April, the western deserts were experiencing massive flooding. Since Afghan village dwellings are built of mud, the water swept away thousands of homes, entire herds of livestock, and many children. We had our hands full carrying out day missions delivering rice and beans, tents, tarps, buckets, and shovels. We flew as much as we could, but sometimes there was no way around it: We had to drive the Humvees over the muddy, unpaved roads studded with huge potholes.

If there is one vehicle impossible to dig out of the mud, it's a Humvee. Fully armored, it weighs about three tons. We'd leave the wire, and sometimes within a half mile of the front gate we'd get stuck in mud. We'd spend the whole day trying to dig it out. Then we'd do the same thing the next day. The locals in whichever area we were stuck in would bring out some green tea and their little cups and say, "Don't worry, relax, have some tea, we'll dig you out." For a while they'd stand there and make fun of us for getting stuck in the first place, then one of them would fetch an ancient tractor to drag us out. Not surprisingly, some genuine friendships were formed this way. Here we were in our huge, expensive vehicles to help the Afghans rebuild their nation—and it was their puny, ill-maintained tractors that rescued us. The irony was not lost on any of us. The effort was cooperative, which made our relationship with the local people seem more equal. The locals were able to hold their heads high and extend the hand of famous Pashtun friendship, without which foreigners can't expect to live for long in Afghanistan.

Spring turned to summer and my six-month contract was winding down. Eric was also nearing the end of his tour. The knowledge weighed heavily on both of us. I was still struggling with so many conflicting emotions when it came to him. Eric had hinted several times that he wanted the two of us to come back to help Afghans as a married couple. I couldn't deny how tempting this was to me. In the way I typically deal with issues I haven't decided on, I ignored his comments. I was worried that things would explode when I went back to Portland and announced that I was going to marry Eric. I wasn't sure that he and I were committed enough to each other to face the centuries-old opposition to this union of a Pashtun woman to a white, Catholic, U.S. Army soldier. But even though I had never believed that it was my fate as a Pashtun woman to find happiness with a man, I didn't want to give up on the idea so quickly. I took to going off alone to sit on my bench to read and ponder the future.

One day I was sitting in the sun, reading a book, and I heard fast footsteps on the small gravel behind me. I turned around to see Eric approaching me with that look of single-minded determination that had made me fall for him. He sat on the other end of the bench—to the rest of the world, we still pretended there was nothing personal going on between us.

He said he'd thought about it and decided we should get engaged before we left Afghanistan. This was the first time Eric had put me on the spot about marriage. Up until then, I had been able to joke about his asking my family for my hand, leaving me out of the equation like a good Pashtun daughter.

"What happened to doing this the Afghan way and asking my family for my hand in marriage?" I teased, putting my finger between the pages to mark my spot.

"We can just get engaged, and get married once we tell your family," he said, undeterred.

"You know there is no such thing as an engagement in Pashtun culture," I said. "Families arrange the marriage and tell the bride and the groom when to show up. The families get a mullah and do the ceremony. You want your family to go talk to mine in Oregon?"

"I'd be happy to call your mother and ask her for your hand," he said.

"I won't be your interpreter for that conversation. And I know you can't ask Omar to do it, since he would then confirm all the gossip around the FOB."

He knew he had a dilemma, but Eric was nothing if not resourceful. He decided to go about it in a different manner. "You know, Saima, you're nothing like any of these Pashtun women. You should decide for yourself, and right now. Don't you want to be married to me and live with me happily ever after?"

I admired his technique, trying to appeal to my independent spirit, but I was not going to fall for it. "You have a point, Eric. I'm not like the rest of the women here or maybe anywhere, but I still have a brother, sister, and mother that I care a lot about, and who I would be pissed at if they ever did something this big without talking to me. You know the American in me wants to jump up and hug you and accept the proposal with teary eyes, but the practical Pashtun in me wants to know if I'm ready to fight my extended family, all two hundred of them, for you. You have to convince me that we're going to be together forever because I am causing this type of drama just once, and then never again in my life. More than that, I have to convince myself I can be with you for the rest of my time on earth. I am only doing this once, and it has to be worth it."

Eric told me that he loved that I wanted those in my family who were close to me to stay close to me forever. He wanted that relationship with my family, too, and would try to be patient. But he also wanted some compromise, which he reminded me would be great practice for marriage because according to him, a successful marriage is all about compromise.

"Can we at least promise each other that we'll get engaged once your family has had a chance to meet me and gotten to know me a little?" Eric asked.

"You mean like a promise-ring exchange?"

"Yes, something like that. I want your promise that you will always be mine, no matter how much pressure you get from your family." Hmm, does he know that the only pressure he needs to worry about is from within me? I thought.

I told him that if he could find a ring I loved, I would consider it, knowing there was nothing remotely resembling an engagement ring at the local bazaar or in the small shop inside the wire.

I wasn't being coy, or playing with his emotions. This really was a decision that I had never thought I would be asked to make. From a very early age, I knew I was not going to marry an Afghan man because I refused to give in that much to another human being, especially one who is himself so controlled by his culture. After my fights with the uncles, I had also decided that I didn't want to face them in another battle, ever. It was not because I was a coward but because I was afraid of what I might end up doing if I heard one more "If your father was alive, he would be ashamed of you" judgment. I knew I was going to lose it. Therefore, my solution was that I would never marry, and no one who knew my father would ever get another chance to say that to me. I was more than happy being in a committed and loving relationship, without making it everyone's business by getting a license for it. Eric, on the other hand, had a different mind-set: You are mine and I want to claim you legally and in the eyes of God. I guess he hadn't counted on our having two different gods.

In telling him to find a ring I would like, I hoped he would take the time to rethink things and realize that marriage was a complication that might best be avoided. A week passed, then two. He showed up at my bench bearing a plain gold-and-ruby ring. I said I didn't like the bright yellow of the twenty-two-karat gold. A few days later he presented me with a small sapphire ring. I said I never wore anything blue—how was I going to match anything to the ring? He told me he would keep trying. I tried to convince him to let me keep the rings just as tokens of his love, but he said he would save them and give them to me when I least expected it, like on our tenth anniversary, or the birth of our first daughter, who would look just like me but would have a sweeter personality, like his (he was sure I was going to change my mind about not wanting kids). I would try not to panic when he would draw this picture of our future; I would tell myself that if he had enough time, he would come to his senses, and I would be spared another painful decision.

One day there was a meeting with Mrs. Sadiqqi, the director of Women's Affairs. She was covered in the black Iranian *hijab,* but her hands were exposed and on one finger she wore a beautiful ring of rose gold and ruby. It was so striking in its simplicity that I couldn't stop staring at her hand as she rearranged her scarf or picked up her teacup. I always translated at meetings with her because she felt more comfortable having another woman in the room. I'm sure my translation was sloppy that day, because I was so distracted by her ruby ring.

After the meeting, I told Eric I might seriously have to consider his offer if he could get me a ring like that.

"You know it's impossible for me to ask her about it," he said. "In Afghan culture it's completely wrong for me to even acknowledge that she's wearing a ring, much less that I like it."

I smiled at him. "You know life with me is going to be one impossible thing after another. If you are not able to take the challenge, just admit it and I will think that this was just a fling for you." He hated it when I would imply that our relationship wouldn't stay strong in the real world outside Afghanistan. Plus, I wanted to see what he would do when faced with an impossible task in an alien and complex culture.

Eric accepted the challenge.

ONE FRIDAY THE governor was called to Kabul for something and there was no barbecue that we had to attend. Fridays were also considered down days, although the soldiers still had to be prepared at a moment's notice to get out there if necessary. Fridays were also the day when the PA played music from 7:00 A.M. to about 7:00 P.M. The choice of music depended on who was manning the desk at the TOC. I heard some interesting music while in Farah; the first time I heard country music was while sitting on a bench under the hot, dry sun of an Afghan sky. That day, I was sitting in my usual spot, with a line of water bottles in front of me on the bench, some empty, others full. One thing I learned very quickly was that if I wanted to sit in the Afghan sun, I had to drink a lot of water to compensate for the sweat pouring down my back. Eric always knew where I was, and he easily found me that afternoon.

"Do you know this song, Saima?" he asked as he sat across from me.

For the first time, I paid attention to the song. "It's country, and you know that I don't really know any country songs or singers. Don't ask me what it is, but I'm sure you can find out whose MP3 it is." I smiled at him. He looked so dashing and handsome in his uniform.

"It's mine, and I am playing it for you. I want you to listen to the words." Eric looked very serious but still had a twinkle in his eyes. I listened and realized how sweet the tune was. The name of the song was "To Make You Feel My Love." Here I was in my father's war-torn country, sitting across from a man whom I felt I could be with for the rest of my life, who had just dedicated a love song to me. No one had ever done that for me. I didn't know what to say, but at that moment I made up my mind that I would be okay with a man who could render me speechless with such a tender gesture.

"I want you to remember that you were listening to this song when you promised yourself to me, and I promised to make you the happiest woman on earth, no matter how many tests you try to put me through," he said. He took out a folded napkin and handed it to me. We were still in public and had to be discreet. I opened up the napkin, and there sat the ring I had coveted on Mrs. Sadiqqi's hand.

He was eager to tell me how he had met my challenge. After the meeting with Mrs. Sadiqqi he had told Omar that he wanted to buy the ring for his mom, and sent him to try to get it. Eric learned something else about Afghan culture that is sometimes puzzling to Americans. When you admire something on someone, like a ring or scarf, they will try to give it to you, and quite forcefully. Mrs. Sadiqqi refused to sell the ring but offered it to Eric as a gift. Eric refused; he knew it was expensive and she couldn't afford to simply give it away. Omar went back and forth several times. Finally, they agreed that in exchange for the ring,

Mrs. Sadiqqi would receive a new generator for the women's center. Eric bought an Iranian generator and a couple of barrels of fuel at the local bazaar with his own money. He hadn't stopped there; he had also gotten the matching earrings, which he told me would be mine on our first anniversary. This was one of the very few times in my life that I became choked up with my own happiness.

And so we were promised to each other.

S EVENTEEN

L
ess than a month later I stood inside the gate at BAF, anxiously
waiting for my cousins. It was difficult to contain my excitement.
I was finally going to be able to live in Afghanistan as just another Pashtun woman among my people. Knowing that I was finally
going to have real interaction with my own family members, no matter
that I had never met most of them before, had made it a little easier to
say good-bye to Eric the week before.

I watched the guards bustle around. Every day hundreds of local laborers are searched before going through the gates of BAF. It took an
hour or more for the cooks, the cleaners, and the local interpreters to
work their way through the Entry Control Point (ECP). While I waited,
I stood around talking easily with two soldiers whose names I only knew
because they were stitched on their pockets. I had become very much at
ease talking to soldiers. In just a few short months my discomfort had
become a distant memory. I knew the two soldiers weren't related to
each other but they could have been brothers, with their blond brush-
cuts and sunburned cheeks. Finally, one of the other guards, his CAT I
trailing behind him, came up to me and handed me a big black bundle.
"It's from some man who says he's your cousin," he said. "He said to put
this on and come outside." I had told my cousin that I would be waiting
at the gate for him and to let the guards know when he was there.

Sabir had arrived and had brought me a burqa to wear during the trip south to Ghazni Province, where they lived. My female cousins and aunts wore the traditional sea-blue *chadri* with the lace grill over the eyes. The black burqa was new. The fabric was heavy and serious.

A few soldiers came to watch as I pulled it over my head. It took me a while to get it right. One very young soldier said, "I've never seen one of these up close. We only see them on the street. How does it feel under there?" This was before the burqa had made its appearance at the local shops on FOBs all over the country, where soldiers bought them as Halloween costumes for just $15, more than three times what the locals paid for them outside.

"Are you going to be able to walk wearing that?" one of the soldiers asked with real concern.

"I don't know. This is my first time," I replied. "I'll let you know when I get back." I wondered if the Afghan men out there looking at their women were ever concerned about their ability to walk wearing the burqa. I found this casual kindness of the American soldiers endearing and touching. I had seen it when they were talking to little Afghan kids, or old Afghan men, or even one another. The war brought out the kindness in most people, although I wasn't naïve about the ugliness it brought out in others.

Outside the gate Sabir stood waiting for me. He had a dark, clean, short beard. He looked me up and down sternly before turning and nodding toward a taxi he'd hired in Kabul. I had not seen him since I was nine years old, and he didn't even say hello to me. There were no welcoming words, no indication that he was glad to see me. It was essential that Sabir maintain distance and authority. Later, I would discover that he had a quick smile. Even though the morning was cool, beneath my burqa I was already sweating—dripping beneath my hair and on the bridge of my nose. I felt like I was suffocating on my own breath and sweat.

Inside the taxi sat two women in their blue *chadri* and one with a huge black scarf covering her from head to toe and her face showing, stern and wrinkly. These were my cousins and my aunt. I got into the backseat without saying anything, but I squeezed their hands. One of them—I had no idea at the time which one she was—held my hand all the way to Kabul.

These were my mother's people. Unlike many Afghan married couples, my parents weren't cousins; they weren't even related. My mother was a chatterbox; at home in Portland she talked loudly on the phone all day long to her friends. But as we drove to Kabul my aunt and my cousins were silent. On the way to the taxi Sabir had warned me not to say a word. He suspected that the cabdriver, whom he didn't know and who kept glancing at me in his rearview mirror, was mixed up with the insurgents. The driver was probably just an Afghan trying to make a living in the war, but it was also likely that he was being paid for any information he might glean from the conversations of his passengers, especially ones he drove to and from the airfield. I was an oddity worth keeping tabs on. I'm pretty sure that in all his years of driving this cabbie had never picked up a Pashtun woman working with the Americans.

I despise wearing anything on my head. Even before I arrived in America, when I was still living in Peshawar, my relationship to the scarf was hostile. Every minute it was on my head I hated it. That light pressure, the bit of friction it always created, the pure nuisance of worrying whether it was going to slip onto my shoulders or even the floor, as if it was a trick by men to keep us occupied—I had no patience for it. When an Afghan girl of seven or eight is told that soon she is going to be able to wear a scarf, she is usually excited. The adults make a game of it, giving girls pretty scarves when they've been good. By the time they're forced to start wearing them, they've already amassed a little collection. Najiba couldn't wait to start wearing her scarves, but I grumbled and complained. My mother would see me without my scarf and ask me where it was, and I would make excuses, saying that Najiba had stolen it or that I couldn't remember where I had it last. She could tell I just didn't like wearing it, and tried not to pester me too much, unless her friends were coming to visit. Then I had to find it and wear it tightly on my head, so none of them could say that my mother was not doing her Pashtun duty by me.

• • •

I SMOOTHED THE fabric of my burqa and tried to relax. Our taxi was clean. Beads hung from the rearview mirror and framed pictures adorned the dashboard. I was touched to realize that Sabir had probably made an extra effort to hire this specific taxi so that he could transport me in style.

In Kabul we switched taxis and drove to a small restaurant, where we ate lunch, also in silence, and then switched cabs. Sabir had a habit of clenching and unclenching his jaw. I could tell he was on edge; traveling with four female relatives was a huge responsibility. At any moment a man could shame him by allowing his gaze to rest on one of us. He would then have an obligation to take some kind of protective and territorial actions. He'd be required to beat up the offender or even kill him, depending on the level of offense. Often Afghans are portrayed as bloodthirsty thugs eager to commit murder, but I could see that for gentle, distracted men such as Sabir, upholding this tradition was a big cultural burden. So he was careful to take precautions. Later, when I e-mailed Najiba back home in Portland, I told her I had felt like James Bond, changing taxis several times, walking quickly through the alleys of Kabul, trying to lose some unseen Taliban spy collecting information for the insurgents, who would use that intelligence to make an example out of me and my family.

I joked with my sister to hide my fear. The fear I felt on my short trip from Bagram to my mother's village was like nothing I had ever experienced. When I was with the army on missions, I knew there was danger, but I had taken calculated risks to be there, because I knew the area and, more important, I knew that I could depend on the arms, weapons, and protection of the American soldiers. Here, in the middle of nowhere, so close to Karzai's palace, I knew that if an insurgent were to attempt to kill me and my family, there would be no one I could count on to protect me. Even praying to God would be useless, I thought, since I was sure God had nothing to do with what was happening in Afghanistan. Afghans always rely on humor to get themselves through uncertainty and danger. This is one of several habits that U.S. soldiers and Pashtuns have in common. I have seen soldiers do the same after dangerous battles.

Ghazni was a green province in 2005, but just a couple of years later, several night letters would be posted by the Taliban in the cover of darkness, messages warning the local people to refrain from supporting the Afghan government—and support meant not only working in the government but also use of any governmental facilities and resources. One of the letters had made it clear that because clinics, hospitals, and schools were all operated by the government, they could be considered targets. A second letter had been found affixed to the forehead of a recently buried soldier of the Afghan National Army. The insurgents dug him up, posted their note on his head, and left him propped against a wall in the bazaar. This clear violation of the Islamic law about respecting the buried was not pointed out by any of the local imams—it was obvious that the message was intended to intimidate, and everyone was clearly intimidated.

If we had been ambushed and I was discovered with my military ID, I would have been kidnapped and probably ransomed, if I was lucky, or killed as an example. The going rate for the head of a U.S. soldier was $50,000; for an Afghan American working with the U.S. Army, it was over $250,000, and I knew that if that U.S. civilian was a female Pashtun, the kidnapper could—*and likely would*—demand more than that, easily. Dead or alive, I was a hot commodity, one most Afghans would have loved to barter to the highest bidder. No one could be trusted to resist the temptation of so much money. I had asked my family not to tell anyone I was coming to visit. I would only meet the people in my immediate family, and no one else could know I was in the compound. However, these relatives were reliable; the fact that they had come to BAF to pick me up meant that if we were caught, they would also be captured and killed.

As we descended from the highlands onto a low river plain, the heat and humidity increased. I could smell my own deodorant and the dry mineral odor of dust. I stared out the window at the crumpled hills, rust-colored in the setting sun, and the mountains in the distance.

One of the things I love about Afghanistan is the mountains. The mountains surrounding them makes Pashtuns feel safe and protected in their remote villages. But these are the same mountains that serve to isolate them from the development and prosperity in the rest of the country. Later I would learn of the tribal disputes that arose over who owned the rights to these mountains, disputes that would claim the lives of hundreds of Afghans and many U.S. soldiers, and continue to do so to this day.

Although this branch of the family had a shop in the city and also a private car, Sabir was concerned that the car might be tracked back to our family. At one of the several *adda* (taxi stations) that day, we transferred into yet another taxi. The sun disappeared over a tumble of distant mountains, and we continued south to our village.

My family's mud-walled compound was secured with huge iron gates that took at least two men to open. Once the taxi deposited us and sped away and the iron gates closed, the courtyard filled with children. They poured from every door and even a window or two. Four brothers lived here with their mother, their wives, and all these kids. My aunt, the mother of the brothers and the matriarch of the compound, confided in me that they sometimes lost track of which kid belonged to which brother, a happy predicament because it resulted in all the children being treated exactly the same. The kids stared at me with their long-lashed, almond-shaped eyes, full of curiosity.

The cousins who had been in the taxi with me shed their *chadri* and hung them on walls and hooks placed all around the compound for that purpose. Now I saw that they were two of my cousins I had never met before. Here, inside the compound, behind the heavy iron gate, the women chattered loudly in Pashtu, gesturing and patting my arm, excitedly telling the others about the sights and scenes on our journey. All of them were talking at once and smiling, and I could finally see the resemblance to Mamai. The kids scampered around my feet. My heart swelled at the sight of such beautiful children. I gathered up as many as I could in my arms.

Even though it was late, they insisted that I have some tea. They wanted to know about my mother. They laughed, remembering her as being so old-fashioned. How was America treating her? Did she like it there? Did she still dress the same? Was she learning English? Did she have any friends? Were there any other Afghans where she was?

I said I hadn't been able to spend much time with her, but that she seemed to be adjusting fine. She was making some Pashtun friends in the area and talked on the phone for long hours to her friends and family around the world. I didn't try to explain how we'd introduced her to Costco, and how her daily walks took her past several Starbucks—she'd noticed that there was one on every corner—where unemployed hipsters blogged and sipped nonfat vanilla lattes. That although she claimed that she didn't like coffee, she would drink all of my double-shot white-chocolate mocha, insisting that it was not coffee. Even though she was in her fifties and had left her father's house decades earlier, Mamai wouldn't have wanted me to share all that with her family. These were still behaviors her family wouldn't have approved of in her. Instead, I told them that America was probably less of a shock than having a daughter like me who forced her to change her ways faster than she could adjust to. I told them that I believed if she wasn't given a lot of time to dwell on the changes, she wouldn't have a chance to resist them, and in a few short years she would become the modernized mother that I needed, in order for her to come to accept what I had become. Both the men and the women arranged their faces to hide their looks of dismay. But since I was their guest, it would be an insult for them to tell me I'd lost my mind.

SOMETIME IN THE middle of my first night there I awoke with a start. My female cousins, with whom I shared a room, were bustling around in the pitch dark. Only a small square window was embedded in the baked-mud wall; it was so dark I could barely see. I pushed myself up from my mattress, half-asleep. As if by habit I listened for the whistle of incoming rockets, mortars, the *pock-pock-pock* of gunfire—anything that would give me a clue about all the commotion at this ungodly hour.

I gave up trying to figure it out and whispered, "What's going on?"

"Go back to sleep," one of them said.

"Are we getting up to pray?"

"No, no. Don't worry. We need to get up and make breakfast."

"But it's the middle of the night."

"It's four o'clock."

So exhausted was I from the strain of all the travel and my anxiety over possibly getting my relatives killed, I fell back onto my mattress and slept as if sedated for another five hours. When I awoke a second time, I was alone and the sun had been up for a while. I got up and walked through the rooms until I found the big bare kitchen, in the center of the compound, shared by all the families. Two of the cousins in their bright scarves stood patting hunks of pale dough into bread and chatting. How could they still be making breakfast? They'd been up for hours. They explained patiently that they also had to take care of the animals, feed the chickens, milk and feed the cows. They collected the eggs, made the bread *and* the butter, because I was the guest and was to be given fresh butter only. A bowl of honey was sitting on a tray with the fresh cream, of course. I wouldn't have been surprised to learn that they had made the honey, too. They had also picked some grapes for the meal, from the vines in the courtyard right outside the kitchen.

My female cousins were beautiful, like my mother, with their heart-shaped faces, almond-shaped eyes, and straight black brows. To me, Afghan men look closed off and wary, although my male cousins looked kind around the eyes. I was looking forward to sitting around enjoying a meal with them all. But even though we were one family, the men ate alone with their mother, my aunt.

"We always eat separately," Bashir, Sabir's fourteen-year-old brother, explained.

"If that's the case," I said, "I'm going to go eat with the women. I'm a woman and am not nearly old enough to be an auntie and eat with the men." I started to stand up to head to the kitchen, where all the women ate.

"No, no, please sit," said Sabir. "We want you to sit with us."

"I don't feel right. It isn't fair. We are sitting here on comfortable cushions, and they are all sitting on the floor in the kitchen."

"They don't really want to eat with us," said Auntie. "It's hard to eat when they have to cover their faces from the men."

I'd forgotten about this. The last time I was in an Afghan village I was one of the long-lashed kids running wild. But I did remember that even though these women didn't have any choice but to live with their in-laws, they were also traditionally obligated to hide their faces from all the males who were at least ten years or older, except their husbands. So yes, they could eat together, as long as they took care to slip their food beneath their scarves and into their mouths, and as long as they ate in total silence. It was all coming back to me: Back in the village my mother ate in complete silence, while my sister and I chattered nonstop to Baba.

The smell of the fresh bread was making my mouth water. I wanted everyone to eat together. I felt annoyed, the same way I did when I argued with Mamai back in Portland over her rabid insistence on continuing to cover her face. She felt she was upholding Pashtun tradition.

When my mother and I argued about this, it was never far from my mind that had I stayed in the village, I would be the one expected to live my life behind the veil, invisible to those around me, until I made the smallest gesture that could be taken as against the customs, and then I would be made into an example for everyone. In the home of a husband I would be expected to say no more than a couple of words a day, and if I were permitted to leave the compound, I could leave only in the company of a male, even if that male was a teenager and I was his mother. I couldn't leave the compound without him escorting me because it would shame my family. I would be waiting for my son to get a little older, so I could find him a young bride and, according to Pashtun tradition, pass the duty of covering up on to her, so I could finally be free to breathe and speak my mind, still within the gender boundaries set by society.

There are moments when my divided self is more fractured than a Cubist painting: Half of me believes that a young woman's desire to cover her face, to uphold a proud, centuries-old tradition, is touching and sweet—while the other half wants to pitch a world-class Pashtun fit over such nonsensical, gender-based limitation on movement and speech.

I sat back down to eat with my aunt and her sons, while the rest of the women ate in the kitchen. The food was fresh and I'm sure delicious, but I couldn't enjoy it because I felt like I was being completely disloyal to Afghan women everywhere, beginning with my female cousins just down the hallway. I felt like I was conspiring against all women and was deeply ashamed about it. I vowed I would not eat another meal without the women, even if I had to hide in the kitchen until the men ate.

Those of us who want to free the Afghan woman are fixated on the veil, and how if we could only lift up the veils, the Afghan woman could do anything she wanted to do. When I was young and naïve, I had thought that if only I were allowed to go outside without covering up, I would be truly free. Just as, years later, in my uncles' house in Portland, I had thought that if only I could stay out past 9:00 P.M., I would be truly happy. Both times I was wrong; the reality is not that simple. What hobbles Afghan women is the endless housework they shoulder, the pre-dawn mornings and late nights—days that end only after everyone is comfortably in bed and all the work is done. They live an entire lifetime of sleep deprivation and monotony. There's so much talk about the importance of sending girls to school, and I agree, it is important, but given the demands of their daily lives, when are these girls expected to study? By the time they are of grammar school age they are already expected to help their mothers with many responsibilities that in the United States even young adults wouldn't be expected to do. In Afghanistan, five-year-olds raise three-year-old siblings. It breaks my heart to see little girls, younger than eight or ten, carrying a three-year-old brother or sister on their hips, feeding them, watching them, being responsible for them in every way. In Afghan villages all over you see young girls, tiny, thin things, lugging heavy jugs of water past groups of boys and unemployed men who are squatting in that impossible-to-copy Afghan way, doing nothing more than wasting time. These girls' childhoods are over before they even start. On top of all that, they are not fed properly, or taken care of by their parents, so they tend to be sickly and look even younger than their age, until they start having children, and then they age years in days. They don't even have time to realize that they should be out there playing, enjoying being children themselves.

Once, when I was going to the bazaar with Sabir, we drove by a group of tiny young girls with water jugs on their heads weaving past a group of men and boys who just sat there and stared at them. I asked Sabir if we could stop, without really thinking about what I was about to do. He asked why, and I told him that I wanted to tell the boys to get up and help the little girls. He locked the doors of the car quickly. I'd never seen him move so fast. He stepped on the gas. "You're crazy if you think you can do stuff like that here. These guys could easily kill you for saying something like that. This is not America, and we have to live here, even after you have gone back." I was appalled by his response, and even more sickened because I actually saw its crazy Afghan logic.

THE NEXT DAY I went to the kitchen when I knew that dinner was about ready and sat there with the ladies of the house. They all looked at me expectantly, questioning me without saying anything. I told them I wanted to eat with them in the kitchen because I was not an auntie who is allowed to eat with the men. They didn't argue much because they said they loved my company and talking to me was like talking to Mamai, their aunt. We were having *shurwa,* my favorite, since I was the guest. This is one of the oldest, simplest, and—in my opinion—most delicious dishes Afghanistan has ever produced. It is simple in that it requires only meat, onions, tomatoes, potatoes, salt, black pepper, and, if you want to get fancy, turnips and carrots. Boil it all together for a long time, over low heat, and soak some bread in it. Put some yogurt on top, and eat it with fresh chili peppers. I had asked the ladies to cook this dish that night. I've made it many times at home in Oregon, but I have never been able to capture the flavor it had that night.

We sent the men their food through my little cousins, but they soon returned, telling me that Sabir and the other men were asking me to come and eat with them. I told the little ones that I was eating where the women ate, and I would have tea with them. This didn't work, and the kids returned with one of the older male cousins. He told me that he had come to ask all the women to eat with them, at least while I was there. I was finally going to eat with my whole family! But I could tell that the women were not excited. Who could blame them? They would have to cover their faces while eating. I felt guilty, but I also felt that at least I would break some silly gender taboo about men and women eating together, even if it was only for a couple of days.

In terms of conversation, we'd already exhausted the one topic we shared—my mother, their sister and aunt—and I struggled to find some common ground with these men. I resented them for the awful way they treated my female cousins while at the same time offering me the care and respect traditionally shown an honored male guest. I couldn't decide if they believed that my female cousins were not human, and therefore didn't have any thoughts or feelings, or whether they saw me as having nothing in common—including gender—with the women at the compound. I was becoming increasingly upset that they wanted to talk to me endlessly about their business, a small gas station in Ghazni City. They made jokes about learning English so they could speak with my mom, in case she became so Americanized that she forgot all her Pashtu. I should have been grateful for their attempts to involve me and entertain me, but I hated that I had to choose which gender to spend time with during my short visit. Why couldn't I be with them all, together?

The soldiers at Farah were so typically American, with their love of Pizza Hut, video games, and country music. As a Pashtun, a female, and a civilian, I was an outsider three times over. I had imagined that when I arrived at my family's compound I would feel a mystical sense of finally belonging. I had thought it would feel like home in the way that Portland, Peshawar, and even Kabul never really did. I was a real Pashtun, so why was I feeling as if I were walking on eggshells, all alone, with no one to guide me or give me some hint about how to behave? I didn't want to insult anyone because I knew that the minute I left to go back to BAF, phones would be ringing in Portland, telling Mamai how I had behaved. I felt pressured to act as she would have because this was her family, but at the same time I felt that it was unfair to treat me so much better than the other females. I sat on the front veranda watching the evening news on TV, listening to everyone talk at once as I sipped my green tea.

I was angry, sad, and hopeless. I felt lonely and confused, like an alien who'd been brought home by the friendly citizens of a new and strange planet. One of my youngest cousins, Bashir, who was lucky enough to go to school during the day for a couple of hours, asked me the English words for apple, grapes, chicken, children, TV, and all the objects around him, but not for women. While the men were amusing themselves, their wives and sisters silently replenished the tea. The men didn't even acknowledge them, much less thank them. It was unthinkable that they would ask their wives and sisters to join us. I felt sick, as if I were giving the entire family the impression that it was okay for these women to be treated this way. There and then I decided that I was going to ally myself with the women. If they woke up at four o'clock in the morning to milk the cows and bake the bread, then so would I.

The next morning I rose in the dark with my cousins. I found Auntie in the courtyard, milking the cows.

"I want to help with everything. For one day I want to be like your daughters," I said.

Auntie wiped her hands on her pale gray dress and peered at me kindly, over the black cotton scarf she'd wrapped around her head and mouth. I think she sensed that I was struggling to try to fit in with the other women in the compound. She took me to the corner of the barn where the cows were stalled beneath an overhang made of dried branches. Shafika was already at work, squatting on her haunches in her lilac-colored *purdugh,* milking a skinny brown cow. She looked up and gave me a brilliant smile. I thought she was amazing, to be able to smile like that at 4:00 A.M. Najiba wouldn't smile like that even at 10:00 A.M., claiming she isn't a morning person.

Auntie told Shafika to let me have a turn. She demonstrated how to pull on the udders, then stepped aside. I squatted down just as she'd done, grabbed the udders, and started tugging. I'd made the mistake of wearing my platform flip-flops, and every time I got some momentum going I couldn't help rocking back on my heels. Not much milk was coming out. The cow exhaled, as if it had lost all patience with my ineptitude, and stamped its foot. It seemed as if the more I tugged and squeezed, the less milk came out. After almost fifteen minutes of struggle, there were a few inches of thin milk at the bottom of the pail. I tried to remember how much milk they used in a day, and thought that if you added up the production of all the other cows, this was at least respectable. Like my cousins I wore a *shalwar kameez,* and as I stood up I stepped on the hem of my *kameez,* lost my balance, and kicked the bucket over. The milk made a little puddle for a moment before vanishing into the parched earth.

I grabbed the bucket and righted it quickly, but it was too late. Auntie saw my distress and began to laugh. She rushed over to help me up and told me that it happened to her all the time. I knew she was only saying that to make me feel better, and that the last time she had wasted milk like that she was probably a very young girl. I felt bad, but since I knew that it was no good to cry over spilled milk, I decided to do something very American: I would replace the milk with store-bought. I sent one of my little male cousins to the local shop with 100 Afghanis and told him to get a half gallon of milk.

When it was time for milk tea, and the store-bought milk was used to make it, Sabir refused to drink it, complaining that it tasted awful. After Auntie told him what had happened, he tried to choke it down in an effort to make me feel better. I told him he didn't have to drink it on my account, and he put his cup down gratefully.

The next morning when my cousins woke up in the dark I pretended to be asleep. After my failure at milking the cow I realized it was best to stick to my role of honored guest. Once the men went off for the day, I escaped up to the roof to get some alone time, an American habit that becomes a luxury in an Afghan house.

IN PORTLAND, I had made a list of items that I promised myself I would one day buy in the Ghazni bazaar, since it was the only place the items were sold. These were silk fabrics that have been the coveted choice for Afghan bridal outfits for centuries—the traditional Pashtun brides still wear these same colors that were worn by their grandmothers and their grandmothers' grandmothers. There were some types of beads and mirrors that were then woven into scarves and dresses. There were silk threads, all the things I had seen when Mamai showed me her wedding outfit. I was very young, but I remember her informing me that one day soon, I would get my own bridal dress ready so I could get married. I had told her, "Mamai, why can't I just get the dress now? I don't want to get married!" and she had laughed. "Everyone has to get married to get the dress. What would people say if you wore it on any other occasion?" she asked me with so much patience, a mother explaining her culture to her daughter. She didn't believe me, and I hardly believed myself then, when I said, "I am going to get the dress, and I am not going to have to marry some man to get it!"

Now I was so close to the shops where these items were sold, and I was getting married, although not to a man who would even know the significance of the dress. Still, I wanted to get it because it meant a lot to me to be married in the same fashion as my grandmother and her grandmother before her, even though I was breaking all the rules by marrying a self-chosen, non-Pashtun, non-Muslim man. I am capable of seeing double standards, hypocrisy, even in myself—maybe more so in myself.

I asked Sabir, the oldest son and thus the man of the compound, if I could please go to the bazaar to get some shopping done. He looked anxiously at his mother for guidance. Luckily for me, and not so luckily for Sabir, my aunt agreed to the trip but said that I would have to go with another female or I would draw too much attention. I thanked her and waited for her to tell me which one of my cousins should come with me.

When my female cousins, who were now back in the kitchen cleaning up after breakfast and preparing to begin cooking lunch, heard about the excursion they were excited. It wasn't every day that there was talk of a trip to the bazaar. They all wanted to go.

Negotiating this was no easier than figuring out who would get to sit down to breakfast together. Like all Pashtun women, my female cousins rarely left the compound. Shafika was eager to buy some beads for something she was sewing. Like her older brother Sabir, Shafika had a quick smile and a beautiful set of white teeth. I could hear her every morning at dawn, singing in the courtyard as she swept the ground and fed the chickens. She had never gone to school, but once I saw her pick up one of Bashir's books when she didn't think her brother was around. She flipped through it, glancing at the pages. It was in Pashtu. I asked her if she could read it. She smiled and said, "Why would I need to read? It is not like I am going to need to read a sign to find the cow to milk!" She laughed, but I didn't have to be a psychologist to know that she was hurting inside and resented her brother for what she could never have. Did she resent me, too? I would never know because one of the strongest pillars of *Pashtunwali* is never letting any insult reach your guest, whether from your own behavior or that of another. During the few hours of the day when Shafika had no chores, she pulled out a battered black-and-gold treadle sewing machine and sat on the floor of the main room. She was making something out of a pretty silken fabric of wide hot-pink, royal-blue, and emerald-green stripes. I thought that it was her own bridal outfit, and felt so sad for her, thinking that she had to make the dress for the day when she would become another man's property. On the day I was leaving, she told me she had made me a present, and it was the traditional silk outfit she had been working on since my arrival.

It was decided that Shafika would go with me to the bazaar. My aunt and cousins didn't leave it at that. They gave me a long lecture on how to behave there. Bashir kept teasing me by saying, "This is not American bazaar" every few minutes, like I could forget that fact once I was surrounded by all the women in their *chadri*. I promised to wait for my cousin to talk to the shopkeeper instead of addressing him myself. I would keep the expected distance behind my cousin. Under no circumstances was I to talk to another man, or look at anyone; I would just look down at my feet. And, of course, I could never expose my face since anyone could tell I was not from there. I wanted to get to the bazaar quickly—otherwise I might have asked what that last comment meant. I know I looked very Pashtun when I saw myself in the mirror, but I'm not sure what they were seeing when they looked at my face.

I found Shafika on the roof, stooped over a cloth on which she was carefully placing bunches of red grapes to dry in the sun. When I told her she could come to the bazaar, she gasped. This would be the first time in three years she had been allowed to go. Although the other women were disappointed that they were not selected, they were genuinely happy for Shafika and gave her their shopping lists. One needed red beads, another a special sort of silver trim. As Shafika put on her blue *chadri* she whispered to me about why the women were excited for us to go: "The men take our lists, but they never get the right things."

Once again my cousin took precautions. We left our car in the compound and walked in the midday sun to the next village to find a taxi. Already, my scalp was sweating. There was no sense in making conversation because everything I said was muffled by my burqa. Shafika and I trudged along behind the men, Sabir, Bashir, and my cousin Daoud. Once we got to the bazaar, the other cousins took off on their own errands, leaving Sabir to take us women to the shops that had what we wanted.

The Ghazni bazaar sits in the shadow of the Citadel, a mud-walled fortress built in the thirteenth century, high on a hill overlooking the city. The narrow shops are part of a larger mud structure. Villages and smaller towns such as Ghazni are bathed in earthen tones. Most of the shops were run by Hazaras, some by Pashtuns, and others by Sikhs, who shockingly, or at least to me, spoke fluent Pashtu. There was one gas station, which barely looked any different from the rest of the shops, nothing like American gas stations with their huge logos. It would be a few years before they would get the American Shell look-alike gas stations. In between the shops wove mud streets that, on a hot day like this one, were full of dust. Every so often one of the shopkeepers would come out with a water bucket and splash some water on the dust so that people could breathe. It was amazing that I noticed all this behind my veil because I was trying so hard not to lose sight of the backs of my cousins in the middle of all those other backs in the tiny view I had from my *chadri*.

Shafika and I needed to go to the fabric shop, but Sabir was in no hurry. He strolled along with the other men, as if they were in a race with an unseen competitor to see how slowly they could work their way through the bazaar. Beneath my *chadri* the sweat was running down the side of my face. Shafika was silent. We shuffled along. Sabir stopped and talked to some friends. My *chadri* fit in such a way that I had no real peripheral vision. The day had become hot. I smelled raw sewage but couldn't see where it was flowing. Men on bicycles wheeled past wearing *shalwar kameez* and white turbans limp with dirt and dust. I felt stifled. I couldn't breathe. Back home, I loved shopping; I could shop for hours. Here I thought I would die if I didn't inhale soon.

We passed a shop with a stack of folded pieces of brightly colored silk standing sentry just inside the doorway. The shopkeeper leaned against the pile with his arms folded. He looked past Shafika and me, careful to make sure we knew that we were invisible to him. I wanted to ask him about his silk, but Sabir strode on ahead.

I stopped in front of the shopkeeper. He continued to ignore me. Shafika stood behind me. She shifted her weight from one foot to the other. I thought I could feel her nervousness. We needed Sabir to speak to the shopkeeper on our behalf, since it was forbidden for us to talk to him directly and I had promised I wouldn't talk to the shopkeeper. I opened my mouth to yell for Sabir before he disappeared into the crowd, but that was forbidden as well. No Pashtun woman's voice should be heard in public. I suddenly realized I didn't have to behave this way. I had an option, unlike the poor women in *chadri,* miserable all around me. I pulled the scarf off my head and gulped a fresh draft of dusty air, laced with the sweet-rotten smell of garbage. I breathed, in and out. The feeling of suffocation was instantly gone.

When Sabir turned and saw me, his look of shock and alarm, which he tried to disguise in order to maintain his composure, was something I will remember until I die. I had done something on impulse, an American quality that could easily get me killed in Afghanistan—worse, it could get all those with me killed. I realized right away I shouldn't have done it, but Pashtun pride kept me from admitting my mistake. I stared at Sabir stubbornly, as if asking what he was going to do in the middle of the bazaar. I knew he wouldn't want it to appear like, God forbid, he had lost control of his women.

"Why would you do that? Do you wish to die and take all of us with you?" he hissed. He reached out to grab me by the arm, then thought better of it. He glared at Shafika. "Why would you let her do this?"

"Don't yell at her!" I said. "It's not her fault. It's your fault. You stood around chitchatting. It's hot under these cursed *chadri*. I asked you to hurry and you ignored me. We finally get to the store I wanted and you keep walking past it. You think we came out here for a stroll with you?"

Sabir was speechless. He had never been talked to this way by a female, and here it was happening in the middle of downtown Ghazni, by a female he knew he couldn't and wouldn't punish. He just shook his head and told me to go to the store and get anything I wanted, but I only had five minutes. Word would travel that a woman had taken off her *chadri* and everyone would likely want to come and see for themselves. I did put the *chadri* back on and went into the shop. The shopkeeper was so shocked that he didn't even bargain with me, and let me buy all the fabrics at rates that even I didn't think I was going to get. I think he just wanted me out of his shop, as soon as possible, before the mob came and interfered with his business.

Back at the compound, Shafika, who'd barely said a word, scooted into the kitchen to prepare tea. I felt horrible for ruining her first trip into town in years, but I really did think that Sabir had been inconsiderate in his treatment of us and should have tried to focus on our needs, since we were the reason he went to the bazaar in the first place. Sabir started to tell his brothers what had happened. I said I didn't like how here, back at home, he talked to me as if I was an actual human being, but in the bazaar he behaved as if I wasn't even there. My cousins and uncles consoled Sabir. They thanked God it hadn't been them in the bazaar with me.

While we were arguing and drinking tea my cell phone rang. I excused myself and went outside, hoping it was Eric. Since I had left Farah, he'd called me every day. My family was curious. Who was calling me here? If it was my mother, they wanted to talk to her, too. I told them it was my boss. It would be impossible to tell them he was my fiancé. My family at home in Portland didn't even know Eric existed. I tried not to think

about this too much. If they thought my taking off the *chadri* in the bazaar could have gotten us all killed, what would my extended family do
when they learned I was buying the fabric for my bridal dress for a marriage to a white non-Pashtun non-Muslim?

Some of the children were playing outside in the garden. I walked to
the kitchen and took the stairs from there to the roof. The kids followed
me; they always did, being unaware of the American concept of privacy
while talking on the phone. Between the rows of raisins drying in the sun
were a handful of pink-and-green woven mats. The roof was surrounded
by a decorative metal fence painted aqua blue. I loved to sit up here and
look out over the garden and courtyard down below. The compound was
surrounded by the customary tall, baked-mud wall, at the base of which
grew enormous sunflowers.

Eric was still in Farah, wrapping up loose ends; his tour of duty was
ending and he would be back in the States in another month. We chatted about how it would be for him to return to Florida and see his kids.
He couldn't wait for me to come home, so we could start planning our
wedding. He talked about what my new life would be like in Florida. We
would buy a house, which I could decorate any way I pleased. He knew I
wasn't really one for cooking, but I would have time to learn.

"You just want to marry me because you think Pashtun women are
submissive, and I'll have dinner ready for you every night when you get
home," I teased.

"Honey, the second I met you, and you told me you didn't belong to
anyone, I knew that you were nothing like the submissive women I had
heard about in Afghanistan. Knowing you, you would probably make me
cook you dinner, *after* I come home from work, while you recover from
shopping all day with my money."

I laughed. One of the things I loved about Eric was his ability to give
as good as he got.

From the day he had mentioned the word *engagement*, I had told him
that anytime he wanted I would give him a Get Out of Jail Free card,
except this would be a Get Out of Marriage to Saima card. He always
refused, but he did ask me to keep offering, in the event that he would

one day want his freedom—to remember how it felt to wear the pants in a relationship. The more tension there was between us, the more we joked; after many tours in Afghanistan Eric had picked up the Pashtun habit of joking about things you can't control.

As I listened to him describe my luxurious future as a Florida house-wife, I started to squirm. I felt something I couldn't define. Awkward-ness? But I had never felt awkward around him before. Guilt for sitting up here on the roof speaking English to my American boyfriend, while my female cousins were treated so harshly down in their own home? I let him talk. He knew something was up, because in the few months he'd known me, I had never been that quiet or withdrawn.

"I love you," he said.

I could feel the pressure for me to say "I love you, too," something that Pashtuns don't do. Soldiers always ask me, "How do you say 'I love you' in Pashtu?" and I have to explain that in a culture where parents don't even develop bonds with their kids until they are much older and there is no danger of losing them to one of the many illnesses that claim thou-sands of infants' lives, we don't have any three Pashtu words to express that sentiment. There are ways you show it, and that is how we like to express our love. We are loyal, and through taking care of our loved ones, we tell them how much we love them. As for romantic love, how could I ever explain to an American that in a culture where almost all of the marriages are arranged by the families, and you meet your spouse for the first time on your wedding day, not knowing if the person is even capable of being loved or loving you, there is no need to say those words? To a Pashtun woman, a husband who doesn't beat her regularly is showing her he loves her. He never has to utter those words. She returns his love by bearing his children and taking care of his family.

It makes me suspicious of a man's intentions when I hear him say "I love you" so casually. It is hard to resist some cultural influences, I guess.

"I miss you, too," I said. I didn't even tell him what had happened at the bazaar or that I had been able to buy all the material for my Af-ghan bridal dress. I knew he would be ecstatic to hear I was planning on having a traditional Afghan dress, and I couldn't handle his enthusiasm right then. He got off the phone because I was not being responsive and he wrongly assumed that I was not in a place to talk openly, so he hung up, making me promise to call as soon as I was able to talk freely.

In two days I would be heading back to BAF. Eric was eager to get on with our life together, but I'd received a phone call from the site manager at Bagram. In mid-September the country was holding its first-ever parliamentary elections, and they needed a Pashtu interpreter at PRT Jalalabad. At first I'd dismissed the idea. I had completed my six-month contract, which was the most time I had told myself I would do when I had impulsively signed up for this.

But I couldn't get past the feeling that I hadn't really accomplished anything. In retrospect, my months at sleepy PRT Farah seemed less like a mission to reconnect with my father's country and more like a camping vacation punctuated with weekly barbecues at the governor's compound. I'm not very good at hiding the truth from myself, and the truth was I had done nothing yet, and I wanted much more. So I signed up for another three months at Jalalabad. Eric was unhappy, but I convinced him I would have regrets if I had left before I felt I had really done something to help my people. He said he never wanted me to have any regrets about marrying him, so he gave me permission. I told him I didn't need his permission, and he said, "I know, honey. I'm just trying to make myself feel good, as your man."

I sat on the roof among the rows of drying grapes and thought about my parents, my siblings, my relatives, carrying on their lives in the house beneath me and in faraway America. Another call came in from Eric, and I ignored it. I felt displaced, yet strangely at peace with my descision.

My female cousins didn't laugh at me for my poor cow-milking skills or for socializing with the men. They treated me with so much kindness, and I loved them for their open acceptance of my limitations. My skills were nothing compared with what they were capable of doing. Their capabilities were feeding tens of children, their men, and so many other relatives who depended on them. I might know how to read in English, but that skill was no good in this village in Ghazni because women were never allowed to work outside their homes. They were always trying to figure out how to entertain me once they got done with their chores. So, the day before I left, I was sitting in the middle of the courtyard talking to several little children when I heard Shafika was looking for me. The women were finished with their chores for the day and wanted to take me to the house my mother had been born in, and then to the vineyard for a picnic.

My older aunt, two younger brides, two single cousins, Shafika, and I donned our long shawls and set out for the vineyard, located not far from the compound. People don't realize that women in the villages have a lot more freedom of movement than they do in cities like Kabul. In villages, families know everyone, and they only socialize with one another—so as long as the women stay within the village, they can come and go as they please during the day. Since during the day, most of the men are also working outside the village, this gives women in the village even more freedom, because there are only other women and children there. I wore an outfit my cousins had sewn for me: a deep-teal silk frock with a wide hem of heavy gold embroidery. The matching pants were made of plain teal silk, and the scarf was chiffon, shot through with gold thread.

I was astounded at how comfortable I felt, strolling along the dusty streets with my female relatives. I felt both free and protected. I felt, for the first time, as if I blended in, as if I was part of my own culture. We had grabbed Bashir, who was on break from school and thus at home on this afternoon, as an escort. Even though it wasn't unusual for a group of women to walk through the village, we still needed a token male. Bashir was only fourteen, wiry and small, his beard just beginning to come in. Even he knew how ridiculous it was, the idea that he could protect us.

"If we're attacked, you'll probably run!" I teased him.

"Yes, but I'll run fast and find a real man to come help you." His answering smile was quick, like he had already figured out what he would do if, God forbid, there were an incident.

Our vineyard was surrounded by high mud walls. Five or six varieties of grapes grew there. I pulled my scarf over my head without experiencing the accompanying storm of conflicting emotions. We ate grapes straight from the vine. We sat in the sun. It was warm, but the air was still crisp. Was it really only five days earlier when I was struggling to put on the heavy burqa (don't get me wrong, I still hated it) inside the gates at BAF?

On the way back we passed the old house where my mother had grown up. Like everything else, it was made of baked mud, surrounded by high mud walls. The doors were gone, the windows removed and repurposed elsewhere. My aunts insisted they give me the guided tour. I saw the room where my mother, as a little girl and then as a young woman, had slept with her sisters, cousins, and aunts. This house had a *kareez* running through the courtyard. It was a sign of affluence; it meant the women never had to leave the compound to fetch water.

I stood in her house and inhaled deeply from beneath my scarf. This was the place I had come from, and these were my people. I felt that strange tug of guilt and pride I'd experienced while sitting at the bedside of the young bride who had set herself on fire, that now familiar internal struggle. I was headed to Jalalabad to work again as an interpreter, but it didn't feel like that was enough. I was an American. I had freedom. I had these women who accepted me and my strange life without question. Shouldn't I be doing more for them, more to fulfill my father's prophecy for me? I had been alive more than half the life span of the average Afghan woman, and I was not even able to help these close relatives, much less Afghans all over the world. Suddenly, I heard the clock ticking, but it had nothing to do with a biological urge to reproduce. It had everything to do with fulfilling what had been foretold by a loving and caring father, about a daughter whom he didn't know at the time and would never have the chance to get to know, but in whom he had faith. I vowed then to spend the rest of my years on earth making his words come true.

EIGHTEEN

In late August 2005, when the Chinook touched down at the Provincial Reconstruction Team in Jalalabad, a sergeant greeted me with a crooked smile. He hoisted my duffel bags onto his shoulder, walked me off the helipad and around the wall that surrounded the compound, and led me to my new home in a barracks next to where the marines were housed. He showed me to an empty room at the end of a row of B-huts. "This should work for now," he said. "I doubt you'll be here long." I tried not to think about what that meant.

If Eric knew I was being stuck in a barracks so close to the men, he would have thrown a fit. I missed him. But even though it was hard to imagine what it would be like to translate for another commander—and a female commander at that—I felt a flutter of excitement in my chest.

The sergeant told me that my new boss, Lieutenant Colonel Judy Cabano, was at a meeting at the governor's, and he wasn't sure when she'd return. I sat on the edge of my bed for a while. I was getting hungry. I wondered what time the chow hall served dinner. I left the barracks and walked around to begin getting my bearings. Jalalabad wasn't a big PRT, but it was bigger than Farah.

I ran into an older Afghan who introduced himself as one of Judy's former interpreters. He worked with the Civil Affairs Team on projects and village assessments. Tall and thin, with short gray hair, he had a serious look, but as another Afghan passed him and greeted him as Engineer-Saab, he smiled and his face became that of any old Afghan man. He wasn't an actual engineer; *engineer-saab* is a Pashtun term of respect for someone who has had the good fortune to acquire some basic education in any field. Engineer-Saab was eager to clue me in about how strict Judy was, how uncompromising. Judy—everyone called her PRT Commander, but when we met she asked me to call her Judy—used to yell at him for mumbling during meetings. She accused him of being a low talker, which simply wouldn't do.

I knew from my own meetings with the governor in Farah that there was no telling how the pace of a conversation would go. Sometimes it stopped and started like a sulking child on the way to school, and sometimes it raced along so quickly it was almost impossible to keep up, much less convey the all-important details, the nuances that contained the most meaning. It would waste time and cause embarrassment for the commander to keep saying "What was that?" If you get the tone wrong, you miss so much nonverbal communication, and these meetings are conducted by U.S. personnel who pay so much attention to the exact translated words that they miss the tone, which often contains the essence. A good interpreter takes time to draw attention to that. The problem I noticed early on was that not only were most of the interpreters poorly trained, but they were too intimidated by the U.S. forces, as well as by the local Afghans, to stop the proceedings and take the time to explain. I never had any problems with feeling intimidated, and never felt bad asking either side to stop so I could do my job. I realized quickly that if the Americans understood the Afghans, there wouldn't be any point in even having the meetings. It was crucial that the two parties understood each other, or we would be in that country forever and no one would benefit from our presence.

Engineer-Saab said he wasn't the only one who had been sacked. Judy had gone through four other interpreters in less than a month. There had been a variety of problems. One of them spoke Pashtu at a third-grade level and kept lapsing into Dari when she got nervous. Another was simply too old and couldn't keep up with the physical requirements of the assignment. Engineer-Saab took a few minutes on his way to the prayer room to tell me this and then said he would find me later to introduce me to the rest of the interpreters, probably after the commander had had her talk with me. His look as he left me was a mixture of pity and glee—surely, I would be the next interpreter to be sacked.

I wondered whether he was right, and if Judy would fire me, too. Perhaps it would be a good thing. I could return to the States, marry Eric, and move to Florida to start my new life. At the same time I was thinking, There's no way I will let her fire me. I will be the best interpreter she's ever had. This was a challenge too personal to ignore.

I ate dinner at a long table with the other CAT II interpreters. Just as I was finishing my tea, Judy walked in. She reminded me of an elf. I don't know what I had expected, but this tiny woman with a heart-shaped face and big blue-green eyes was not it. She scanned the room and when she spied me, the new girl on campus, she came over and introduced herself.

"Maybe when you're done here you can stop by the office," she said. My first impression was that she was uptight and angry. I wasn't surprised. By then I knew that she hadn't gotten to where she had in the army by being sweet. It was dark outside when I arrived at her office in the TOC. I sat down on the sofa in front of her desk. She asked me where I had interpreted before. I tried to stress that I was not a professional interpreter.

"If my experience is any indication, it looks like none of the interpreters are professionals," she said.

"I just spent six months in Farah," I said. It sounded so meager, even to my ears.

"I think it's a matter of personality and attitude," she said. We talked for a while about the difficulties of interpreting in a language that differed so much from region to region, and the fact that there was no training that any of us interpreters went through, or even much rigorous testing to screen out the bad from the mediocre. I spoke in a concise manner, at what I thought was the perfect volume to let her hear that I was capable of communicating clearly with her and for her. She must

have liked what she heard because she said that I could go with her to
the morning meeting at the governor's.

Before I left, she asked about my accommodations. When I told her
where they'd put me she called in the sergeant with the lopsided smile,
who apparently was the PRT sergeant major, and told him to get me out
of there immediately. "I don't care what time it is," she said. "I don't care
if there are no empty rooms. Move your soldiers around and give Miriam
the room on the floor above mine."

I could tell that the SM wasn't thrilled to receive an order to move his
people around after they'd all bedded down for the night. And he wasn't
about to say that he'd only dumped me there because it was convenient,
and he hadn't thought I'd last more than a few days. I smiled at him;
aware that as a civilian he thought I was a nuisance. Still, an order was
an order. He'd been tasked to move me, and move me he would. Before
he left, Judy, sensing his displeasure, said, "Cultural sensitivity starts at
the PRT, Sergeant Major."

I was moved to a room inside the dilapidated building known fondly
as Motel 6. A former resort built by the Soviets for short in-country va-
cations, it had been repurposed as the hub of PRT Jalalabad. My room
was on the second floor, directly over Judy's. It had a private bath and
a deck with a view of a stand of tall trees and an enormous swimming
pool. The pool, which had been dug at least eight feet deep all around,
was empty, and served as a makeshift basketball court; a hoop and back-
board were affixed to one side of the pool.

UNLIKE FARAH, DOZING beneath the sun in the far west like an old
frontier town, Jalalabad, in Nangarhar Province in eastern Afghanistan, was a happening place. The main road from Pakistan to Kabul
ran through its center, and much of the food that fed the country was
grown on the fertile, irrigated lands around the city. Palm trees lined
the streets. The wind carries the tangy scent of basil and citrus. Jalalabad was Afghanistan's own sensual Mediterranean city. Unfortunately,
it was also infamous for sheltering insurgents.

Most Afghans hold a negative view of Arabs. There is no love lost between the two ethnic groups. When Osama bin Laden was expelled from Sudan in 1996, he sought refuge in Jalalabad. The predominately Pashtun city was quiet and prosperous; the economic freedom gave the people the luxury of practicing *Pashtunwali* in its strictest form.

To Westerners, *Pashtunwali* is an utter mystery. Literally, it means "the way of Pashtuns." It is a set of principles that guide the behavior of Pashtuns in everyday life and unites them with other Pashtuns spread out all over Afghanistan and, after the Russians attacked, to those who emigrated as well. The Farsiban—the main minority ethnic group in Afghanistan—in their inherent contempt for the Pashtuns, have simpli-fied *Pashtunwali* into three words: *zan* (woman), *zar* (gold), and *zameen* (land).

Although this Farsiban judgment of *Pashtunwali* as being barbaric is meant to be insulting, these three words do hold great importance for any Pashtun. The main principle revolves around the concept that a man's pride is directly linked to his possessions and how he protects them. His possessions are twofold: his land and his women. Anyone who tries to take either of these from him is his enemy; avenging any wrong-doing is a duty, and the only honorable way to exact revenge is by death of the enemy, or of oneself, if one fails at the former. This is not neces-sarily a passionate act; it is not vengeance taken in the heat of the mo-ment. A true Pashtun will take years to plan his retaliation, with a cool and calm head. And, if he dies trying to restore respect for his family and himself, then it becomes the responsibility of his sons to carry on the mission. Families may take centuries to avenge their lost honor, and during that time the sons are unable to enjoy everyday life. The simple fact that their enemy—or their enemy's children or children's children—continues to live and breathe without having paid for dishonoring them makes life unbearable for a Pashtun.

A man's honor is linked directly to the conduct of his women; thus, the females in Pashtun society carry the heaviest burden of *Pashtunwali*. One careless action from a silly teenage girl—such as starting a romance with a boy—can easily trigger a family feud that may take the lives of hundreds of men and women over generations.

But what most non-Pashtuns don't realize is that if you ask a Pashtun for forgiveness, and you follow the customs of *Pashtunwali* while asking him, he will be obligated to forgive you for all you have done to him and his family. His forgiveness exacts a price, however. In exchange, you have to give him your most precious belonging: one of your women (or more, depending on the severity of the offense being forgiven). It is called a blood bride, and my grandmother was one. The life of most Afghan women is difficult, but the life of a blood bride is insufferable. When a woman marries, she leaves her own family and moves in with her husband's. A blood bride is surrounded for the rest of her life by people who were the sworn enemies of her family and who most likely have killed her close relatives. She is forced not only to live with them but to take care of them for as long as she lives.

As ancient and seemingly intractable as *Pashtunwali* may seem, even it has changed with the times and with the past forty-plus years of war in Afghanistan. Due to the Soviet invasion and the resulting Pashtun diaspora, its rules as practiced by the younger generation are far more lax; they tend to forgo family agendas and revenge seeking, although they still hold their women to a strict code of conduct (which I feel has less to do with *Pashtunwali* and more to do with misogyny and the belief that their women belong to them).

That being said, there are pockets of Afghanistan, such as Jalalabad, that have enjoyed relative peace even over the last thirty years of national tumult; in these places, strict Pashtun communities still flourish. A visitor to the region, savvy to the ways of the Pashtuns and well aware that a single village can protect you better than an entire company of Afghan National Army soldiers, could easily exploit Pashtun *melmastia*, or hospitality. This is what Osama bin Laden did.

Bin Laden knew *Pashtunwali*, and what it would mean if he sought *melmastia* from a Pashtun village, which in its simplest form can be defined as protection. Regardless of whether the Pashtuns to whom he presented himself as a guest agreed or disagreed with him and his fledgling movement, Al-Qaeda, the code of *Pashtunwali* required them to treat him as a guest and assure his safety. Bin Laden was shrewd. He knew Afghan culture and used it to his advantage. He knew the Pashtuns would be unable to refuse him, especially in Jalalabad, where the practice of *Pashtunwali* was still relatively strong. He hid out there for those first few years of Tora Bora fighting and later was rumored to have moved across the border to Pakistan.

In the fall of 2005, Jalalabad, despite what was going on in the rest of the country, was among the safest cities in the country. The Taliban was anemic, still recovering from having been ousted four years earlier. That year, there had been only a single suicide bomber. All over the city men fearlessly shaved their beards. There was even a gym in the middle of the city, with a large banner out front depicting a muscled man posing. A few small music stores had opened and were doing big business in Bollywood CDs and DVDs. But as I write this, a mere six years later, it's as if we have gone back in time. The city is nervous. Just a few months ago, a group of seven militants entered a bank in downtown Jalalabad and killed eighteen ANA soldiers who were getting paid that day— something none of us in Jalalabad in 2005 would have ever predicted.

I AWOKE WITH a start. My room was dark and filled with a weird electronic buzz. Outside, the sky was lightening. The buzz resolved itself into an amplified throat clearing. It was at once like no sound I had ever heard and deeply familiar, from another time. It was the mullah calling the city to four o'clock morning prayer. In Farah the PRT was far away from the city; here the loudspeaker for the neighborhood mosque was right next to Motel 6. The acoustics of the place made it sound as if it was right outside my window.

Without success I tried to go back to sleep. I'd tossed and turned most of the night. My room was stuffy, the air heavy. I lay awake wondering what I was doing there. I missed Eric, our long talks, and how we teased as a way of finding out things about each other. Still, I knew that the pull he had on me had weakened compared with the pull of the Afghan people who surrounded me at that time. There are times in the night when you cannot hide from the truth, and at that point I could no longer deny that my feelings about happily ever after were changing every day. Once again I was feeling my airway closing in as I lay there listening to the mullah call my countrymen to prayer, inciting their sacred response, as they had for centuries, no matter the hour of the night. How could I have thought that I'd be able to live a normal American life? How could I have changed so much in a mere fourteen years when the rest of my people behaved as they had centuries ago?

SINCE IT WAS my first morning in Jalalabad, I had assumed Judy would want to meet for further debriefing, but when I arrived at her office she was arranging a green silk scarf on her head.

"Are you ready to meet the governor?" she asked.

I must have appeared sick because she smiled and patted my arm. So far she'd been nothing but kind to me, but I kept thinking that she could still fire me at any moment.

"Don't worry," she said. "He's loud and overbearing, but he considers me his sister. He's just another one of the characters in Afghanistan. Anyway, Jawed will do most of the interpreting. Your job today will be simply to observe." Jawed was Judy's current CAT I interpreter.

The Governor's Palace was not far from the PRT, less than ten minutes by Humvee. We passed through the gate and drove up a gravel driveway lined with olive trees through the ANA compound. It was so long it seemed as if we'd turned onto another road. We drove through a small bazaar. Little kids stood on either side of the street gawking at us, while the men loitering in front of the mud shops stared as we rumbled by. We passed immense green lawns studded with jacarandas and palms, until we came to an enormous square pale-yellow building with a turquoise-blue tiled façade. It looked as if it belonged in Beverly Hills. I couldn't help but compare it with the governor's house in Farah, a basic mud structure furnished with a sofa and a few chairs.

One of the PRT FORCEPRO soldiers led Judy and me through the mansion's foyer. Rickety scaffolding hugged one wall. A dozen or so workers were affixing tiny blue tiles to the ceiling, an elaborate mosaic in progress. I wondered where Jawed was. He lived in a village just outside Jalalabad, and I had assumed he was going to meet us here.

We were ushered into an enormous room. It was bigger than ten average-sized American living rooms put together. In the center stood a table that could easily seat forty people. A half dozen seating areas, with sofas, chairs, and low tables, were scattered around the periphery. At the far end of the room several Afghans stood smoking near an open window. The walls were covered with the same small tiles used for the foyer ceiling, arranged in an intricate geometric pattern of dark blue, turquoise, red, and orange. Crystal chandeliers hung from the cathedral ceilings. The rugs were staggering in their beauty. Afghans love their rugs. The most modest village home has at least one on the floor of the room where guests are received, but usually they are small and machine-made. The governor's rugs were hand-loomed, made from the finest wool and silk, in rich shades of red, beige, and cream. The rug beneath the large table must have cost several million Afghanis. Every inch of concrete floor was covered. I would soon learn that this governor could not bear to have his feet touch cement, even when he was wearing shoes. This was luxury, I thought. Not just Afghan luxury, but world-class luxury.

Judy and I were shown a spot at the big table. I stared at the door, willing Jawed to walk through it. Time passed. The governor didn't appear; nor did Jawed. I folded my hands in my lap and looked out the window, through which I could see a blue-tiled swimming pool. It was the biggest swimming pool I had ever seen. In the center there was a fountain. Judy fiddled with the ends of her scarf. At this point we had both realized that Jawed wasn't going to make it to the meeting. Finally she said, "Do you want to give it a shot?"

"Sure," I replied bravely. "This is what I've been hired for."

Gul Agha Sherzai strode into the meeting room, the legs of his pants tucked up in such a way as to reveal his beautiful black dress shoes. He roared his *"Salaam alaikum"* and sat down. With his bright turban, his kohl eyeliner, and his sparkling white *shalwar kameez*, he looked like a Hollywood Pashtun.

I knew a little about Sherzai. It's safe to say that everyone who knew him knew only a little about him. Gul Agha was not his real name. He was born with the simple name Shafiq in a poor section of Kandahar. When he joined the mujahideen he changed his name to Gul Agha; when his father was murdered by the Russians he added Sherzai, which is Pashtu for "son of lion." But he was more like a bear than a lion, with his enormous head and shoulders and thick limbs. Sherzai had a long history both of opposing the Taliban and of "acceptable corruption," a term coined by the coalition forces after they had been in Afghanistan for a while and had seen that their previous stance of "no corruption" was unrealistic. They realized that there was no way to control the nation's Sherzais, men who were a little corrupt but who were also our only allies, much better than the alternative. I would get upset when someone would use the term "acceptable corruption," and I would ask, "To whom is this corruption acceptable?" Not the regular Afghans, and certainly not the American taxpayer who was funding this war.

The exact nature of Sherzai's corruption was unknown. What *was* known is that he took the PRT into areas where the PRT had never been before. He eased the way for us to build schools and clinics in places we otherwise could not even have visited. He displayed generosity to the people of the province and was beloved in Jalalabad. In the evenings he liked to walk to the bazaar, where people would line up on the streets waiting to talk to him.

Sherzai had big black eyes that were constantly sizing people up. As he looked around the table I felt my stomach twist. Sherzai was not above inflicting public humiliation. My predecessor, the interpreter who'd nervously lapsed into Dari, had made him hysterical. "I'm a true Pashtun of Kandahari Pashtu!" he'd cried. "Bring me a real Pashtun!"

I summoned this memory as a way of calming myself. I was a real Pashtun. If he had a problem with a female Pashtun, he should have been more specific in his demand.

He looked at Judy and in English asked, "And how are you?" Then his eyes rested on me, and in Pashtu he said, "And *who* are you?"

He turned to his young assistant, Masoud. Like Sherzai, Masoud had style. He had a small goatee and wore an expensive-looking polo shirt with khaki pants. He rephrased the question in English, as if I wasn't there. "And who is she?"

"I am the new *turjuman*," I said, addressing Sherzai directly, in Pashtu.

He raised his heavy black brows. I'd amused him. "Look at this!" he cried. "She speaks Pashtu. Look at her. Just look at her. She is one of us."

Judy laughed. Later she told me that she had had a feeling he would have a field day with me. She hadn't told him she'd snagged for her new interpreter that rarest of creatures, a female fluent in both Pashtu and English.

"This meeting cannot proceed until I get to know this Pashtun sister," he said, flattening his palms against the table.

I told him my name was Miriam and smiled a little. It was the name Eric had given me in Farah, to protect my identity as well as that of my family. I told him, roughly, how it was that I found myself at PRT Jalalabad, working for an American contractor.

"So you come from America?" he asked.

"I was born in Kabul," I said. I never mentioned the village. "But yes, now I come from America."

"Tell me," he said, "is America really as crazy as people say it is?"

"Crazier," I said. "But still not nearly as crazy as your country."

He laughed and slapped the table, then looked at Judy. In Pashtu he said, "I am so happy you brought a Pashtun and a female sister to me. I am so happy that she is not from here. Your other interpreter is from a village nearby, and I am never comfortable talking freely. Now we may speak openly, as friends, and now we can do some real work on some projects I have in Jalalabad."

Judy had warned me in the Humvee on the way over that Sherzai's normal conversational style was speechifying. He liked to hold forth, and he rarely took a breath. My challenge would be to hold everything he was saying in my head until he paused. I soon learned that I could just ask him to stop, reminding him that I had a job to do, and that I needed him to take a break to do it right.

"I'm very happy," Judy said. "But you better be nice to her, because I don't want you to scare her away!"

Sherzai wagged his finger at her. "Oh, Judy, have I ever scared anyone away?"

Back at the PRT Judy confided that it was just as well Jawed was unable to make it that day. The evening was warm. It was so humid that I could feel my hair growing wild with frizz as we sat in her office and drank tea. The two windows in her office were wide open. The air of Jalalabad smelled green, fresh, and very different from the dust and sewage of other big Afghan cities.

Judy told me what I was already figuring out on my own—that the trouble with CAT I interpreters was that one never knew who their cousins might be, or who their relatives might know. Afghans are famously interrelated. Jawed was not simply a random Afghan who spoke English, he was also the nephew of the chief of the border police, who was in charge of the border patrol at Torkham, the busiest crossing point on the border between Afghanistan and Pakistan, at the top of the winding Khyber Pass.

At the border there are no neat and orderly highway lanes, no agent patrol booths, and no big signs welcoming you to Pakistan. It's the same at Khost, at Kandahar, and at every other place where the two countries rub shoulders. The border is porous. Anyone, including and especially insurgents, can cross anytime. They never have to explain if they are there for business or for pleasure or—in their case—for jihad.

At Torkham the border is an ant nest, a big, noisy bazaar, crowded with small shops selling everything you can imagine: sandals, soap, drugs, weapons, and, in the last few years, U.S. Army uniforms. For me, the only thing that distinguished this place from any other border town was the army of small children with their rusty wheelbarrows. Afghan taxi drivers drop their fares off at the Afghanistan side of the bazaar, where the kids would take over, loading suitcases, groceries, chickens, and grandmothers into their wheelbarrows. For a few Afghanis they'd transport the stuff to the other side of the bazaar, just a few yards away in Pakistan, where a Pakistani taxi would wait to take you to your destination.

Later in my deployment Judy and I would visit an American base under construction at Torkham. We left our Humvees at the base and walked through the bazaar. We stopped at a small eatery that sold chai and pomegranate juice by the cup and *chapli kabobs,* fat patties of ground beef fried in oil that had been sitting there for weeks, then wrapped in a *doughdi.* It was the best *chapli kabob* I've ever tasted. I attribute it to all the dirt, dust, and grease that found its way into the oil. I wouldn't let Judy taste mine, for fear she might be sick for weeks.

To the displeasure of the coalition forces, weapons dealers and drug smugglers did business in the open here. The American forces had to collaborate with the Afghan government if they wanted to crack down on the smugglers. Here is where this particular CAT I dilemma came into play: When Sherzai wanted to discuss a possible crackdown with Judy, he was hindered by having to communicate through Jawed, for fear that Jawed might tip off his uncle, the chief of the border police, who was rumored to be on the payroll of the smugglers. So they never discussed it.

Later it came out that Jawed also had relatives in the construction business. When Sherzai discussed projects that required a bid, Jawed would skip that part of the translation. Then, when it came time to start building the clinic, the community center, or the school, only Jawed's uncles would show up to bid for the job. Judy realized that Jawed scrimped on his translations when it suited his purposes, but she couldn't bring herself to fire him: He was the only interpreter—CAT I or CAT II— whose English she could understand.

Jawed may have been sneakier and more unreliable than most, but the presence of even the most upstanding CAT I could be a problem. As the decade wore on, working for the Americans became more and more dangerous for the average Afghan. Even though many meetings with governors and government officials involved nothing more than discussing what the people of the province needed, outside the walls of the governor's compound, in the street and in the villages, lived the *perception* that these were top-secret meetings where valuable information was exchanged. No governor or PRT commander wanted to be held responsible for the kidnapping and torture of a CAT I, and so they held their tongues. This is what Sherzai meant when he said "real work." Not only was I not related to anyone in the province, I was from Portland, Oregon, a place most Afghans had never even heard of. Plus, I slept on the base at night, and never needed to leave there unless I was flying out to return to the United States.

That night, even though I was exhausted from having been awakened at 4:00 A.M. by the call to prayer, I couldn't sleep. The window was open, and although there was no breeze, I could smell Jalalabad's unique earthy scent of night jasmine and citrus flowers. I'd made it through the day without being fired, but I felt no sense of triumph. I got up and looked out the window. Beneath me was the empty swimming pool. The sides cast long shadows on the bottom, beneath a full moon. I stood there for a long time, looking into the empty pool, as if the answer to my restlessness was lurking at the bottom.

NINETEEN

Outside Jalalabad a handful of big refugee camps languished on the desert plain that extends into Pakistan. Without plumbing, heat, or electricity, they were bursting with tens of thousands of people who were forced to return to Afghanistan after the settlements where they'd lived for decades in Pakistan's North-West Frontier Province were demolished and closed. Most spent their meager savings buying a space in a truck traveling over the Khyber Pass, only to find that once they arrived in Afghanistan they had no place to go. Often, their homes and villages had been destroyed by the Soviets, or the mujahideen, or the Taliban. But just as often, their land had been confiscated by the current government officials.

Most Pashtun tribal land is passed down from son to son, and has been for centuries. When the Soviets began carpet bombing Afghanistan in 1979 and millions of Afghans were forced to flee to Pakistan, the government was in chaos. No one thought: Before I flee for my life I'd better go to Kabul and see if there is some public office still open for business where I can file the deed to my family's ancient village, so that when we return I can prove it belongs to me. When the refugees returned to their villages, after the war was over, they assumed they would be able to resume the lives they'd left. Then someone would show up from the governor's office and say, "Sorry, this isn't your land." It cost only a few hundred dollars to forge a genuine-looking deed, and many provincial governors drew them up to claim the most attractive, fertile tracts of land in their province, and would put it under the name of a brother or cousin. The rightful owners couldn't produce any paperwork, and so the family land was lost.

One sultry morning a few weeks after I'd arrived, we set out for a refugee camp just after breakfast. It was stuffy inside our Humvee. Even though summer, with its triple-digit-degree days, was waning, it was going to be hot—the soldiers were already sweating.

Judy liked going on missions to refugee camps because the problems there were easier to solve, hence the visits were known as quick-impact missions. You need some HA, some human aid? Sure, here are some bags of rice, some pencils, and clean, bottled water. Here is a portable mosque. The missions were low-effort but high-impact. I'd learned in Farah that often a PRT's missions—for better or for worse—were determined not by what needed to be done but by what could, realistically, be done. It's not much of an exaggeration to say that the whole of Afghanistan could benefit from reconstruction, but whereas it might take years to rebuild a stretch of road, in an afternoon you could cure a dozen ear infections.

This camp huddled on a rocky plain near the border. It was crowded, a flat sea of blue U.N.–issued tents. Some families had strung plastic sheets around their tents to create a kind of courtyard; the sheets flapped in the wind, fanning random pieces of garbage. Some people had lived there so long they'd built mud walls around their tents, creating a makeshift compound.

As soon as we stepped from our Humvees we were swarmed by children—the little boys in dirt-colored *shalwar kameez* and plastic sandals, tiny girls in dresses of turquoise and lime green, all of them covered in dust. There was dust on the bridges of their nose and the tops of their feet. They were curious about us, but they did not ask us for anything. There were no high-pitched cries of "Pen, mister! Pen, mister!"

We waded through the crowd of children; I was taken aback, seeing men and women walking together or chatting between their respective tents. I'd been in Afghanistan long enough to have forgotten American street life—the boys and girls at bus stops, men and women strolling arm in arm in broad daylight, a whole constellation of couples and families out and about. The men wore Western jackets, donated by various NGOs, and kicked at the rocks on the clay-hard ground. The women wore scarves carelessly tossed over their hair. Occasionally the wind blew the tattered squares of fabric off their heads and onto their shoulders. There wasn't a burqa in sight.

A woman with sharp cheekbones and deeply wrinkled skin stood outside her tent and stared at us. Her dress was black-gray, permanently dusty. I called to her in Pashtu, "Hello, *adhai*, how are you?" The literal translation of *adhai* is "mother," but the word is used for older women, such as grandmothers.

"Oh! You speak Pashtu, daughter. I have so much to talk to you about. Come, sit in my tent. It's big enough for all of us." She smiled. She had no teeth.

The woman eyeballed us: I was wearing my dark-rinse jeans, tennis shoes, and windbreaker, while Judy wore her army fatigues and matching green head scarf peeking out from beneath her helmet. I used to tease Judy about her avid scarf wearing, saying she made me look bad, as an Afghan woman.

I told Judy that the lady wanted us to come inside. Judy hesitated, calculating the proper behavior. Behind us were six FORCEPRO soldiers. They would have to come with us, even though *Pashtunwali* forbade any Pashtun female to invite a man who was not a relative into her house. Was this old woman inviting just Judy and me into her tent? Did she understand that the FORCEPRO guys would have to come too? What if Judy declined her invitation altogether? Would that be more insulting than trying to enter the tent with our security? These were the days before the military fully understood how easy it was to offend an Afghan, but Judy knew that even with the best of intentions it was possible to undo months of constructive interactions in a few seconds. She glanced at me again.

"You sure we won't be causing a scandal here?"

"I think we're all right," I said.

That day I learned something I hadn't known about my father's people. When you are poor and living in a refugee camp, the rules of *Pashtunwali* are lax. To practice *Pashtunwali* to its full extent requires a life of luxury. A woman must enjoy a certain amount of affluence to be shielded from the world. She must live in a walled compound, and have a lot of men to do outside work, to go to the shops, to do the errands. If she wants to go out, her family will have to have a car with curtains on the windows to protect her from prying eyes. There was none of that at the refugee camp. Women coexisted with men however they could. As a result, women in refugee camps, ironically, were among the freest women in Afghanistan.

As we filed inside, I thought about my own refugee experience. In Peshawar we'd been lucky enough to rent a house. My uncle's brother-in-law had moved to Peshawar as soon as the war started. He worked for the ANA and was helping with the resettlement. There were tent camps not unlike this one, at the edge of our neighborhood. Our family was relatively affluent, which meant that my mother and aunts were expected to practice a stricter version of *Pashtunwali*. I was forbidden to go to this part of the settlement because the men and women mingled freely there. My sister and I were driven to school each day in a car with curtains, so no one could catch a glimpse of us.

Judy and I and our FORCEPRO ducked inside the tent. Judy started when she saw not just five or six children sitting on their haunches on the bare floor but also several goats, a skinny, sad-eyed cow, and a manic-looking chicken furiously pecking at the dirt.

The woman shooed some of the kids away. Judy and I sat down on the bed. The mattress was thin and lumpy. The soldiers squeezed in behind us. The woman wasn't apologetic about the crowded conditions of her house. It was what God had decided to give her. She prepared some tea, which she cooked over a small fire in a pit on one side of the tent. The wood was dry; there was little smoke. The children stared at us, as did the livestock. The chicken pecked at the dirt, ignoring the human commotion.

The woman wanted to discuss a land dispute the camp had with Sherzai. She begged us to tell Sherzai to give them their land back. She didn't want anything else we had to offer. We could keep our pens and paper, our antibiotics, our sewing classes. She wanted us to convince Sherzai to return the land that rightfully belonged to her children. Her scarf was casually pinned beneath her braid. As she worked, it kept slipping.

Judy gave the woman her word that she would talk to the governor, and at our next meeting she did. Sherzai said he had no idea what she was talking about. And anyway, he had already given his people plenty of land. True, it was arid and rocky, and even poppies struggled to grow there, but it was something, wasn't it?

The soldiers remained standing by the door. The air smelled of dust, animal hide, and milk. Judy took out her notebook and pulled a pen from her front pocket. She began asking the woman questions about her life. The tent flap opened, and three new women squeezed inside. Word had gotten around the camp that the Americans were there, doing the inexplicable things that we do.

"Do your children go to school?" Judy asked.

The women all laughed. I felt my heart lean toward them. "We can barely feed them," said a woman with a faded red scarf draped over her braids, "and you're asking about school?"

I glanced back at the FORCEPROs who accompanied Judy and me every time we left the wire. I was used to their passive, businesslike demeanor. This was different. They'd never had to pull security in a refugee's tent crowded with goats, a chicken, kids, a cow, and a clutch of feisty Afghan women cracking jokes. Their faces looked alive. They were intrigued, interested in where this conversation might go. A goat ambled over and began sniffing at one of the soldiers' pant legs. The old woman watched as Judy scratched away in her notebook.

"Put your notebook away. We don't expect anything from you. We are grateful for what we have. We're fine, really, as long as you don't shoot at us."

I'd hoped we were going to be served a simple cup of green tea, but our hostess reached for a battered tin pitcher of goat's milk. It was most likely the family's milk for the day. Who knew how long it had been sitting there?

Judy asked quietly, "Should I drink this stuff?"

"I hate to say it, but you're going to have to drink a little. In Afghanistan we only serve milk tea to our most honored guests."

"I'll be fine," she said. "When I get back to the PRT, I can get something from the medic."

In the long history of milk tea, that was perhaps the worst pot ever made. I feel confident saying that. It was warm, oversweetened goat milk on the verge of souring. The women seemed pleased to be serving it to us. I felt as if to them I was a representative of the United States, and to Judy and the soldiers, a representative of the Pashtun. So I braced myself and swallowed the tea in several big gulps.

The old woman must have thought that the speed with which I drank meant I enjoyed it. Before she could offer me more I said, "*Adhai*, you must have the next cup of tea."

"But I only have these two cups," she said.

"Take my cup," I quickly offered.

"But you are my guest. You know that in our culture we make sure our guests always have everything they want."

"In America, which is also part of my culture, we like our hosts to be comfortable, to join us in drinking what we're drinking. As an American, I want you to join me."

Even then it was important not to stay in any one place too long. The more time we spent at the camp, the more dangerous it became for us. In Afghanistan gossip travels like a flash flood. Within moments of our arrival everyone in the camp knew that the Americans had arrived. After a half hour everyone in the surrounding villages knew. In less than an hour's time every villager who'd been slipped five bucks by an insurgent would have found his benefactor and revealed our whereabouts. We left the camp around noon, promising once again to the old lady that we would bring her request about the land to Sherzai. Walking to the Humvee, I could feel the sun burn the part in my hair. The milk tea bubbled in my stomach. I imagined the sinister brew of a cartoon witch.

That night in the chow hall I was having dinner with some other CAT II interpreters when I overheard the soldiers at the table behind me talking. There had been an improvised explosive device on the road that we'd taken to the refugee camp. We'd returned via a different route and so had escaped it, but a nine-year-old boy riding his bike home from school had ridden over it. In 2005, this was unusual.

"But no one else died, just a little kid," said one of the soldiers.

I spun around. "How can you be so insensitive? Do you really think it doesn't matter when an Afghan dies? There are local laborers working here, around you, who know enough English to understand what you're saying. As an American, I'm ashamed of what you just said."

The soldier looked over at me, mildly embarrassed. He was nineteen or twenty, and he looked like a little boy to me. He had razor burn on his neck, pimples on his nose.

"I didn't mean that, Miriam. I'm not happy a kid died. I meant that none of our friends died. No one we know. Of course I'm sad a kid died. Of course I'm sad."

"I understand you're happy we escaped casualties," I said. "But anyone dying is horrible. Look at this little boy. He was coming home from school. He was dreaming of a better future and hoping going to school will make it happen. We are here to give him a better life. And now he's dead. What good are we going to be able to do for him if he is dead?"

I sounded like I was lecturing, even to myself, but I couldn't help it. I was fuming, feeling so hurt for the little boy. I am not naïve enough to pretend that in war no one dies, but the news of children dying is always the hardest for me to accept. I remembered being in the middle of falling bombs, running for my own life at an age when I should never have had to worry about the constant threat of death. Every time I heard of a child dying, in addition to the horror anyone feels about a life unjustly ending at a young age, I was also reminded that I easily could have been a child casualty of war, and that I owed a debt to someone or something for being alive today. A debt that I knew I had not paid back.

LIKE SEVERAL PROVINCIAL reconstruction teams all over Afghanistan, JBAD, as it was known by soldiers, had several dogs, and I befriended a yellow puppy with dark eyes. I love dogs, but remembering how hard it was as a child to let go of our cat when we had to leave the city, I had refrained from getting pets. In Muslim societies, dogs are allowed only as outdoor pets and even then should only be used for protection purposes.

But in Jalalabad, for the first time I wanted a pet, something that I could take care of and talk to, knowing there would be no talking back or advice giving. I was lonely, having only Judy to talk to, and she was my boss. I saw the appeal of that unconditional love, that look in a loyal dog's eyes. Like everyone else, I fed the puppy pieces of steak from the chow hall and used to tell him that he was the most spoiled dog in the whole of Afghanistan because most Afghans could not afford to feed steak to their kids, much less their dogs, if they had any dogs to begin with. Soldiers weren't allowed to have pets in their rooms, but there were no restrictions on me, a civilian. I wanted the puppy to sleep in my room at night, but no food bribes could coax him into the courtyard, past the swimming pool, and up the stairs at night.

I didn't think much about it, until one evening when Judy hosted a dinner for Colonel Hussein, the liaison officer from the Ministry of the Interior. Colonel Hussein wore his green-and-brown camouflage ANA uniform. His hair was shiny and well groomed. You could tell he enjoyed his job, and Judy liked hosting him. The PRT was believed to be there, in part, to mentor the government, and sharing some roast lamb and rice was proof that that was happening.

Somehow the topic turned to the number of dogs on base and how much Americans loved them. Jokes were made about how even though dogs weren't technically allowed on the PRT, the sergeant majors tended to look the other way, because even they needed someone to whom they could unburden themselves without having to worry about being asked to write a statement about it later. I reported that in the true American spirit I had made friends with the yellow puppy with the dark eyes, but that in the true Afghan spirit he was only my friend during the day. At night I was all on my own. Both Judy and the colonel got the inside dig at Afghans. The villagers said that during the day they would come out and talk to us, and even host us, but at night, when we Americans went back to our bases, leaving the insurgents to come out and rule the area, they would tell us we were on our own and would not be seen as our friends.

Both Judy and Colonel Hussein laughed hard, and Colonel Hussein wagged his finger at me. "It's not you, Miriam, it's that swimming pool. The little dog knows what happened there."

"What happened there?"

"Horrible things," he said, and then elaborated. He had been involved in Afghan politics for many years. "During the Soviet occupation that very pool was the site of hundreds of executions. The Russians would gather up the mujahideen, line them up in the bottom of the empty pool, and execute them. Then they would order more mujahideen into the pool, forcing them to step over and onto the bodies of their fellow fighters, and then execute them as well. This would continue until their blood reached the lip of the pool, at which point the Russians would haul off the corpses and begin again."

I should have known it was something like this. Most Afghans would tell you that the country is haunted by the ghosts of lost mujahideen from decades of wars. Some would even claim that the dead Russian soldiers roamed the land they had tried to conquer. I stopped trying to coax the yellow puppy to come to my room. They can smell fear, love, despair, and also—if the yellow puppy was any indication—the terror of the long-since dead.

THE MORNINGS WERE difficult. I was awakened every day at four o'clock by the crackling of the loudspeaker, then the call for prayer. Once awoken, I would stare at the ceiling until sunrise. The underside of my eyelids felt like emery boards, and there was a heavy feeling in the pit of my stomach. I spent my nights at the MWR, chatting with Eric on one of the few computers or talking to him on the phone. Noon in Flordia was nine o'clock at night for me.

Eric had left the army after seventeen years and was living with his parents in Florida, waiting for me to come home and marry him. He was anxious; he had all the time in the world to correspond. At night, after we'd logged off or hung up, I had my walk past the swimming pool/ execution spot and my three hours of shallow sleep to look forward to. He wanted to talk about our wedding, about the guest list, our out-fits, the menu, the kind of house he would buy me in Florida. Mostly he talked about how amazing our life together would be. Eric had so many fantasies he'd never been able to fulfill because of his dedication to the army. I had told him that I didn't want to be married to someone who was already married to the army. He had completed every mission he'd ever wanted to do and, after being a commander of a successful PRT, was open to changing things around. When he talked about leav-ing the army, I encouraged him cautiously, not wanting him to resent me later for supporting it too loudly. We talked about our shared desire to come back to Afghanistan someday to work and to live here with our family—a desire that I think I knew even then would always be a fantasy.

To celebrate the fulfillment of these dreams in our future, he'd bought several pieces of jewelry at BAF. There was the jade set he was going to give me for our second anniversary, and the gold-and-ruby bracelets I'd admired that he said he planned to give me when I gave birth to our first child. He hoped the baby would be a girl, a little Saima. I said if he couldn't handle one Saima, how was he going to live with two of us?

"Our daughter will always be on my side and will force you to be nice to me," he said. I could hear the yearning in his voice.

All these conversations about kids, houses, and special celebrations should have made me feel excited to hurry back to the States, but for some crazy, totally Saima reason, they didn't. I felt uneasy, and the more Eric talked about our magical future, the faster I wanted to get off the line. Then he would get hurt and say that I was changing. I didn't argue.

He was right, I was changing. For a crazy minute in Farah, I had thought I could find the kind of eternal happiness found only in marriage with Eric, my perfect partner. But the minute was over. I was turning back into the Saima who knew that she was going to have to look for her happiness independent of any man. For a second, I had indulged in the type of romantic daydreams I had always scorned in the movies or in others' lives. But once I had distance from Eric, I grew frightened of and repelled by the power he had had over me. I saw that if I didn't break it off, I would end up in a home in Florida, taking care of five children, in full makeup, waiting for Eric to get home every day. That was *not* what my father had envisioned for my future.

This was much like what had happened with Greg, with one big difference: Now I knew what I needed to do to make myself happy. I had to find a way to get out of the marriage that Eric was waiting for. I knew that in the end Eric was not going to like my transformation, but I hoped that I would at least find a way to be at peace with myself.

One morning I walked into Judy's office. She looked at me and sighed heavily.

"Do I remind you of those pushy Pashtuns you have to deal with, and that's why you sighed so loudly?" I asked.

She laughed. Over the weeks I had come to realize that she was not going to fire me the first chance she got, and I'd grown comfortable enough with her to tease her. Whenever we went to one of our many meetings with Sherzai, before he made his grand entrance, we'd engage in small talk. When she began to joke with me during meetings, I felt even more relaxed.

That morning Judy had been waiting for me to arrive. Her green scarf was folded over the back of the chair beside her desk. "There's a park opening today," she said.

"Oh, good," I said. "I could use a picnic in the park."

"Oh, this will be no picnic!" she said. "We've got that meeting with Hazrad today, too."

Hazrad was the other larger-than-life Pashtun in Jalalabad.

In every province in Afghanistan the same ridiculous relationship existed between us and the governor, the chief of police, or the chief of the border police. Every time a new PRT commander rotated in, each of these men was eager to be the first to meet with, impress, and convince the new commander that the other two were corrupt beyond measure. The reason they were so eager to make an acquaintance is that word had gotten out, all across the country, that Americans tended to trust the first person they met.

Thus, the governor would swear on his children's heads that the chief of police and the chief of the border police were high-level smugglers of car parts, television sets, or opium. And the chief of police would show up and plead with us not to be swayed by the lies told by the governor and the chief of the border police, who were robbing the people of Afghanistan blind, and providing a safe haven for the insurgency, and anything else he could think up that sounded disreputable and corrupt. The chief of the border police would show up and tell the same tales about the governor and the chief of police.

In Jalalabad, one of the busiest crossing points between the two countries, Hazrad held the very powerful position of chief of the border police. He oversaw the comings and goings across the Khyber Pass. He was tall and movie-star handsome, with fine, dark features. The moment I met him I thought, Eric would have hated this guy. With Judy I could whisper, in English, "Wow, he's handsome," and she would agree. If I had ever ventured such an opinion to Eric, he would have told me to go wait in the Humvee until the meeting was over.

Hazrad's money came from smuggling who knew what. Every few months he built himself a new house somewhere in the leafy Jalalabad suburbs, and each time he completed a house he would have a housewarming party. I went to at least four of them in the short time I spent there. The thing he loathed most about Sherzai was that occasionally he would wear a nice double-breasted suit, with a dress shirt, cuff links, and shiny Western loafers. Hazrad mocked Sherzai's fancy suits, believing they proved that he wasn't a true Pashtun and was dressing just to impress his Western allies. Hazrad was never seen without his turban. Come to think of it, I never saw him in his Afghan Border Police uniform, either.

By late morning we were on our way to the park. The PRT was obligated to show support for any and all reconstruction projects, and we assumed our appearance was going to be the usual formality. But Sherzai was Mr. Last Minute. He believed in whims and spontaneous inspiration, the importance of carrying out every stray idea that entered his head. It was part of his charisma. Before we left the PRT, Judy got word that the park opening had become a celebratory picnic for the local villagers. Sherzai wanted to see squares of colorful blankets dotting the newly sodded lawns, lamb kebabs grilling on open fire pits dug just for the occasion. He wanted what he usually wanted: a photo op, music, and good food, in that order.

The park had new sidewalks that glinted in the midday sun, rose beds newly turned with dark, rich earth, a grove of cypress and orange trees. Of course, no women were anywhere to be seen. In the more conservative Pashtun areas, such as Jalalabad, it's highly unusual to see women in the parks and other recreational arenas. It is too much work for their men to protect them from harassment, and thus, to protect the virtue of their entire families. It is easier for the men to prohibit their women from going to parks. Even Sherzai, with his grand ambitions for his province, could not bring any Afghan women, other than me, to this picnic. So, as usual, Judy and I were the only women there.

Big sand-colored tents had been erected, and inside were rugs, blankets, and bright silk pillows. They were places to recline, to chat. Sherzai circulated, shaking hands, patting shoulders, doing the universal politician's duty. He wore a bronze turban, flowing white *shalwar* pants, and a white embroidered Kandahari-style *kameez* beneath a black vest. He was in high Pashtun mode.

He saw me and rushed over, his big hands in the air. "Miriam. My decorator tells me you want to buy a chandelier just like the one I had put in."

"You're talking about that seventy-five-thousand-dollar chandelier, right?"

"No, the expensive one!" he exclaimed, before rushing off to greet someone else.

My exchange with his decorator had been in Pashtu. I often thought that whenever Sherzai saw me he said the first thing that came into his head. Judy looked mystified. She leaned into my shoulder. "What was that?"

I told her. Sherzai had an interior decorator, a Pakistani with gold-rimmed teeth, who was overseeing the remodeling and renovation of the Governor's Palace. During our last meeting at the palace, when we broke for prayer, I had wandered into the vestibule where he was supervising the creation of an elaborate ceiling mosaic. A dozen workers labored on the scaffolding that lined the walls, reaching to affix the postage-stamp-sized tiles. Other workers were hanging a huge crystal chandelier, like something that belonged at Versailles.

"I love that chandelier," I said to the decorator.

"It's one of a kind," he replied, watching while the workmen tugged on the ropes that would hoist it clear to the ceiling. The chandelier swayed, its crystal prisms tinkling.

"How much did it cost?" I asked.

"Seventy-five thousand," he said.

"Not bad," I said. "Where did you find it? I'd like one for myself."

Suddenly, his gaze shifted from the chandelier to me. "You must make a lot of money."

"Not that much," I said.

"Enough to buy a seventy-five-thousand-dollar chandelier like it is nothing!"

We both laughed. I had thought he meant 75,000 Pakistani rupees, which is about $875. Then, since we were laughing, I wondered aloud where the governor got that kind of money for a chandelier. The average Afghan is lucky if he earns a dollar a day.

"Why, Karzai gave it to him to build the palace!" said the decorator in a tone that suggested I should know this already. Anyway, he couldn't care less where the money came from; he was happy to be hired and paid.

It was difficult for the soldiers to pull security while Judy and I circulated through the crowd. Since we were going to be there for a while, we found a place in one of the big tents. The tent was open, with all the sides rolled up and tied beneath the roof. We sat down on one of the blankets and engaged the locals passing by in small talk. Some men wandered into the tent. Even in the heat they wore sports coats over their *shalwar kameez* and black plastic sandals. They'd heard there was a female Pashtu speaker at the PRT who could also speak English. We engaged in small talk, both the visitors and the conversation drifting here and there. No one was in any hurry. The park was close enough to the PRT that it was unlikely we would be ambushed if we took our time, and so we just sat chatting and drinking tea, and trying to connect with locals in a way we had never done before. The sun lazed across the sky; the breeze carried the medicinal scent of eucalyptus. Someone mentioned that they'd planted some on the other side of the park. A few men dozed, and I would have too, had I not become aware of something unexpected.

The army's standard approach to interacting with regular Afghans is to devise a mission: Let's go to village A and see whether they need a school, and complete that mission in the shortest time possible, preferably the same day. The mission might include counting the number of school-aged children and figuring the distance to the closest school. Afterward, a storyboard of the mission is created, usually heavy on pictures and light on text, describing what happened on the mission and whether or not the goals set out were met. Most PRT missions are designed to be short, featuring a straightforward goal that can be measured at the end of the day. If the mission happens to be a meeting or public appearance, once the event is over, everyone hops into their Humvees and races back inside the wire to work on the storyboard that inevitably concludes with "Mission accomplished!"

But this casual gathering was something else entirely. It didn't seem to have anything to do with anything measurable. Judy, the commander, the soldiers pulling her security, and some local agronomists were just sitting around talking, getting to know one another, becoming acquainted with one another's culture.

Sherzai blew into the tent and reached his arms wide, as if trying to gather up the scene for future reference. "I like this!" he cried.

This may not sound like much. Today we have a greater understanding that building long-term relationships with the Afghan people is critical, but in 2005 it was very unusual. To most soldiers, Afghanistan was just a tour of duty. Their only goal was to get through it alive, so they could be promoted and move on. Even now it's unrealistic to expect soldiers to think differently. I remember counting down days on my wall calendar a couple of months before my contract would end. And I was there by choice, not to mention the fact that I wanted to be among people with whom I share roots. The average American soldier viewed Afghans as poor, uneducated, and often crazy men who bullied their women. They wanted to do their time and return to their families and their regular posts, where they wouldn't be shot at as much. If, in the meantime, they lost a buddy in a firefight, an ambush, or an IED explosion, they'd resent Afghans even more, failing to understand how allegedly innocent villagers—people whose lives the soldier was risking his own to improve—would allow the insurgents to plant IEDs in their roads.

The missing link was a genuine relationship with the local population. If the villagers felt connected to us, they would be more likely to cooperate with our missions, warn us of any impending danger in the region, and avoid providing shelter and support for the insurgency.

This tactic of forging relationships is part of the counterinsurgency, or COIN. In 2005 the U.S. Army was not practicing any COIN that I observed. The marine corps released its COIN Manual in 2006, with its focus on Iraq; and the special forces and the marines were practicing some COIN, but it was not yet the official policy of the regular army. Most army members at the time thought that COIN was unnecessary in Afghanistan because the regular army was there on a reconstruction effort, and not just chasing the bad guys. I imagine the thinking went something like this: Since the United States had been invited to Afghanistan by the government, COIN wasn't necessary because GIRoA is a democratically elected entity, meaning, essentially, that the Afghan populace wanted us there and we would and should not have to fight for their hearts and minds.

Soldiers didn't realize the importance of relationship building in the success of U.S. reconstruction efforts. This is not to say that villagers would be able to stand up to the insurgents directly just because they were supportive of the U.S. mission, but if they felt that the company commander was a friend, they might find a way to pass on crucial information that could potentially save the lives of his soldiers.

Once established, these relationships could be passed on to the incoming units, because one of the characteristics of being in uniform is that you become interchangeable with the soldier who replaces you. If one company commander stresses the importance of good neighborly behavior to newly arrived troops and introduces them to local villagers, he creates a foundation that can be built on when the next unit arrives, and so on. The result is trust, and a long-term relationship, principles that are a big part of Pashtun culture.

This picnic felt like the beginning of a new type of relationship between Afghans and Americans, and the beginning of the idea that led General Petraeus to encourage his soldiers to mingle more, to drink more cups of the world-famous Afghan green tea.

SEVERAL DAYS LATER Judy and I arrived at Sherzai's palace to find him in the grip of a new idea. It had come to him in the middle of the night, and by 10:00 A.M., he was busy implementing it. Inspired by the success of the park-opening celebration, he'd invited five hundred *mullahyaan*—the Pashtu plural of *mullah*—to his compound for an impromptu meeting, in the hopes of endearing himself and his government to them and showing them that he was approachable. This was pure Sherzai, who was all about scoring points—with the *mullahyaan*, Karzai and the central government, Judy and the PRT, even me. When he learned that I'd admired the beautiful white embroidered Kandahari *kameez* he wore to the park opening, he immediately sent me two, one in white, the other in beige. When I told Sherzai that my fiancé, Eric, had always wanted one and would love it, Sherzai said, "Well, Miriam, if I had known that you were going to be marrying a non-Pashtun, I wouldn't have given you those; I don't want to be giving a gift to a non-Pashtun who is marrying a Pashtun woman!"

The meeting with the *mullahyaan* was news to Judy and me. I'd arrived wearing what had become my uniform, a pair of Express jeans and a plain, short-sleeved T-shirt. Judy was in her standard fatigues. Sherzai stood by the window, grinning and rubbing his hands together like a movie villain.

"We've been waiting for you," he said, nodding out the window.

A hastily erected tent stood in the courtyard. *Mullahyaan* were arriving in twos and threes, prayer beads dangling between their fingers. I stared down at the tops of their white turbans.

"Wali Sahib, why didn't you tell us about this? We didn't bring our scarves." I used his title in Pashtu, which I did when I wanted him to remember that I was there as an American.

"Didn't you tell me you refuse to wear the scarf, Miriam? Or has the sight of these *mullahyaan* finally put the fear of God in you?" He grinned at me.

"It's a matter of respect. I'm not going into a tent full of mullahs without a scarf." I didn't want to offend these men unnecessarily. It was one thing to make a point with the average Afghan man by not wearing a scarf, but there was no need to rub the *mullahyaan*'s noses in it.

Sherzai collared one of his assistants and sent him searching for a pair of scarves for Judy and me. I stood at the window, watching the *mullahyaan* file into the tent. The day was overcast, a uniform ho-hum Portland gray. Judy and I would be the only women in the tent. I looked at her. She was glancing at her watch, unconcerned. As a woman in the army she was used to being the only female in a room full of men. My situation was considerably different. To be the only female Pashtun in a room full of religious men meant that I was going to be judged, and judged harshly.

The assistant returned empty-handed, unable to locate the nonexistent secret trove of scarves Sherzai seemed to feel existed somewhere in the compound.

"Take this." Sherzai pulled his black-and-white-checked scarf from around his neck.

"Are you joking? They'll know it belonged to you. That would be even worse."

"You know, Miriam, you are more trouble than all the *mullahyaan,* all five hundred of them combined."

He called over one of the guards and sent him to the bazaar. The guard returned with identical pale-green scarves, the hems stitched with pale green thread. They were prettier than anything in my duffel bag at the PRT. Sherzai escorted Judy and me into the tent, where we sat in folding chairs near the front and listened to two and a half hours' worth of speeches. Regardless of their tribal affiliations, *mullahyaan* love to make speeches and are true politicians at heart.

Afterward, Judy and I wandered outside into a warm drizzle. One mullah, a frail old man with black eyebrows, white hair, and only two upper teeth, said, "Daughter, I feel it's my Muslim duty to tell you that you will go to hell for what you are doing here."

"I'm thankful for your concern, Baba." I used the title of grandfather in hopes of reminding him that he was supposed to be kind. "I will make sure that when God is sending me to hell He knows you did your Muslim job, telling me the error of my ways. I am hopeful that He will be merciful and not hold you responsible for my sins." There is a belief of most Muslims, especially the more conservative ones, that if they see another Muslim doing un-Islamic things, it is their duty to point out the error, and if they don't, God will send them to hell with the one committing those crimes. This puzzles me, as I've read the Koran and know that there are many restrictions on one Muslim's duty to question another Muslim's faith and intentions. I would never understand how a Muslim could justify questioning my faith, but it has happened a hundred times to me, not just in Afghanistan but even in a convention center in Portland.

Sherzai invited us to his office for tea, eager to hear us reassure him that the afternoon had been a success. I told him about the old mullah who'd told me I was going to hell. Sherzai narrowed his eyes, something he did before he lost his temper, and went to the window, as if the offending mullah was still out there.

"Who said this to you? Show me who insulted my guest."

According to the strict interpretation of *Pashtunwali,* Sherzai had every right to kill this mullah. He would receive no punishment for murder; in fact, he would be viewed as a good and honorable Pashtun for defending the honor of a guest. I suddenly felt tired from my long nights of little sleep.

"I don't think that's the point, Wali Sahib. It was a fine event. They were all happy. But the bigger point is that these *mullahyaan* are not ready to mix with Western females. So next time, don't invite us, please."

"These *mullahyaan* need to adjust, Miriam. They must accept the realities of the modern Afghanistan."

"And we want to be accepted by them, Wali Sahib, but this makes it seem as if we are invading their space and disrespecting the culture. We'll never be accepted under those circumstances."

"I suppose this means you're not going to tell me which mullah showed me disrespect by insulting my guest?"

"The American in me won't let me tell you, especially if you're going to beat him up. You have to let it go."

"He told you you were going to hell, Miriam. It's hard for me to let that go."

"It wasn't the first time I have been told that," I said. "And I am sure it won't be the last."

TWENTY

At night the CAT I interpreters who worked next door, at Jalalabad Airfield, came over for tea, television, and conversation. The CAT II interpreters at the PRT had a tearoom for sitting and talking. It was furnished with a TV, a table, some chairs, a hot plate, and a mini-fridge. Because it was at one time someone's quarters, there was also a set of metal-framed bunk beds. There was a maroon-and-black, machine-made rug from Iran on the floor. Interpreters and U.S. soldiers (invited by interpreters they worked with) all hung out here before and after dinner. Sometimes we'd bring food from the chow hall and eat there. It was the first place where I really saw U.S. soldiers and interpreters socializing during off-hours. The soldiers loved laughing at the local TV shows, where if any female was wearing short sleeves, her bare arms would be blurred out. Or they would see some woman on TV and say, "Hey, look, we *can* see Afghan women during our deployment." The interpreters would reply, "Yes, but they are not Pashtun women. They are the Kabuli women, and it is not the same. Real Pashtun women are not allowed to be seen by men!" They would argue back and forth, and I would sit there in my jeans and T-shirt, watching the interpreters telling the soldiers the difference between a Pashtun woman and a Kabuli woman. Were they trying to insult me by having this discussion in front of me? I honestly didn't think so. Like myself, they didn't see me as belonging to either group; for that moment I was an American.

Most of the interpreters were like me, Afghans who'd been forced to flee to Pakistan, where they'd grown up to become men and women who belonged to no one culture completely. Haaroon was my favorite. He was around twenty-two, long-faced and serious, the youngest child and only son in his family. He had long, slim fingers, like a musician. He was careful with his words and spent most of the time sitting quietly, observing his surroundings. I immediately thought of him for my sister. Unlike me, Najiba said she would not marry an American, and wanted to be with someone of similar background.

I'm sure they had a TV-watching room at the airfield, but Haaroon and a few others, all Afghans with heavy brows, white teeth, and a slight smirk always playing on their faces, liked to come to the PRT and hang out with the other PRT interpreters.

Most days I wouldn't show up at the tearoom until long after dinner. I would have had a meeting with Judy after dinner, or I'd find myself in a conversation with some soldiers at the chow hall, or Eric would have called me. I'd arrive to find them slouched in front of the TV like a bunch of retirees. It looked as if they'd been sitting in those chairs, or reclining on that slim mattress, for many years, bored and unmoving. I couldn't keep myself from laughing. If there's one thing an Afghan is good at, it's sitting and waiting, a must-have quality in a U.S. soldier. The similarities between Afghan culture and U.S. Army culture baffle my mind.

When I finally showed up, one of them named Ahmad, who had bright black eyes and a fat black mustache, would say, "Oh, good, now the talking can start. When it's just us guys it's so boring."

"That's your own fault," I'd reply. "If you allowed your women to be CAT I's, they could be here talking to you, like I do."

"Ah, no," they'd say. "Our women are not like you."

Whenever I could wrestle the conversation around to the topic of their women, I did. So much attention is paid to building schools for girls, but their men refuse to allow them to go. In a culture where women are so dependent on the goodwill of the men, how can we expect to move women's rights forward without getting the men to bring them to the new age of liberty and democracy? Without my realizing it, this had become a personal mission of mine, to keep a running conversation about Afghan women.

Haaroon seemed to be more interested in the subject than the others were.

"Women need some freedom," I'd insist. "You need to let them go to school, to support them in their studies."

"They don't want to go to school," Haaroon would say. "They're not like you."

"Perhaps they need a little encouragement."

"Perhaps," he said, doubtful.

Some nights Haaroon showed up by himself. I think the other men had wives back in their villages, but Haaroon was alone. On those nights we'd discuss philosophy, politics, and Bollywood, for which Haaroon had a secret passion. Other nights, the group would discuss issues of the day, but gradually everyone but Haaroon would leave, and he and I would sit drinking tea and talking. He could talk for hours, his soft voice never seeming to tire.

"Do you ever speak with your sisters about the things we talk about?" I asked one evening.

"They're only interested in women stuff," he replied. "Not the rest of the world."

"Explain to me this woman stuff. What do you mean? Am I not a woman?"

"Once I tried to talk to my sister about Karzai, and she couldn't figure out what was going on. It made her nervous and stressed out, so I stopped."

"You stressed her out, trying to talk about politics."

He frowned, confused, as if I'd asked him to solve a difficult math problem. I thought he was cute. I told him I would love to have met his sisters and to be there while he talked to them.

"I know it's strange for me to be saying this, Haaroon, but I think you would be a good match for my sister." As a Pashtun female, I was not supposed to offer up my sister like that because his family was supposed to beg for her hand—in fact, I wasn't even supposed to acknowledge the fact that I *had* a sister of marriageable age. Still, there was an American matchmaker in me. Najiba had begun getting to know (since it was not dating in the true American sense) a young Nepalese man named Kabir, but I didn't know at the time that it was serious, and found Haaroon to be handsome and earnest. As soon as the words left my mouth I realized my cultural blunder and wanted to explain.

"My sister is very Pashtun. She's not like me. She has no idea I'm saying these things."

At that moment Ahmad came back with a couple of soldiers from his unit. They wanted some tea. One of them turned on the hot plate and set about making it. A plate of green grapes sat on the table. Haaroon stared at it and was silent. What had I done? Clearly, he was upset. Before he could open his mouth, another CAT I appeared in the doorway. He was one of the regulars. He loved to tease me about being a rich American.

"What about you, Miriam? Don't you want to marry a nice Pashtun?"

"I'm already engaged," I answered without thinking. I could have gone all deployment without saying a word: I'd shipped Eric's beautiful gold-and-ruby ring back home, for fear it would be stolen, and as far as anyone knew, when I took personal phone calls they were all from my family in Oregon.

Miriam is engaged! This was breaking news. I rarely shared anything personal about myself. By the next evening word was out that I was not simply engaged but engaged to an American soldier. Pointing out to them that he was an officer and not a soldier was going to be irrelevant. In the tearoom, there were shouts of *Woo-hoo!* and fist pumping from the Americans, as if they'd scored one for their team. The CAT I's were dumbfounded. How could I do this to Pashtun men? How could I betray them so? Our evening gatherings became combative. For Pashtuns, arguing is like a sport. The interpreters argued with me mercilessly, and I argued right back, all in good sport. Don't take it personally, I assured them. You're all great, but even if I wasn't already engaged, I would never marry any of you; you're too controlling. You can't help it; look at how you're trying to control me right now! We were arguing in English, for the benefit of the soldiers, who were watching, mesmerized.

Once, while we were going back and forth, my cell phone rang. A smile must have crept onto my face as I looked at the caller ID, because Ahamd cried, "It's him, it's him!" And the others chimed in, "We are your people! You belong with us. He's a foreigner. He doesn't understand you. Don't talk to him!"

I excused myself and took the call from Eric. He wanted to know if I'd given any thought to our guest list. It took me a minute to figure out what he was talking about. The guest list? The interpreters were just teasing me about Eric, but they were right. He was so different, which was part of his enormous appeal, part of why I couldn't help but love him. He had lived a life totally different from that of the men from my country. True, he had lived amid missions and bombs and tanks, just like the Afghan men, but he had chosen to join the army and to be in that environment. The Afghan men were forced to live there in war. Having had no choice about that had made them bitter and angry to a degree that frightened me. Eric could separate the violence around him from within him; the Afghan men's violence became them; you could see it hovering behind their dark eyes.

Once I returned to the party the other interpreters cried, "Did you break up with him?"

"Not today. Ask me again tomorrow."

Haaroon never joked about my engagement, nor did we ever mention my sister again.

Judy already knew I was engaged to a soldier, although I hadn't divulged that he was a fellow PRT commander. Shortly after I'd arrived, when I saw she wasn't going to fire me, I had told her, to explain all the time I was spending on the computer and the phone in the evening.

She was married to a fellow commander, and she cautioned me that it wasn't easy. I think she was genuinely concerned. One day not long after, I was sitting on a bench beneath the *narange* trees, and an older U.S.

Army officer I'd never seen before sat down beside me. He was tall, slender, and blue-eyed. His hair was completely gray. I thought he was just a nice officer out for a walk, but he turned out to be the army chaplain. He said that he heard I was engaged to marry an American.

"Is he Christian?"

"Catholic," I said.

He asked if there was anything he could explain to me, anything he could help me understand.

"To be honest, I'm not very religious, and my fiancé respects my religion enough. We both pretty much feel the same, that it's important to be good and to do good, and if you don't, there are consequences."

"I can't argue with that," he said. Then he told me that he'd done several tours in Iraq and studied Islam; he felt it was important to know the religion of the host country. He said he deeply admired my faith and certainly wasn't going to encourage me to convert; it sounded as if I was going into my marriage with my eyes open. Then he asked about Eric's ethnic heritage. I told him he was half Italian and half Argentinean.

"Oh, boy," he said, and began to laugh.

"Why are you laughing?" I asked.

"It's just that Afghans are volatile, emotional, and expressive, and so are Italians. And so are Argentineans. I don't envy your neighbors. You're going to be screaming and yelling one minute and making up the next. Your friends will never know if you two are getting a divorce or going to live happily ever after."

"That's pretty much it," I said. We sat for a moment without speaking. I asked him who had told him I was getting married, and he said that Judy had sent him. She was concerned and wanted to help. During those early weeks, it was empowering just to feel that I'd made a friend who cared about me.

$\mathcal{T}$ WENTY-ONE

In 2005, Ramadan, the month of fasting, began on October 4. It started with an unsettling occurrence. I was sitting in the yard when a soldier on desk duty in the Tactical Operations Center came to get me because Judy was looking for me. There was a fight in the bazaar that some were saying was instigated by the Taliban. Judy quickly told me what had happened. A teenager who'd refused to honor the fast had been beaten. All Muslims are required to fast. It doesn't matter how observant we are the rest of the year—for one month we must go without food and drink from sunrise to sunset, the better to empathize with people who are less fortunate, who don't have a choice about when they can eat and drink. It's also meant to strengthen the community. Each day after dark we invite people into our homes to break the fast; or we take food from the home to the mosque. It also cleanses our bodies to fast from food, and to give them a break from eating. During Ramadan we're also supposed to refrain from lying, stealing, or having impure thoughts.

Judy's CAT I, Jawed, went into the city to see exactly what had happened. The boy, who was clearly old enough to be fasting, had been chewing gum—another indulgence prohibited during Ramadan. The locals called him out. He shot off his mouth, saying the Taliban was no longer in power and that he could do whatever he pleased. According to Jawed's report, shopkeepers then tackled him and beat him severely.

It was the talk of the tearoom that day. I said to one of the CAT I's that I felt conflicted about it. "That boy was old enough to have an opinion and to speak his mind. And he was right—ultimately fasting was his own choice, something between him and God. At the same time, I can see how his behavior was insulting to traditional and fasting Muslims."

The CAT I looked at me coldly. "He deserved it," he said. "If you choose not to fast, then don't fast, but don't show it in public. We don't have that kind of freedom in Afghanistan."

In October Judy was called away to a meeting of PRT commanders. I loved my job and I loved staying busy, but I felt relieved when I heard she would be gone. Her absence would give me time to go on missions with the Civil Affairs Team and the United States Agency for International Development (USAID), where I would meet villagers, and not just attend the governor's meetings.

During the month of fasting, Muslims are encouraged to read the Koran from start to finish, a little bit every day. Mosques in the cities use public speakers to read the Koran in Arabic, as it is traditionally read by Muslims worldwide, but they go a step further; they not only read out loud the translation in the native language but also preach in between the verses. Because it was in Arabic and Pashtu, the soldiers could easily block it out. But I knew what they were saying and I was tormented by it.

The morning it happened I was lying in bed, listening to the Qari (one who has memorized the Koran) talk about hellfire and how everything we do here on earth will be judged by God, and how we will be held accountable for it. Even though the rational side of me knew better, I couldn't help but feel that the Qari was talking to me directly, telling me that for marrying Eric, an infidel, I would burn in hell for eternity.

Then, at 8:50, the ground started shaking. I saw the time on my travel clock just before it fell to the floor. I could feel the earth's roar in my joints and bones. I leapt up from my bed just as it was being heaved into the air, causing me to stumble when my feet hit the floor.

My room was on the second floor. I ran down the curved cement stairs, petrified as they groaned and swayed with each step, filling the air with dust. By the time I had staggered to a bench near the edge of the swimming pool, the shaking had stopped. Soldiers were streaming from their rooms, barefoot, shirtless, cussing.

A little boy, who worked as a janitor at the MWR, sidled up to me and whispered, "Do you know you're not wearing any shoes?"

"I'm just glad I'm wearing clothes!" I replied.

"I didn't feel anything!" he said. He sat down next to me. "You should put some shoes on." The earth rocked and shivered again. I grabbed the side of the bench. The boy giggled and ran off. God, how I wished that I was so fearless about death.

THAT SAME MORNING, Judy's deputy commanding officer, Captain Christopher Malm, asked me to accompany him to the hospital in Jalalabad. We wanted to know how many people had been injured or killed in the earthquake and he thought the hospital should know. Much later we would learn that the epicenter had been in Kashmir. It was said to have been as big as the 1906 earthquake in San Francisco. In Pakistan, close to seventy-five thousand people were killed, but in Afghanistan only four died. In Jalalabad a small girl was crushed beneath a crumbling wall.

At the hospital there weren't as many injured victims as we'd feared. A handful of men with bloodied foreheads sat in the small waiting area. Chris and I waited with the hospital director. Chris had barely uttered one sentence when suddenly it felt as if the building had been hit by a massive truck. It was yet another aftershock, the worst one so far. I cried out. I hated that I was acting like a scared little girl, but earthquakes terrify me like nothing else.

The director cleared his throat anxiously and folded his hands. We began again. Chris repeated his sentence. I cannot remember what it was. Distressed and distracted, I couldn't keep my eyes off a crack in the wall. It was a delicate crack, winding its way from ground to ceiling like a lazy river. It wasn't new, but I knew with complete certainty that the next time the earth shook, the room would split in half right there, and our skulls would be crushed by chunks of falling concrete.

Just as I was thinking that, the earth rumbled again. Now my knees were shaking. I am an educated American woman who speaks five languages. I know how to drive a car, hop on a transatlantic flight, manage my credit, purchase my own property, and choose my own husband. None of that mattered. Suddenly, I was the little girl who knew beyond all doubt that God was angry with her. Earthquakes mean one thing in Afghanistan, in Islam: God is angry. God has had it with you. God had had it with *me*. He was on the side of the CAT I's: I was marrying a non-Muslim and it was wrong. This earthquake was my sign from God.

Chris passed me his water bottle. My hands were shaking. I couldn't drink without spilling. "Let's get you back to the PRT," he said with real concern.

There was a basketball game in progress in the empty swimming pool as I made my way back to my room. The men called to one another, passed the ball, couldn't have cared less. They weren't being shot at, so life was good. I envied them then. I thought of Eric, and wondered whether his Catholic god was as angry at him for marrying me.

I lay down on my bed, on my back, my arms folded over my chest like a dead person. I stared up at the ceiling, relieved to see that there were no cracks. I tried to close my eyes, but every time I did I felt the room shake. I was comforted slightly by the basketball game outside, the rhythmic sound of the ball bouncing on the pool floor. I'd start to drift off but would catch myself. If I could just keep my eyes open, I convinced myself, the earthquakes would stop.

And I needed to stop them. Even though I'd already moved my bed away from the window, I knew that if another quake hit, the glass would shatter and the entire side of the building would collapse on top of me. Who knew how well it had been built? The Soviets had constructed it using local workers who had probably wanted the building to fall on top of the Russians and kill them all. Who knew what shortcuts they'd taken, what interior beams and joists and whatever else holds up buildings were missing? It could be a death trap. I had a little deck off my room. I would never step out onto it again.

A few days passed. I was fine in my room during the day. As long as I could hear soldiers outside, playing basketball, or talking as they sat around, I could at least rest. Napping was out of the question. I felt that if I closed my eyes for an instant, there would be another huge aftershock. It wasn't rational—but knowing that feelings are irrational does not give you the power to control them.

In the evenings, after sunset, there was a heavy presence in my room. I knew it was there when the air became heavy and cold. Sometimes it smelled like roses gone bad. I told myself for the first few evenings that my mind was playing tricks on me and that I was all shaken up about the earthquake so was imagining the eerie presence as a result of lack of sleep and stress. I tried not to think of the ghost stories I'd heard, stories told in the chow hall or tearoom before the quake, when I could still find that dark enjoyment in a good, scary ghost story.

My room had two beds, the bed I slept in and the daybed, where I sat and read, worked on my laptop, and talked to Eric on the phone. One night, as I was sitting on the daybed reading, I suddenly sensed another presence in the room. The feeling was so intense that I swear I could hear it breathing. The daybed was by the door. I didn't even look around the room to confirm that there was a ghost I could see. I was sure that there was, and I didn't want to see it. Grabbing my cell phone, I bolted out of my room, down the stairs, and past the empty swimming pool to the MWR. My hands shook as I called Eric. It was after midnight, and the moon was high in the sky.

"Why are you up so late, honey?" he asked in lieu of a hello.

"Eric, there's a ghost in my room! I can't sleep there. And I'm afraid there's going to be an earthquake again. And that's what brought out the ghost, and there will be more!" I blurted out.

Normally this would be Eric's cue to tease me without mercy. My fierce Pashtun is afraid of a ghost? Ha-ha! But he could hear, for the first time, genuine fear in my voice. "Honey, you need to come home to me," he said.

But I realized then that I wasn't sure I wanted to go home, or to him. I didn't like having a ghost in my room or the feeling that God was angry at me, but I wasn't ready to face Eric and our wedding, either. I replied that it was good to hear his voice, that I'd just needed to talk to him, that I would be fine, and that he shouldn't worry.

So back to my room I went. I never should have said the word *ghost* aloud. I cautiously walked back past the swimming pool. Judy would be back soon. She was the voice of reason; she had more common sense than anyone I knew. But she wasn't there now. What was still there, in my room, was the ghost. I spun around and bolted back to the MWR. I decided I would sleep there until Judy returned.

The next evening after dinner Haaroon and the other interpreters showed up at the tearoom as if nothing had happened. Earthquake or no earthquake, tea must be drunk. Ahmad, who liked to badger me, said, "Miriam, you look distraught. Are you dumping your American boyfriend after all?"

"There's a ghost in my room," I said.

"They're all over the place here. Think of all the mujahideen who were slaughtered steps from where you lay your head each night. The ghosts were probably sleeping until the earthquake woke them up." Soldiers and CAT I's alike swore they'd seen at one time or another someone in all white walking among the *narange* trees. When they'd called out, asking who was there, the spirit disappeared.

I covered my ears, told them to stop. I confessed that I'd slept on the couch in the MWR, which started them on a chorus of "Miriam, that's just not right."

I couldn't bring myself to pass the swimming pool and climb the stairs, so I didn't return to my room that night. I was like the yellow puppy. I sat up all night in the MWR. There was a small lending library there. I curled up on a nice sofa and read *The Da Vinci Code,* which I had been meaning to read.

A version of this night repeated itself several times. By the time Judy returned, I'd convinced some female medics to sleep in my room, occupying the ghost's bed. The three of them had shared small quarters and were happy for the additional elbow room. Judy was upset when she discovered this arrangement.

"That's not going to work," she said. "There is the issue of accountability, in case of emergency. They have to go back to their room. We assigned them a spot, and that's where they need to be." Instead, she sent me to the medic, who prescribed some herbal sleeping pills that did nothing but upset my stomach—or maybe it was the stress that did that.

I became nocturnal. There was a landing outside my room, big enough for a chair. One day I asked Haaroon whether he would mind sitting there for a few hours so I could take a nap. He agreed without a word. He sat on the landing all afternoon, reading a book or playing a game on his phone while I tried to sleep. Finally, having finished his book and grown bored with solitaire, he said, "Look, you need to get over this. The ghosts won't do anything to you. They've been here for a long time."

"Haaroon, you're not making me feel better, talking about this like it's real."

"It was the earthquake that got them agitated, not you," he said with a sigh.

Once Eric had voiced his desire for me to come home, he started lobbying for it every time we spoke. He reminded me that I'd said that all I wanted to do was fulfill my contract, and I'd already done that. I'd signed on to interpret for six months, and it had been almost twelve. I'd had no break between my postings at Farah and Jalalabad, with the exception of the week I'd spent in the village with my family, which wasn't much of a vacation. I didn't tell him that I had been asked to do another three-month extension, and that I had been seriously considering it until the ghost appeared in my room.

He was right, which I hated to admit. Still, I was secretly proud of myself for managing to continue my duties despite my lack of sleep and terror of ghosts and tremors. Life was difficult but not unbearable. Masoud, Sherzai's stylish assistant, invited me and two other CAT II interpreters to break the fast each day down at the Kabul River, by the Darunta dam.

The dam was built in the 1960s to provide hydroelectricity for the city, but with the buildup of silt in the river and the damage done during the various wars, it no longer produced electricity. Instead, the green, slow-moving river had become a popular picnic spot. Each afternoon fishermen went to work catching and cooking fish to sell up and down the riverbank. They served the fish with bread and chutney made of garlic, tomato, and mint. I wore a long tunic and khakis and would roll up my pant legs to wade in the cool, shallow water. The smoky smell of the fish and garlic, the chatter of people happy to be eating amid such beauty, the breeze that formed tiny white frills on the river's surface all made it a heavenly scene.

One CAT II from Kandahar, looking at my ankles and lower calves, said that I could get stoned for my behavior. I didn't think so. I was a guest of Masoud and, by extension, Sherzai. Now such an outing would be too dangerous, but in late 2005, it was still safe. Or safe enough. At the time Sherzai was trying to get the dam fixed; he eventually succeeded, and today it produces all of the electricity for Jalalabad.

These trips to the river each evening sustained me and reinforced my love for Afghanistan. While I was there, enjoying the freshest fish I have ever eaten, the sound of the pale green river, the birds chirping away in the last light of the day, and the company, I could comfortably straddle the horns of my dilemma: I missed Eric and felt anxious being so far away from him, but I was also relieved to be separated, because I was coming to the conclusion that I wasn't ready to get married.

Now that I'd been in Jalalabad for several months, it was clear that Farah had been an idyll, a time out of time. The PRT was so small, relaxed, and peaceful beneath the eternal gaze of the orange mountains. Eric and I were like two kids who'd fallen in love at summer camp, and now it was time to go back to our respective schools. The relationship had been amazing in fantasyland; would it be the same in the real world? Every time he asked how I was and I told him I wasn't sleeping, he told me to come home. I heard something in his voice that sounded very much like an order. And I knew all too well how I felt about men ordering me around.

One morning while getting ready in my bathroom, I looked in the mirror and realized that I looked as harassed as all the other women in Afghanistan. I had what had become permanent circles beneath my eyes and had lost weight. My hair, once lustrous enough for a shampoo commercial, was brittle and dry.

Judy could also see that I was flagging, but she was angry with me. At the PRT conference she'd attended before the quake, someone had been gossiping about the PRT commander who had fallen in love with a CAT II interpreter, and Judy had put two and two together. When she returned, she was different. Her green eyes were cold. She stopped chatting and joking with me between meetings. Had I broken some kind of unwritten rule by seducing a man of her pay grade? Should only an 05, a lieutenant colonel, be able to marry another 05? Or was I mistaken about her disapproval, and was it just my sleep deprivation that made me feel that way? I would never find out, but I did know one thing: She was no longer on my side.

Matters did not improve between us when Sherzai invited me to his Eid party. Eid ul-Fitr is a big three-day holiday that marks the end of the month of fasting. The Eid celebration took place in early November. Sherzai sent a personal invitation to me at the PRT. The note said, "Miriam, this is not work. I want you to not have to translate, so please, do not bring Judy. I will send my car to get you. The dish you love will be served."

Months before, when I had just arrived in Jalalabad, Judy and I had joined Sherzai for lunch. He served grilled eggplant topped with yogurt and fresh cilantro. At the risk of looking like a greedy American, I asked for seconds. And I asked Sherzai to please let his chef know that it was the best eggplant I'd ever had.

"So you think my cook did a good job? I should keep him around?"

"Yes! Even my mom doesn't make it this good," I replied.

During the month of fasting it's a tradition to send people you know gifts of food at the end of the day. At least twice a week during that month a messenger from Sherzai arrived at the gate with a plate of eggplant for me. It really was too much—which never stopped me from accepting it. I always sent back a warm thank-you and complimented the cook.

One of the times Judy and I went to the Governor's Palace for a meeting, I asked him whether he would mind if I asked his cook for the eggplant recipe. Judy was out of the room on a phone call.

"Sure, Miriam, ask!" That day he was dressed in a white polo shirt. He could have been one of my uncles in America, except they are not so big and burly. Plus, he smiled at me, and they never did. He had a devilish look that made me wonder if the rumors about him behaving as if he were above the law were true. Then he said, "I am the cook. But don't tell anyone."

"You're the cook?"

"I love this dish, and I love making it for you. No one else can make it right. As a Pashtun you know that we grew up eating it. I can tell you did, too, and it made me happy to make it for you so you can think about your country and its cuisine."

At that moment Judy returned, and the meeting resumed.

I went to Judy's office to tell her about his invitation. I couldn't go without her permission. She had agreed with me wholeheartedly about the importance of building relationships, and that it happened during ordinary moments, when Afghans and Americans were given the chance to interact without an agenda. An Eid party provided exactly this sort of opportunity, and we both knew it.

"Everyone from Jalalabad and the local villages will be there," she said. "It won't be safe. You'll have to take a security detail."

I didn't say anything. She busied herself with some file folders. I knew I would be perfectly safe. Sherzai would be my security detail. She knew that showing up with a dozen armed American soldiers would ruin the party for everyone else. I knew she wasn't thrilled about Eric, but I suspected that she also felt as if I'd replaced her in Sherzai's esteem. If I hadn't shown up at the PRT, she probably would have been invited to the party. She would have dragged Jawed along to interpret.

I called Sherzai on my cell to tell him that I was sorry to have to decline his invitation, but I was busy with some urgent matters here at the PRT.

"But this is your first Eid back with your people!" he cried. "I want you to celebrate it properly."

"Please don't worry. I'll come over in a few days and celebrate with you then."

"I will never cook for you again, Miriam. You rejected my invitation. I had them buy all the ingredients, just for you. Now I am going to throw them away."

He was such a drama queen. "No, you're not going to throw it all away. Cook the eggplant like always, and serve it to your guests."

Sure enough, that night his messenger arrived at the gate with another batch. The next morning the same messenger arrived at the gate, staggering behind an enormous basket of Pakistani sweets. It must have weighed at least twenty-five pounds. I needed a soldier to bring a truck to the gate to transport it back to my room.

I put the basket on the bed that belonged to the ghost. I hadn't slept at night in this room for weeks. I sat on my bed and stared at the basket, filled with dates, cookies, doughnuts, and candy.

Many Afghans enjoy a life of extreme disappointment, of endless labor and boredom. A few, like Sherzai, know no deprivation. Once Sherzai joked that he would like to make me his fourth wife. I responded that being the fourth wife is indeed a good position to be in, because then you are the spoiled wife. He said I shouldn't be so sure; his other wives were older and would expect to boss me around. They might make me do all the work. We joked a lot about my marrying him, but never in front of other Afghans. Sherzai knew how disrespectful it would have been for him to joke about something like that with a Pashtun female in front of other Pashtun men. I had never for a minute thought Sherzai was serious. But now, as I stared at that ridiculous basket, I thought perhaps I had been wrong.

I tracked down Judy, sitting in a chair outside her office, reading some reports in the sun. It was November in Jalalabad and it was still hot. The air still smelled of basil and orange blossoms. I sat down beside her and closed my eyes. The sun's rays felt heavenly on my face and closed eyelids.

I told her I wanted to throw an Eid party for the soldiers. I had been in Afghanistan for almost a year, and I had never shared anything special with the soldiers. I knew they'd been trained to respect the rituals of Islam, but mostly they were mystified by the religion and those who practiced it. An entire month of fasting seemed extreme to them.

"That's an awesome idea," said Judy. Her eyes still on her reports. We sat in silence for a moment. "I suppose it would ruin the fun if I showed up?"

"Of course you must come," I said. "I'll give a little explanation of Eid. Come for that, then we can hang out afterward."

The day of the party was sultry; a golden haze nestled against the feet of the mountains. I wore a white outfit embellished with silver embroidery that I'd purchased at the PRT bazaar. I wore silver bracelets, black eyeliner, and glittery powder on my cheeks. I had taken no makeup to Afghanistan the first time I returned. I had thought it would be silly to wear it while at war, but I did find some makeup in the local bazaar. Like most things sold in Afghan bazaars, it was past its expiration date, but it was better than nothing.

For Eid I had asked one of the PRT shopkeepers to bring me some silver sparkles. This was the army. No one looked like this, ever. I felt so dressed up beside the soldiers in their beige uniforms.

The chow-hall cook had made milk tea for the party. I brought Sherzai's enormous basket of sweets and supplemented it with some cookies from the bazaar. We set up a table in the MWR and announced the celebration over the loudspeaker. I gave a short talk about the month of fasting and the reason behind it and how we celebrated Eid. I taught the soldiers the proper way to wish someone a happy Eid in Pashtu: *Akhtar de mubarak sa.*

"Although you didn't fast, we won't hold it against you and will still let you celebrate with us," I teased the soldiers.

"Sometimes we did," said one of them. "Just the other day we had a meeting in a village and for the first time no one offered us tea!"

"Okay, I think that counts as fasting." I was always generous in giving the soldiers credit.

The party was a success. In a few hours the basket of sweets was empty, not a crumb left, and for the rest of the day I was heartened to hear several soldiers wishing the local laborers *akhtar de mubarak sa*. The laborers thanked them, often offering a quick lesson in proper pronunciation. This was progress.

The wind picked up in the evening. The sound of it rustling in the palms reminded me of being near the ocean. Judy said that the party had been an excellent idea. I reminded her it couldn't have happened without Sherzai and his determination to be larger than life.

The only thing that marred an otherwise perfect Eid was an incident with some of the local laborers. On the way to the MWR I passed several young guys from a nearby village digging a trench. They'd straightened up from their work and openly ogled me. I was worried about how the party would go, already exhausted from my eternal lack of sleep and the heavy, damp heat. I lost my temper.

I told Judy what had happened. "I just don't know how long I can stay in this country," I said. "In the beginning, it was all right, being gawked at by everyone. I thought people would get used to seeing me. But still, wherever I go, everyone stares. I can't take it anymore." Although it upset me to be stared at in any country, it upset me a lot more in Afghanistan. I think it's because I knew that the men doing it would be risking their lives if they were to stare at other Pashtun women outside the wire. So it was insulting on a different level, that they would feel free to look at me like that without fearing the consequences. Usually, I would take matters into my own hands and tell them to stop staring and remember that we were all Pashtuns, hoping to shame them. But that day I was also looking for an excuse to blow up. I missed everyone back home, and wanted to be with my family on Eid.

"I'll take care of it," Judy said.

"Don't worry about it," I said, as soon as I realized that I would be better at yelling at the local men than Judy. "It's Eid day. Things can get a little crazy. I probably overreacted."

The next day, without telling me, Judy called a meeting of all the interpreters and local laborers and told them to stop staring at me. She told them it was not permissible to even look at me, and that if she caught any of them so much as glancing my way, they would be fired instantly. I only knew this because I bumped into Haaroon. Quite literally. He was staring down at his shoes. For extra measure, he shielded his eyes with his hand.

"What's wrong with you?" I asked.

"The commander said if she caught us looking at you, we'd get fired!"

I found Judy in her office, shuffling papers, her green scarf folded on the back of the chair beside her desk. I said I appreciated her effort, but that this was even worse—now I looked like a prima donna.

"If I have to fire a few local laborers to hang on to you, then I will," she said.

"There's no need to fire anyone."

"I can't let you go," she said, in a tone that told me she knew I would be leaving. "I don't know what they'll send me if you leave."

THE LAST TIME I saw Sherzai before I left Jalalabad he was the star of a local TV-news story. The story concerned a mission we'd undertaken that morning at a nearby refugee camp. It was the same camp where Judy and I and our security detail were invited into the old woman's tent to partake of the worst milk tea in the history of the nation.

During the months I'd spent working in his province Sherzai had been in hot water with the refugee population, over the land dispute we'd first heard about on our previous visit. The refugees claimed he'd been unfair. It was said he'd favored certain people, depending on their tribal associations, not to mention the fact that he was rumored to have just flat-out kept some of the land for himself. This disturbed him. He was beloved in Nangarhar and he didn't appreciate any gossip.

We'd agreed to meet him at the settlement camp, but that day we'd had word that there might be an ambush planned for us. Our convoy moved slowly, stopping at each point of watch, radioing to one another that the road was clear, that there weren't going to be any nasty surprises, no ambushes or IEDs.

By the time we arrived, Sherzai was already there. Judy and I found him standing atop a small hill, dressed in his Pashtun photo-op gear: his dove-gray *shalwar kameez,* his black vest, and a gold-and-black turban. A crowd of people pressed into him. Children scampered around the periphery hopping and waving their arms. Dust hung in the air, disturbed by all the bare, stamping feet.

We watched as Sherzai extended his big arm, the gold watch on his wrist and in his hand a wad of hundred-dollar bills. Another hand snatched it from him. The crowd jostled. People ran toward him, shouting.

In 2005, $100 equaled about 5,000 Afghanis, more than an average Afghan made in a year. It would be like someone showing up on your doorstep with forty grand. And Sherzai passed out hundreds to everyone, to six-year-old girls and shifty young guys and stooped grandfathers who probably wouldn't live long enough to spend the $100. This was his solution to the land-distribution mess.

Judy and I stopped. People pushed past us in their rush to get to Sherzai. Most didn't seem to know who he was, this big Pashtun with the hundred-dollar bills. If they knew, they didn't care.

"Judy, did we know he was going to do this?"

She shook her head. I knew she was wondering how she was going to explain this to her superiors, Sherzai passing out hundred-dollar bills like paper napkins at a barbecue. We were there to support and mentor the local government, and he was the local government. Even if she could make herself heard over the chatter and cries, she couldn't stop him. It would have been violating his authority.

Behind the crowd a very old woman, bent nearly in half from a lifetime of sweeping dust from dirt floors, crowed, "Where is the man with the money! I want my hundred-dollar bill!" Her head was raised and tipped at an angle peculiar to the blind.

Sherzai spied her and hollered, "Step away, people! Everyone step away!"

He pushed his way through the crowd. The performance was about to begin.

"Where's my hundred dollars?" she called again, aware, I imagine, that the mood of the crowd had changed, that something was about to happen.

Sherzai stepped in front of her. It was difficult to tell whether he could see that she was blind, or whether he was so caught up in what he was about to do that he didn't notice. "*Adhai,* how are you today? I am Sherzai. I am the governor of this province."

"Son, I do not care who you are. I heard you were giving out money, and I want mine."

Sherzai laughed. I saw his eyes narrow as they did when he was angry or amused. And most of the time he was amused. Amused by the passing parade, by his lavish, absurd lifestyle. I thought of his immense crystal chandelier swaying over the foyer in his palace, his compulsion to make eggplant, his outlandish stunts, like this one. He was an Afghan warlord, and many people thought he was bad—and just as many didn't care. Sherzai said, "You do not even care what I am doing here, *Adhai?* Why I've come to see you today? You do not care what I have to say?"

"As long as you give me my money, you can say anything you want."

Sherzai slapped his thighs. He was caught in that loop of laughter, where you laugh and then laugh at yourself laughing. He pulled another roll of bills from his pocket and peeled off five. Five hundred dollars, counted into her cracked and dusty palm.

Judy gasped.

"I know," I said.

In his eagerness to make a lavish gesture he'd put this grandmother's life in danger. Tonight, after he was long gone, someone would probably rob her, or even kill her for those five crisp bills. And there would be no one to report her death the next morning to the police, even if there had been police in the city.

$\mathcal{T}$ W E N T Y - T W O

When I left Jalalabad, I didn't tell Mamai I was coming home. I wanted to surprise her. Najiba and her boyfriend, Kabir, picked me up at the Portland airport. They were slightly late and rushed right past me on the way to the gate.

I knew I didn't look like the Saima who had left them nearly a year before. I was too tan, like a homeless person or a prophet lost in the desert; the points of my shoulders were visible beneath my tunic and the whites of my eyes were dark pink. I blamed my failure to use sunscreen, the pork-heavy army cuisine, which meant I missed more meals than was healthy, and my dirty contact lenses, which I had worn throughout the long flights. Later, Kabir, who would become my sister's husband, would tell me how shocked they'd been at my appearance. They blamed Afghanistan and always would. What they couldn't have known was that I was also stressed not only from having hidden my engagement to Eric but also by the simple fact of him.

Mamai slept with her door open. When I arrived she was sleeping on her back, her thick black hair threaded with gray coiled into two braids.

"I'm back after all these months, and you're sleeping like it's no big deal?" I said, standing in her doorway.

"Shrenghay? What's going on? What are you talking about?" Mamai sat up and blinked. Shrenghay was Najiba's childhood nickname. She'd mistaken me for my sister.

I turned on the light. She sat up in her nightdress and blinked, then started to cry, then started to laugh. She leapt to her feet, hugging me and slapping my shoulder at the same time, both upset and overjoyed to see me. "Why didn't you tell me you were coming home?"

It was midnight, but she insisted on warming me up some dinner and making tea. I said I only wanted a little tea, that I was too tired to eat, but she wouldn't hear of me not eating.

While they were in the kitchen warming the food and making tea, I went to my bedroom. I dropped my bags on the floor, then tucked into the bathroom, closed and locked the door. I had missed my bathroom as if it were a close personal friend. When I'd phoned Najiba with my flight information I'd asked her to please make sure there were fresh towels in my bathroom and told her I was going to spend hours in there. At the time she thought I was joking. She had also gone to the trouble of scouring the sink. I could smell the cleaner. I closed the toilet lid and sat on it. I inhaled the good smells. I pressed my face into one of the clean towels.

Almost an hour passed. I had been showering in tepid, overchlorinated water for a year. I looked at my shower with affection. I thought I could easily go to sleep in the bathroom, curl up right on the bath mat. It was so safe and clean.

There was a soft knock on the door. "Are you okay in there?" asked Najiba.

I came out, only because I knew it was upsetting them that I was staying in there, and drank some tea. As long as an Afghan can choke down some tea, all is well. My cell phone rang. Mamai and Najiba looked at each other. Who was calling at this hour? I mumbled some excuse and left the room to take the call.

"I'm coming out to Oregon. I've got to see you." Eric had been living in Florida with his parents. They didn't know about me yet, either.

"Can't we wait a little? I just got home. I don't think I can talk about anything."

"What do you mean?" The alarm in his voice annoyed me.

"I mean, I just flew halfway around the world, and I need to chill out for a while."

"For how long? I don't understand. I thought you'd be glad to hear I was coming to see you. Don't you want to be together anymore?"

It went on like that for a few minutes. I felt myself growing frustrated. He'd been in the army for years. Didn't he understand that I needed a week or two to get reacclimated, that it wasn't about him, or us, or my feelings about the wedding? He jumped to conclusions. He wondered if I'd met someone else. He kept asking me if I still loved him.

Looking back, I realize I was probably suffering from post-traumatic stress disorder. Most Americans who are lucky enough not to live in a combat zone don't understand PTSD. There are so many forms and shapes of it that it even surprises those of us who are very much aware of it in ourselves and others around us. A lot of people I have talked to think that unless you are caught in a firefight or survive an IED explosion, you can't have PTSD. But just the trauma of living in an environment where you never know whether you might be bombed the next day, or if the person you are talking to while eating will be there tomorrow, is emotionally stressful enough to create the kind of extreme anxiety that leads to PTSD. On top of that, there are loud noises—outgoing mortars, incoming rockets, helicopters landing steps from where you are sleeping—and when you return to a place like Portland, a car backfiring on the street will take you back to Afghanistan instantly. And the feeling stays with you. Waking up and telling yourself that you're at home and out of harm's way does little to help allay your fear.

For the next week I spent most of my time reading in my closet. I had a walk-in closet with good lighting. My bedroom was simply too big. I felt too exposed, and if I heard noises from other parts of the house, I would be forced to investigate. It was nerve-wracking. My closet had just enough space to contain me, and the clothes muffled the sounds of the rest of the house. It also reminded me of my B-hut.

I rearranged my bedroom, pushing my bed into one of the corners farthest from the door. I could only sleep if my back was against a wall and I could keep my eye on the door. One night in late December, just as I'd started to drift off, I heard gunshots. I leaped out of bed before I was fully awake. My heart felt as if it was trying to break free from my chest. It banged in my ears; my head was swimming. I couldn't think of anything to do but text Najiba, who was out with Kabir.

"Naj!" I typed. "There are gunshots. Someone's shooting up the neighborhood."

Our house was on a cul-de-sac. My bedroom faced the street. The gunshots were loud.

"It's New Year's Eve," she texted back. "Those are fireworks. Are you okay?"

Sure enough, I peeked out the window and saw a gang of older kids lighting strings of firecrackers in the middle of the street. I had totally forgotten that it was New Year's Eve. Days blend together when you're trying to hide from everything around you.

"I can come home!" she texted again.

"I'm okay. Enjoy ur night," I texted back.

Eric called four or five times a day, wondering if I felt better, wondering whether we could now get on with the wedding, wondering whether I'd talked to my family. He was relentless, and the more I dissembled, the more I begged for time, the worse he got. I thought that if only he had called to check on me and ask me how I was dealing with being back, I could have unburdened myself to him—who better to understand me than Eric, who had been dealing with PTSD for years? But he didn't. He was worried about the wedding and my reluctance to talk to him. His behavior was making me feel like I had a cause to be questioning our compatibility. In Jalalabad I had been concerned that we were of two very different cultures, but I had been more concerned with making our families understand and accept us. I had never worried that we would be having this issue with each other. But now, back in the States, he acted like he had no clue what I was going through and was in such a hurry to start our lives that I felt like he was rushing me into making a mistake.

● ● ●

ONE DAY NAJIBA asked, "Who *was* that? Who is this person who calls you so many times a day?"

"It's funny you ask," I said slowly. "It is actually my fiancé."

My sister looked at me a long moment to see if this was yet another Saima joke. I assured her it was not.

If I'd stopped and listened, I might have heard Wahabs the world over calling one another and shrieking in disbelief. In Portland, London, somewhere in Germany, Peshawar, and Ghazni Province, Sunday meetings were called to figure out what was to be done. Saima was getting married! Saima was marrying an infidel, and not just any infidel, but an American infidel, and not just any American infidel, but a soldier, a commander, a man who was in charge of invading and further ruining Afghanistan.

When it became clear that Sunday meetings were not enough, emergency midweek sessions were held. The uncles summoned Najiba, Khalid, and Mamai. To my brother they said, "You are a good-for-nothing brother if you let your sister do this." To my sister they said, "This is the worst thing that your sister could have done. If you are still talking to her, that means you are okay with it, and you are just like her." To my poor Mamai they said, "Your daughter is out of control; you're a horrible mother to allow her to get away with this." Not surprisingly, they never asked for my presence at these meetings.

I had not spoken to the uncles in years. But when I saw Mamai's tear-stained face after they had lectured her, I knew something had to be done. I contacted an aunt who lived in the States and was still on speaking terms with me, and who in the past had served as a messenger between the uncles and me. "What do you think you're doing to my mother? You guys washed your hands of me and kicked me out in the middle of the night because you weren't able to control me. Do you think that makes you all good Pashtuns? How do you expect Mamai to do something you men weren't able to do? You had every resource in the world, and you weren't able to control my behavior at the end. Why do you expect my mother to succeed where you failed?"

Mamai went to the meetings because her brothers-in-law demanded her presence, and Khalid and Najiba were there in order to support her. But Mamai had not been surprised to hear I was marrying an American. She remembered that declaration that I'd made when I was nine or ten: "I'm never going to marry an Afghan man!" Mamai's friends were over for tea, and had told Mamai that it was time to start thinking about finding a husband for me. I was still a little girl. I had no idea what it was I was saying no to, exactly. My father was gone, and my only brother was a reasonable boy, a low-key observer of life. I had no real sense of the ways in which a man could take over a woman's life. There were distant female members of the family whom I occasionally saw with fear in their eyes and bruises on their bodies. These girls would say, "Oh yes, my brother beat me up, but he stopped when I promised not to upset him again." I remember wondering why anyone would willingly give someone else the right to do this to her. Where were the mothers of these girls? I didn't know at the time that the mothers were treated just as badly and wouldn't have been able to defend their daughters. When I wouldn't shut up about never marrying an Afghan, Mamai told me to find something else to do and not come out when her friends were visiting. I embarrassed her.

Word came down from the uncles that since Mamai could not control me, they did not want to have anything to do with her. Mamai is not stupid. Even while they were ordering her to tell me this and tell me that, they never offered to take her in. Mamai finally said to hell with them. She realized that her children were her true allies, and that her future lay with us, not with the uncles. One day I heard her say to someone on the phone, "My future is with my daughter." It was the first time in my life I felt as if my mother was on my side. I had waited almost thirty years to have my mother on my side, and the happiness I felt hearing her say that was inexpressible.

Mamai refused to go to any more meetings, and one night, while I was making tea, she stood in the middle of the kitchen and said, "Marry whomever you want. I am okay with your decision."

Still, the gossip reached us. All day long, from inside my walk-in closet (where I still retreated on occasion), I could hear the phone ring. It would be my aunt calling to urge Mamai to disown me. Or someone from Kuwait or Peshawar with other ideas on how to force me to obey. The uncles were beyond displeased and unhappy. Word got back to me that at one of the meetings the idea of an honor killing was raised, but they would have to have someone else do it because they didn't want to get caught.

I heard this and laughed out loud. "They are Pashtun enough to decide on an honor killing but they can't do it themselves? They have to outsource it? How American of them!"

I called Eric. "Don't get too attached to me," I said, "I might be stoned any day now."

"I'm calling your uncles to talk to them," he said. His voice shook with anger.

"They don't mean anything to me. Don't give them the satisfaction."

"Then I'm reporting them."

"To whom? You know these people. They'll just side with each other. They'll deny everything. I'm just telling you because I thought it was funny."

For weeks it seemed as if all I did was talk on the phone, pausing only to eat Mamai's delicious *parakay,* fried in butter, stuffed with potato and leek. I felt exhausted by the whole subject of my wedding, even as I began to plan it. I was American enough to know what needed to be done, but the Pashtun in me was at a complete loss. A bride planning her own wedding is unheard-of in my culture. The family organizes everything, and the bride is only told when to appear. Why couldn't I have been more like the other Pashtun girls of my family? I would agonize over the stress of wedding planning, but in the next breath I would thank God for giving me the ability to plan my own wedding.

Still, I pressed on. Things fell into place. I wanted to be married in a room with a view of the mountains and the river. The Marriott downtown had the perfect room, and it was actually available on the date we'd selected, February 14. More amazing was that when I told the cook at the Marriott that I wanted to serve Afghan food, he was all over the idea. He was going to learn to cook every dish I wanted to serve.

Our wedding was going to be small—no more than fifty people— and my wedding colors were deep burgundy, gold, and beige. Wedding colors! Could I have been the first Pashtun female in the recorded history of my tribe to have deliberated over wedding colors? The invitations were beautiful, printed in gold, with a Koranic verse at the top, in Arabic, and the rest in English. I loved the way the invitations had turned out, and couldn't wait to mail them.

My spirits started to lift. I felt good enough to taunt my brother, a sure sign that I was returning to my old self. "What kind of a Pashtun brother are you?" I teased him. "Why are you not planning my wedding and telling me just to show up?"

"If you want me to be a good Pashtun brother, I will tell you not to marry Eric," he replied, half joking.

I ran into problems trying to find a suitable wedding dress. White was out of the question. Farsiban wear white; I wouldn't be surprised to find out that every white prom dress from the 1980s had been shipped to Central Asia, catering to the Farsiban taste for shiny, poofy white dresses. Pashtuns wear colors, and I wanted to wear a traditional outfit, the most elaborate I could find. I saw it in my mind's eye: royal-blue, emerald-green, and hot-pink silk, decked out with beadwork, mirrors, and lace. There was nothing like it in Portland or even Seattle. In Afghanistan they are all made by hand; little girls work on those dresses for many years so they can wear them on their wedding day. I ordered something I thought was similar from a tailor in Nepal suggested by Kabir; when it arrived it was all wrong—not silk but chiffon, and decorated on the front but not the back.

I'd been told by my American friends that brides always feel this way, but I took one look at the failed chiffon wedding outfit from Nepal and called Eric. "I can't do this. This is a sign from God that I am not supposed to be getting married."

"Honey, everything is going to be just fine. Please don't bring God into this—your god, my god, any god."

To prove his point Eric tracked down several shops in Florida that specialized in wedding clothes for people from the Near East and sent me a plane ticket.

I had only seen Eric in uniform and in Farah, where no one knew we were together and we had to act like we meant nothing to each other. Seeing him in sunny Florida, wearing a flowered, short-sleeved shirt, walking toward me at the airport, I almost didn't recognize him. Until he smiled. I'd have known that smile anywhere, and suddenly I felt a heavy weight lift off of my shoulders. I had been worried that I wouldn't feel the same way about him, and I was happy to be wrong.

We found ourselves at a bridal shop specializing in Indian wedding clothes. What was I doing there? Even though it wasn't what I thought I wanted, I found a deep-burgundy silk skirt and top, heavy with gold embroidery and Swarovski crystals.

"Go try that on and come out and show me," said Eric.

"You're not supposed to see me in my outfit before the wedding. According to your culture it's bad luck."

"Honey, we're breaking so many other cultural traditions here I don't think one more will matter." He never got tired of calling me honey.

Eric lived near Orlando. That evening we took a walk in a park near Disney World. As the sun fell toward the horizon, it turned cold. The air smelled odd, like rotting vegetables. I felt my hair frizzing around my ears. It put me in a bad mood. Eric's urgency to marry felt like a pair of strong hands on my back. We passed a family wearing Mickey Mouse hats, arguing about their favorite ride. The tops of their cheeks were pink from the sun. This was important to them.

"There's nothing worse than a tourist!" I cried.

"You're a tourist," said Eric.

"I'm not," I said. "I would never go to that Disneyland place."

"What's wrong with you?"

"I want to go back to Afghanistan," I said. We stopped in the middle of the path. An airplane flew overhead. The wind picked up. I told him that I'd already researched it. I'd found a company that would be happy to hire us back as a couple. Since he'd been a PRT commander he could write his own ticket.

Eric considered the idea. He said he liked it. I could see his military mind ticking away, figuring out how to use my enthusiasm. On the way to the airport we reminisced about Farah, about Country-and-Western Fridays, Ping-Pong tournaments, and the late nights we spent sitting beneath the Milky Way on my bench. We were encouraged by the memory to believe we had a future.

The idea that we'd be returning to Afghanistan distracted me from our impending marriage. The wedding became something that needed to be accomplished in order to redeploy. After weeks of meetings (arguments, debates, crying), my extended family decided they had no choice but to allow me to marry my infidel. But I had yet to meet Eric's parents.

A week before the wedding Eric called and said he wasn't sure his parents were going to be able to come. When I asked him whether they objected to my being Muslim, he cleared his throat. I hummed with irritation at his hesitation.

"Just buy the tickets and tell them they're going to Argentina. When they arrive in Portland they'll have no choice but to come," I joked. I didn't feel like joking, but this was how Eric and I operated.

"That's an excellent idea!" he said. "Problem is, he's not supposed to fly at all."

"He's not?"

"Because of the stroke," he said.

This was the first I'd heard of any stroke. For a minute, I had to think. Stroke of the hour, golf stroke, to stroke the cat. The stroke he meant was like a heart attack of the brain.

"Your father had a stroke and you didn't tell me?"

"It wasn't really a stroke, it was just . . . he can't fly right now."

"Was it a stroke or not?"

"It's fine, honey, it really is."

"Did he have the stroke before or after you told him you were marrying a Muslim?" I asked.

For the first time I could remember, Eric had nothing to say.

I CALLED OFF the wedding. Perhaps it was inevitable. I canceled the hotel, the caterer, the cake. I put the lovely deep-burgundy dress away in the attic. There were many qualities that Eric and I shared, and the most important ones were that we were both hot-tempered and prone to be impulsive. He put everything he owned in storage in Flordia, except his computer, his printer, and a duffel bag full of clothes, which he threw into the back of his car. Then he drove to Oregon.

He had his own unacknowledged PTSD. He refused to fly. He couldn't bring himself to get on an airplane, to sit wedged in a seat in economy class between a crying baby and a snoring fat man, at the mercy of the commercial pilot and his crew. He believed he could drive straight through, almost three thousand miles without a break. He called me on the phone when he started getting sleepy. I told him to pull over to get a hotel. He refused.

After he arrived, he sat in my living room with his hands on his knees. While we went through the motions of arguing, while we wept and held each other, a part of me felt lighter. I closed my eyes and saw Afghanistan, the blue dome of sky, the big-shouldered mountains, and the mud houses huddled at their feet, the stars and moon bright enough to read by.

TWENTY-THREE

I knew I had made a full circle of the last two years of my life, sitting at the passenger terminal, PAX in Bishkek, Kyrgyzstan, waiting for my flight to Bagram Airfield. It was the middle of the night. There would be no flight for hours. I had a small bag of cold popcorn and a book. I was impatient. The longer I had to wait, the more time I had to think, which I didn't want to do. Thinking meant replaying the mess I'd made of my life, and of Eric's.

It was a year after I'd called off my wedding, and I was returning to Afghanistan; I couldn't believe it had taken me this long to find courage to face what lay ahead of me, again.

I RETURNED TO Afghanistan with a company that had a contract to provide interpreters for a small section of the country. Unlike my first time, when I had to wait at BAF for over a month to be sent out to my site, I was assigned to Asadabad in Kunar Province within hours of arrival. BAF had grown bigger and had more of a city feel now. There was a Jamba Juice, which I thought was just too much. Were we trying to fool the soldiers into thinking they were in a mall in the United States instead of in the dry desert of Afghanistan?

The next morning I caught a ride on a Chinook headed for Asadabad, where I was supposed to be yet another PRT commander's interpreter.

The helicopter took off, then hovered for several long minutes over BAF. Out the window, I could see the row of battered Soviet tanks by the runway that had been abandoned decades ago. All over Afghanistan abandoned Soviet vehicles decorate the landscape, commemorating the time when the Afghan people brought a superpower to its knees. When an ordinary car breaks down and is left by the side of the road, within minutes it is stripped for parts. But these same people would not touch Soviet machinery of war scattered all over the vast landscape of Afghanistan. It's as if Afghans had an unspoken understanding that the sight of all the tanks and other vehicles left behind by the fleeing Russians as they exited from our country was worth more than the money they would get by stripping them. I've experienced this same feeling while driving down roads throughout the country. I see the old rusted tanks and I feel a surge of Pashtun pride, a reminder that we are strong and have defeated many fierce enemies.

Suddenly I felt my stomach drop as the Chinook descended. We weren't going anywhere. Mechanical problems, we were told.

I WAS HAPPY to leave BAF so quickly, even if I was being sent to Asadabad. At the time, in March 2007, Kunar was one of the hottest spots in Afghanistan. The Korengal Valley, a few miles to the southwest in the neighboring Pech district, was known as Ambush Valley. As if I could have missed this detail, a few days after I arrived at the PRT I went to the Morale, Welfare, and Recreation center and turned on one of the computers. The home page had been set to Yahoo!, and the pop-up news headline read: THE HOTTEST SPOT ON EARTH: KORENGAL VALLEY. I clicked away from it. I had learned some of the soldiers' tricks while in a combat zone; one of them was not to dwell on the news when you're the news.

While I waited for the Chinook to be repaired, I stood on the tarmac with the other passengers, soldiers deploying to different parts of eastern Afghanistan. The one standing beside me introduced himself as John. Tall and burly in all his army gear—the armor vest, weapons, and a dozen other gadgets hanging off of him—he was a newly promoted lieutenant, and full of friendly optimism.

"What were you doing at the retirement center?" he asked.

"What's that?"

"That's what we call Bagram. There are interpreters who are too old to be sent outside the wire, but their company won't send them home. So they lounge around, drink tea, and take lots of walks. Just like retirees at a community retirement center in the States."

"You think I belong in a retirement community?"

"No, you're far too young to retire. Plus I don't know if you speak any other languages, but your English is great, already something that most those interpreters lack," he said with a grin. He told me about the few interpreters they had at Asadabad, including a CAT II who was quite popular with the younger CAT I men. It was rumored that she bought them alcohol, and spent most of her days doing her hair and makeup, and smoking like a chimney. "We have no real evidence that she speaks Pashtu," he said.

That sounded familiar. "Is her name Suraya?" I asked.

"No clue," John said. "Never got close enough to find out."

Late that night when we arrived at Asadabad PRT, I was shown to my B-hut by a sergeant major, where I unpacked my sleeping bag and alarm clock and went to sleep. Just as I was drifting off—*kaboom!* The flimsy walls of my hut shook. Things started falling around me; my clock broke. I could feel my heart pumping in my chest. Another earthquake? Was God still upset with me? I threw on my jacket and ran outside in the dark.

On the other side of the B-huts, not far away, was a shallow, circular ditch reinforced by sandbags. The mortar pit. Two soldiers worked in the pit, their beige T-shirts bright in the moonlight. *"Outgoing!"* one of them hollered. I saw a white flash; right after that the earth rumbled. *Kaboom!* The sound of the explosion set my teeth on edge. Making sure there was no incoming, I ran back to my hut and tried to go back to sleep, but it was no use.

The next morning I walked outside my B-hut, and there, sitting on a plastic patio chair with her legs crossed, a cigarette dangling from her lips, was Suraya, my first roommate in BAF. I recognized her perfect hair. It was dyed light brown, then highlighted. She wore lipstick, eyeliner, and eye shadow. Even though it was 8:30 A.M., she looked ready for a night on the town.

When she saw me she leaped up from her chair, knocking it over. "Oh, Saima-jan! It's you! We're roommates again! This is going to be so great!"

Suraya's use of *jan,* a Farsiban term of endearment, didn't help her case. I've always hated this faux-friendly term that Farsibans throw around so casually in conversations that it has lost all endearing qualities. It implies the kind of familiarity that I had never had with Suraya.

Suraya had been one of the first people I'd met in Afghanistan, back in 2005 when I was new.

We had been roommates at BAF with two other interpreters in our wooden B-hut. Even there she sat outside and smoked a lot. She'd been a hairdresser in Southern California, and she liked to give the soldiers free haircuts.

One day, soon after I had arrived at BAF that first time, she had presented me with some *doughdi.* I hadn't adjusted to the food in the chow hall and was always hungry. Suraya had made it her business to know all the CAT I interpreters, who regularly brought her Afghan food. I told her I loved the bread and was so happy to have it.

She said that she could get us an entire Afghan meal for dinner. I offered to pay for it, but she wouldn't hear of it. Then she went outside to have a cigarette. The walls of the B-hut were only plywood. I heard her say, "There's a new female here. You should come by tonight."

Later, a bunch of Farsiban guys showed up to share the meal. I thought perhaps it was always this way, that BAF was just a warm and friendly place, with interpreters mingling, sharing tea, and hanging out. Then I began to notice a pattern: These large gatherings always happened on the nights after Suraya had made a series of phone calls, telling her callers that I, the "new female," was going to be there.

I began to avoid the B-hut on those nights. I would go to the MWR and use the computer or watch a movie. If it wasn't too cold, I would take a walk. The first night I did this she was annoyed when I finally turned up. "Everyone was here waiting for you," she said.

"I left my family in America so I wouldn't have to constantly check in with people!" I half joked.

She laughed the loud, forced laugh of a person who is not amused. I was never sure what exactly was going on with Suraya. Was she using me as bait to get male interpreters who normally would not be interested in her? Or was she simply lonely and inept and trying to make her life a little more interesting?

I'd heard that there were interpreters who didn't speak the language, people the company had lost track of, who got paid for being a name on a list, who spent their days sitting around BAF, but I hadn't given it much thought. Apparently Suraya was one of them, one of the "retirees" John had mentioned. Now I was going to be her B-hut-mate again. Maybe God was still mad at me.

THEN I HAD a piece of good fortune. I was sitting on my bed reading while Suraya, as she had done at BAF, lounged outside smoking and calling to people as they passed. She hated Asadabad. If BAF was New York City, Asadabad was a town in Wyoming, high in the mountains. The rumors had already started that Suraya blamed me for her posting here, for having pointed out to a site manager over a year earlier that she had somehow fallen through the cracks, that she was collecting a fat paycheck for giving the occasional free haircut.

I could hear her talking to someone outside. I concentrated on my book. The door opened, and in walked a pretty woman with a head of springy reddish curls and freckles scattered across her nose. I looked at her with disbelief.

"Haseeba!"

"Saima!"

We embraced and started jumping up and down like a couple of high school girls. Haseeba had been on a mission when I'd arrived. I'd heard there was another female CAT II here, but I had never imagined it would be the only real friend I'd made in years.

Before I deployed for Asadabad I had been required to take a two-week training seminar at Fort Bragg in North Carolina. Haseeba and I were the only women in the program. We bonded one night when some soldiers and a few other CAT II's going through the training took us out to allegedly the best place in town for wings: Hooters. Haseeba was in her late thirties, a housewife from Houston with five children. We were both appalled at the sight of the waitresses in their skimpy shorts and tops. We kept our eyes on our chicken wings, and the soldiers laughed at our discomfort. They insisted that the only other dining option was one of the many strip clubs.

Haseeba and I realized we had many things in common. She was from Peshawar, and we talked of growing up there. Like me she had also moved to the States at a young age and had spent spent her entire adult life here. She was also fleeing a complicated situation with a man.

When the training session ended and we parted company, we never imagined we'd be lucky enough to be posted at the same PRT. Female Pashtu-English speakers were rare. There were females at the so-called retirement community in BAF who spoke Pashtu but only rudimentary English, and there were, of course, Farsiban who claimed to speak Pashtu but didn't, and almost no one spoke both with equal expertise. When I had first arrived in Afghanistan two years earlier, I was told I was the only female in the country who could claim fluency in both languages. Haseeba's mother language was Pakistani Pashtu, but she had trained herself to speak as an Afghan Pashtun.

Suraya wandered in, cigarette in hand. She watched our reunion from beneath her carefully fluffed bangs. I released Haseeba and introduced her to Suraya, forgetting that they already knew each other.

"This calls for some tea," Haseeba said.

We invited Suraya to join us. There was no reason to exclude her, no reason to be impolite. I made a toast with my teacup to old friends and new ones.

"Pashtuns don't believe in toasts, do they?" asked Suraya crossly.

"No, but Americans do," I said. "Here's to the female interpreters of Asadabad!"

But Suraya could not be jollied. She didn't speak Pashtu, and when Haseeba and I conversed, she was excluded. Matters were made worse by the fact that Haseeba was a Pakistani Pashtun.

Afghans and Farsiban alike hate Pakistan, which they believe, not unjustly, is more than a little responsible for the current war. Afghans are well aware of the role that Pakistan plays in the instability and unrest in Afghanistan. They see with their own eyes Pakistani intelligence agents crossing the border to recruit and train Afghans for their cause, which creates chaos in Afghanistan. This would be one of the topics that Afghan villagers would want to discuss with me to no end years later when I was no longer an interpreter and free to carry on discussions. To most Afghans, the Pakistani role in the war and the destruction of Afghanistan is unforgivable and when the United States looks away from the stark knowledge of Pakistani influence, it loses credibility in Afghan eyes on every front.

Although Afghans know that not all Pakistanis support what their government and secret intelligence agency do in Afghanistan, using the notorious Pashtun logic, they still hate all Pakistanis. While the Pashtun in me shares the Afghan feeling about Pakistan, the American in me believes individual Pakistanis should be treated as individuals. Haseeba came to America when she was nine years old. She grew up in Texas and Michigan. She was just a woman trying to make some money and have a life. As far as I was concerned, she had no hidden agenda. She was a very good friend.

DURING THE FIRST few weeks at ABAD, as soldiers called Asadabad, Larry LeGree, the PRT commander, was still on R & R, which left me on my own. This was one of many things about working as an interpreter that I hated—being on call, never having your own projects or missions, but also having a lot of free time to sit around doing nothing. There were many administrative duties that a PRT commander performed that did not require an interpreter, so most of my time was spent just walking around trying to keep myself busy. Every unit would claim one or two interpreters and train them according to how the unit worked. This meant that by the time I got there, the PRT commander was the only one waiting for an interpreter, and so if he didn't use me for a meeting, I had nothing to do. Like everything in Kunar, the PRT was built on a steep hill. The members of special forces that shared the installation with us zipped up and down the hill on dirt bikes; the regular army soldiers struggled on foot.

The local Afghan National Army base was right next door. It shared a wall with the PRT and used the PRT entry gate. The ANA soldiers, who were high on danger—or something stronger, as was rumored—used to roar up and down the hill in their Datsun pickup trucks at high speeds, ignoring the SLOW DOWN signs. I joked with the sergeant major, who'd ordered the signs to be posted, that maybe they didn't speak English. He asked me to write new SLOW DOWN signs in Pashtu, which I did, but there was no noticeable difference in their speed. The only time the ANA soldiers slowed down was when they saw one of the few females on the PRT walk by—I guess there are some traits all guys share, regardless of differences in cultural backgrounds.

I hiked up to the farthest point of the PRT, and there I found my new favorite bench. The view made me forget my exhaustion, my sadness at having left Eric, my frustration at being stuck living with Suraya again. This PRT looked down on a blue river right out of a children's book. Rising behind it were huge mountains, brown and orange and green. There were no radio towers, no power lines, no planes flying overhead. Just some mud houses clinging to sides of the mortar-pocked mountains.

Moments after I sat down I felt the earth tremble. Before I could go into a full-blown earthquake freak-out, I saw the mortar hit one of the hillsides and an avalanche of earth and rock cascade into the valley. I wondered whether there were any *Kuchi*, nomads, passing through the valley and hoped they'd escaped being buried by the debris.

An older sergeant walked by. He stopped and asked me whether I was a bird-watcher.

"Not so much," I said. "But I can see some birds in that tree there."

"There's a bird I sometimes watch from this bench. It's turquoise, as bright as a piece of tile. I haven't found it in any guidebook. It's only here, in this part of Afghanistan."

"There are a lot of things around here that aren't in any books," I said.

"It could be a new species," suggested the sergeant.

We sat silently and watched the shadows change as the sun moved across the mountains. For a few minutes it was quiet—no outgoing mortars—and we could hear bird calls, and from below, the soothing sound of the river. I felt at peace.

LARRY RETURNED FROM R & R, and the first order of business was meeting with the governor. The PRT had erected an administration building for the governor's office and the other departments that made up the provincial government. It was a simple building with a courtyard and a little pond in the middle. There was a small mosque to one side and a kitchen to the other, where a male cook made green tea all day long. There was also a Civil-Military Operations Center there, where a couple of the local PRT staff members lived because their homes were too far away to go to every night. It was too dangerous to travel after dark, and it got dark pretty quickly those days. Assadullah Wafa, the governor of Kunar, was very different from both Wasifi of Farah (the Afghan American onetime pizza-franchise owner) and Sherzai (the larger-than-life Pashtun warlord).

Wafa was slim and serious. He wore wire-frame aviator glasses and reminded me of Al Pacino. The moment he set eyes on me he frowned. Before I showed up they'd been using a male CAT II who spoke only Farsi.

"I wish you were a man," he said. "As a Pashtun woman you should not be sitting here with the men."

"What do you need to talk about that a female can't be present for?" I asked.

He waved his hand at me. He could hear the teasing in my voice. "It's not the topics, Miriam, but there are certain things a Pashtun woman should never do, and sitting in the middle of men is one of them."

I had expected hostility from Afghan men, but I had not expected resistance from an official of the central government, who had pledged with the United States to improve the lives of Afghan women. How was the governor supposed to do that if he wasn't even comfortable with me as an interpreter? This was a rude awakening, and I wanted to share it with the PRT commander, who was to mentor the governor and assist him in finding solutions. Well, here was the number one issue, as far as I was concerned, and I wanted to see what solution they would come up with. I leaned over and in English told Larry what Wafa had said, so he could see his closed-mindedness firsthand. I didn't know anything about Wafa's background. Americans think that because these men are in positions of power, they are highly educated and well traveled. It is possible Wafa had only a middle school education and that he was there because he was a relative of Karzai.

"I understand that this is shocking to you," I told Wafa, "that this is not something that your daughters would do or that your wife would do. I respect that. However, I am also an American and am going to continue to do this because this is what I was hired to do. If you are really uncomfortable, I will ask for the other interpreter to come back, but he is going to speak Farsi, so it is up to you who you want to work with."

"That is not really a choice," he answered impatiently. "Of course I would rather have a Pashtun interpret for me. But I am uncomfortable with you being a woman, and if I act awkward, that is why."

ONE DAY I was hiking up the hill to what had become my favorite bench at Asadabad PRT when John, the soldier had I met on the Chinook ride from BAF, drove up beside me in his truck.

"I have a proposition for you."

I laughed. "Aren't you happily married with, like, seven kids?"

"It's not that kind of proposition." He grinned.

John and I had become friends. He had been stationed in Fort Lewis, near Seattle, and had already served a tour in Iraq. He was the first of many soldiers I'd meet who loved Afghanistan deeply and already talked about coming back for subsequent tours there.

John's proposition involved doing a mission where he and his men would be able to sit down and talk with real Afghans. He wanted me to help his soldiers experience Afghanistan on a personal level. Most of them only interacted with the ANA soldiers with whom they went to the shooting range. The Americans might chat with their Afghan counterparts between turns at the firing line, and during reloads, but that was the extent of their interactions. John also didn't want a formal meeting at the governor's, where his men would only be pulling security.

Once he'd mentioned a village he passed through on the way back to the PRT. Like many Afghan villages it was a collection of mud huts that didn't appear on any map. Every time John went through this village, the elders would try to stop him and offer him tea. But this was the army. There was no stopping for tea. There was a schedule to be met, a timetable to keep.

I reminded him of this village. "We could go there, don't you think? They already like you. We could sit down and drink tea." I hadn't heard about General Petraeus then, but this is exactly what he would tell us to do years later: *Go and have tea with the villagers. That should be your mission. Have tea and get acquainted with Afghans in your area of operation.*

It made sense that I would be John's interpreter, and he knew that he couldn't hope to socialize with the villagers without having a Pashtu speaker by his side. I said that before we left, we should sit down and talk a little about how to behave, what to say and what not to say.

The soldiers I'd met at BAF, Farah, Jalalabad, and now Kunar wanted to do the right thing by the Afghan people. They wanted to show the Afghans that they were there to help them in rebuilding Afghanistan. They wanted to convey their natural American friendliness, but they didn't know how to do this in an alien culture without being able to speak the local language.

Whenever possible, the PRT included the ANA in their missions. There was a first sergeant named Kevin, who led the Embedded Training Team (ETT) that oversaw the training of the Afghan National Police, and he had asked John if his guys could be included as well. Although it hadn't yet become mandatory to include the Afghan National Security Forces in U.S. missions, we saw the benefit of bringing the ANA along, not only to link the locals with their government but also to keep the village children from getting too close. I had seen again and again how kindhearted American soldiers had a difficult time being tough on the children, whereas the ANA soldiers had no such issues, literally beating them off with sticks—they were from a culture where the whole village really does raise a child, and disciplining them was part of that.

This was the first time I was going to formally talk to the soldiers about my people. I was energized, excited, and nervous. I had some time before the briefing, so I thought I'd pull myself together a little, change my tunic, comb my hair, and maybe put on a little makeup. After putting on some mineral powder, I wanted to rinse out my makeup brush, but there weren't any sinks near my room. The bathroom, which was a long walk from my B-hut, reeked of raw sewage and harsh disinfectant. However, there was a small sink outside the chow hall, so I walked down to the chow hall with the brush in my hands.

A soldier wearing dark sunglasses was walking in the opposite direction. The day was hot, the sun so close. The soldier's hair was longer than army regulation allowed, spiky and black, with some gray peppered around his temples. He sized me up, then released a brilliant smile that I could tell he'd used to good effect for his entire life. It lit up his face and took years off his age.

"What's that for?" he asked, nodding at the brush.

I glanced at the name sewn above his pocket and recognized Kevin's last name. He was the head of the ETT I was about to brief. Oh, great; he is going to think that I am just a civilian more concerned about makeup than what was going on around me in the country. My cheeks grew hot.

"This brush . . . ," I began. "I am painting an art project in my room, and I just needed to rinse this out."

"You're painting with that? I'll ask my CAT I to get you a real paintbrush from the local economy." He was always very generous.

"Oh no, I can't ask you to do that!"

"It's no trouble at all. You can't paint anything with that little brush!"

"Okay. Now I feel guilty for lying to you. This is actually my makeup brush. But if you tell anyone, I'll deny ever seeing you before!"

He burst out laughing, and I knew then that we would become great friends. "You must be Saima," he said, pushing his sunglasses on top of his head, getting a better look at me.

"Why do you say that?"

"You're the bossy, frank, opinionated, impossible-to-please Pashtun."

"Is there any other kind?"

"You're the one keeping everyone on their toes."

"Well, what do you expect? I am Pashtun and I am female; it is my job to make you all nervous and stressed."

He laughed easily and introduced himself as Kevin. I said I already knew who he was, just as he knew who I was. This seemed to amuse him.

The brief was held in the Tactical Operations Center. All the soldiers going on the mission were required to attend. I was not used to being alone at the front of a room, addressing others. Later, I would become so at ease in this role, I would wonder why I was ever so nervous. Until that moment, however, my standard spot had been at my commander's elbow. I didn't want to sound as if I was lecturing, but I had so much to share.

I tried to keep it simple. I said that the main thing was to remember that what might seem to be a normal, friendly question to Americans might be insulting to Pashtuns, who in general are a lot more reserved around outsiders. It was important to let the villagers lead the discussion. We were there to talk about their concerns. The mission was to get acquainted, and to allow them to see that we, as Americans, were interested in what they had to say and what their priorities were.

"If they say anything that could get you riled up, if they question why you are in Afghanistan, explain that you are here to help, that it was not your decision. Remind them that you are not here by force but that the Afghan government asked the U.S. government to assist in the nation's reconstruction.

"If they offer you tea, accept it graciously. Even if you don't really like tea, please drink a little. They love talking about the antics of their children, and you can talk about your children too, but do not talk about their women, and refrain from talking about the women in your lives. Do not discuss religion.

"The meeting will most likely be outside, but if they invite us inside, pay attention to whether or not we're entering a mosque. In small villages like this one, the mosque might not be obvious. It will look like any other house, only there will be a loudspeaker on one of the walls. That's how you'll know it's the mosque. Since you are soldiers, you are not required to take off your boots when entering the mosque. However, because you are visiting with me, a female, I doubt they will ask us inside the mosque." The soldiers were listening. They wanted to do this right.

As I spoke I thought about the tiny village just down the road, the mud houses with no electricity or indoor plumbing. The women were behind those mud walls, living a life that none of the soldiers could imagine. What's more, I couldn't even imagine it, and I was from there. The men sat beneath the trees, the sky blue and daunting overhead. With that sky, these mountains, who could believe in anything besides an all-powerful God? How could we ever sway them to our way of thinking without using the power of God Almighty?

The next morning we assembled in front of the TOC. The ANA soldiers got one glimpse of me and gawked and giggled like eleven-year-old boys. "Is she Afghan? Look how she speaks Pashtu and English. Do you see her hair? There is nothing covering her hair. She talks to those men, those American soldiers. Is she Pashtun? Is she?"

I pulled Kevin aside. "You've got to have a little talk with your guys; they're acting very unprofessional," I said.

"Do you want to yell at them yourself?" he asked, grinning.

"I don't even want to acknowledge their presence. But I'll do it. I'll tell them what I think of what they're doing, and then perhaps you can back me up."

I stood before them. They fidgeted, not quite sure what was happening. I said, "Look, one of the complaints you Afghans have is that Americans don't respect your culture. Right now, you're not respecting your own culture. You're acting in a way that says it's okay to harass females. So if one of these Americans harasses one of your women, you'll have yourselves to blame. Just because I am behaving outside of the boundaries of the Pashtun culture for whatever my reasons might be doesn't mean you are free to behave inappropiately, too. Don't use my behavior to justify yours." Then I walked away. Kevin dressed them down, and it would have humiliated them had I stuck around to watch. Kevin said later that they were ashamed and wanted to apologize in person. I told him to let them know that I accepted their apology but that I would not meet with them again and give them yet another chance to make me feel as if I were a circus attraction.

WHEN WE ARRIVED at the village, an old man scurried out to greet us. He was white-haired, stoop-shouldered, and toothless, with a creased smile and a long white beard. He could have been a jolly, if skinny, Afghan Santa Claus. He reminded me of my beloved Baba—he had the same captivating smile and a white turban on his head.

I called to him in Pashtu. "Hello, Baba! How are you?" John and Kevin stood on either side of me, a couple of steps behind. The soldiers and the ANA pulled security, forming a half circle around us, their weapons at their sides.

The villager's mouth opened, then closed. "*Looray*," he said, addressing me as daughter, "did you just speak to me in Pashtu, or am I suddenly understanding English?"

"I don't know, Baba, but it's never too late to learn a new language."

"I like these guys anyway," he said to me, "but now that they've brought you here they have become my favorite people. Come, come and have some tea."

It was early morning, the sky was a brilliant blue, and the sun was already hot enough that standing beneath it and talking was uncomfortable. Thankfully, he led us to a deep shadow beneath the village's largest tree, just outside the mosque. "What's going on here? What brings you to us today?"

John said, and I translated, "We have no mission, we are just here to talk to you. John loves your village. He loves the feeling he gets when he passes through, but he has never before today had the opportunity to sit down and talk with you. You are not far from the PRT. We are neighbors, and just like in Pashtun culture, it is an American custom to get to know your neighbors. In case we need to borrow sugar or eggs some day."

"*Looray,* we don't have any chickens to lay eggs! And we get the sugar only if someone goes to the city to buy some. How are we going to give you any?" He looked stressed that he would have to refuse us if we did show up at his door.

"Baba, he's just saying that! It just means that he wants to get to know you and have some kind of ongoing relationship with you." I realized that we always focused on the American lack of Afghan knowledge, when in reality, Afghans could equally benefit from learning more about the Americans.

Within five minutes we were sitting beneath the trees, U.S. soldiers, Afghan soldiers, village elders, a nice big crowd of cute little kids, and one woman—me—all conversing at once.

John, Kevin, and I sat on the ground across from the elder and a few other villagers who had appeared from their huts. Baba told us about their new project, converting half of the mosque into a school. At the time in Kunar there was no Ministry of Education in the villages, and no one in the Afghan government to help them, so the villagers hired one of the locals to teach. Each house in the village contributed a small amount to the teacher's salary; those who were too poor to give money gave butter and flour. John and Kevin expressed their admiration. The elder proudly showed us around. He didn't ask us for anything. His village had learned to be self-reliant. We walked around the mosque, and while he didn't invite us inside, he gestured to the place where the classroom was being built. A gang of kids trailed behind us. The elder grabbed one by the shoulder and told him to tell the women that we needed our tea now.

We finished our brief tour of the mosque-school, and as we returned to our tree, children appeared carrying small pots of tea and cups full of sugar. Apparently, someone had gone to the city. Sugar is quite expensive, but offering it is a sign of hospitality. Afghans don't stir sugar into their tea; instead they fill the bottom of the cup, then pour the tea over it. For special guests, the cup is nearly half full with sugar. Our cups were nearly filled to the brim, a clear message of profound hospitality. John was quiet, overcome. "This would never happen in Iraq. In Iraq they would throw stones at us."

Kevin was also pleased. He had told the ANA that this was a mission of getting to know your neighbors, and they were asked to mingle with the villagers, ignoring my presence and building relationships. The ANA had listened to him. The noonday heat settled in. Flies buzzed. Children hovered around the circle of adults drinking tea. A breeze kicked up, and nothing could have felt nicer.

We finished the tea, were offered more, and finished that as well. As the noon sun moved toward the other side of the sky, we decided to head back to the PRT. There was a war to be fought. This get-together had been a small but significant success. As my new Baba uncrossed his legs and stood up, I went to him and thanked him for his splendid hospitality, for inviting the PRT to visit, for showing us the new school, and for the delicious tea instead. Soldiers talked among themselves about how they could get their family back home to send some school supplies for the village.

Behind me, suddenly, I heard a burst of laughter. The kids were giggling, the soldiers guffawing. It was like an unexpected gust of wind. I turned to see John holding his notebook over his front. The soldiers were hooting now, and the kids were hugging themselves, giggling so hard they could hardly keep from falling over.

I must have looked startled. In Pashtu, Baba asked me what was going on.

A soldier told me that when John stood up his pants ripped. Before that moment I hadn't known that sometimes soldiers don't wear underwear. Apparently, if they were stuck outside the wire on a mission, or were deployed to some tiny installation where there weren't any showers to speak of, it was more hygienic not to wear underwear. When John had stood up, his pants had ripped, and every local of his beloved PRT had been treated to a view of his privates.

This was bad for me. The elders had accepted me as an Afghan American, but this would be too much.

"Go sit in the Humvee and wait for me. I will say good-bye for you," I told John.

I made our good-byes, but Baba wouldn't have it. He wanted to shake John's hand and thank him himself for taking the time to come to the village. I brought him over to where John was sitting in the vehicle, legs crossed, his green notebook secure on his lap. Baba didn't see anything, but after we left, I'm sure the kids told him everything.

John apologized until it became a joke. From that day forward every time he asked me to accompany him on a mission I would ask whether he was wearing any underwear. He pulled me aside a few times and said, "Please don't ask me that in front of my soldiers. They're going to think something is going on between us."

"I just want to make sure," I'd say. "I don't want the Afghan people to think that every time Miriam shows up they're going to be treated to more than just the sight of a Pashtun female."

TWENTY-FOUR

With each passing month it was becoming more dangerous to leave the PRT. I never paid attention to news reports about Afghanistan, but I knew Mamai was sitting back in her little room in Portland, listening to *Voice of America* and the BBC in Pashtu and worrying herself half to death. I didn't like her knowing of the danger I was in. I would tell her everything was different where I was, that things were not as bad in Asadabad. Still, every day it was more evident that the coalition forces were wearing out their welcome. The insurgents were eluding us during the day and returning to the villages at night to intimidate the locals, while we were safely back at our FOBs. In trying to catch them we were turning villages upside down and sometimes killing civilians who the villagers would later claim were innocent bystanders. Of course this created resentment toward our soldiers, and the villagers started avoiding our presence for fear of the nighttime knock on the door some of them were getting from the insurgents. We were becoming less beloved. Kids still greeted U.S. convoys when they rolled into villages, but instead of scampering along the road shouting, "I love you!" like they had when I'd first arrived in Farah in 2005, they were now yelling "Fuck you!" These sentiments, it seemed, were shared by the adults.

Afghans in villages all over the country would tell you the same thing: Taliban rule was merciless and cruel, but at least people knew where they stood. They knew that if they obeyed the many unforgiving rules, at least they would be secure. Cruel certainty provided cold comfort. The central government claimed to have rules, too, but they were not enforced with any consistency. People were uneasy. From day to day, no one knew what to expect.

Once, returning from a medical operation at a local village, where we'd gone to deliver Band-Aids, aspirin, and antibiotics—the usual for any med op—our convoy was speeding through a stretch of barren landscape. Most of the roads in Kunar are a series of dizzying S's carved into the sides of mountains, but not this road. We were making good time. I had stopped seeing the sand and empty space in front of my side window and instead was daydreaming about how nice it would be if there were green trees like the ones back in Oregon, when suddenly there was a muffled explosion and the Humvee rocked to one side and stopped.

We got out. There, splattered on the side of the vehicle, were the remains of a suicide bomber. We would learn later that he'd been detonated remotely by someone watching from a far-off hillside. From the angle at which the insurgent had been watching, he had misjudged the distance and hit the button just before our convoy was in range.

Most villages are not a part of any master urban plan in Afghanistan, but are a collection of *qalats* built near the road by people whose livelihood depends on the road in one way or another. They might be families of drivers who decided to settle around the road for easy access. When we'd arrived in this area, there were a few *qalats* and a couple of shops around the main road. Later I would learn that if you drive through an area like this and there are no children around, something bad is about to happen. If the shops are closed, something even worse is about to happen. The locals have likely seen the suicide bomber, who most of the time is stoned before meeting his maker; they have seen the bad guys lurking around, up to no good. They know that when these people appear, an IED, a roadside bomb, a suicide bombing, or an ambush will soon follow. The villagers don't want to be in the middle of any of it. So they take their children and hide.

In 2007 the insurgents were still perfecting their suicide-bombing methods. They were not yet using suicide bombers as casually as they do now, especially in remote areas like this one. The time had not yet come when the initial attack—usually an IED—was the first step of a complex ambush, where the soldiers were drawn out and away from their vehicles, the better to be targeted with small arms and RPGs. By 2009, this had become the common method of insurgent attacks and it remains so to this day.

Slowly, the dust began to settle. The breeze picked up the smell of burnt flesh. We decided to stick around until the National Directorate of Security, Afghanistan's version of the CIA, showed up. There were pieces of the suicide bomber everywhere I looked. I moved off the road to get away from the smell. I was watching my feet, to make sure I didn't step on any bloody chunks of flesh. When I thought I had left the worst behind, I almost stepped on the head. The explosion had blown it clean off the body. His eyes were open, and he was staring at me. It wasn't even slightly burned. He looked no more than twenty years old. He had eyebrows and eyelashes. I noticed his hair—it was long, chin-length, and curly. Perhaps it was my mind's attempt to deny what I was seeing, but he reminded me of an *Attan* dancer. *Attan* is an ancient Pashtun dance and the national dance of Afghanistan. It is known for, among other things, the long-haired male dancers. Sherzai loved *Attan*. Every Friday night he would host a performance.

I was enjoying the new respect I'd earned from John, Kevin, and the soldiers. Word had gotten around that I had more to contribute to our fight there than just my language skills. I didn't want to scream like a girl, like a civilian, so I calmly called to the sergeant, "You probably want to see this."

I was an interpreter. My orientation never covered anything related to suicide bombing. The soldiers inspected the Humvee. My ears were ringing. My eyes stung with the still-flying dust. Standing by the side of the road, I looked around and saw that there was no one in sight. I had been in many firefights by then, but the personal nature of a suicide bombing was very different and harder to take in. At least it was for me.

Someone wanted to kill us so badly that he was willing to give up his life in the process. That was hard to take in when I felt that I was truly there, with all the young soldiers, to help the Afghans stand on their feet. But this was not the last time I would be baffled by what had gone wrong in Afghanistan. How could two nations who had helped each other defeat a superpower less than twenty years earlier get to this point? Something had gone terribly wrong, and as I looked at the severed head of the youth, I vowed to find out what it was.

ONE NIGHT I was awakened at 3:30 A.M. by my team and told to come to the clinic. I pulled on a tunic and jeans, grabbed my jacket, and stumbled down the hill. There was no moon—it was a dark FOB, which meant there was no other light allowed either, and there was shouting in the distance. The soldier who fetched me said someone had just arrived, a civilian who'd been injured by one of our outgoing mortar rounds.

Most likely he was an insurgent. This was not uncommon. The PRT would have been attacked by rockets or mortars, we would have responded with outgoing, using technology to locate the point of origination, and within a couple of hours Afghans would appear at the front gate, bearing their wounded. We were always told, "This is my cousin. He is an innocent civilian, and you bombed him while he was sleeping!" More often than not they were the insurgents themselves, knowing we would have no choice but to take them at their word. We never turned away an injured Afghan, and they knew it. It happened more in mountainous areas where there weren't any local doctors that the insurgents could intimidate into treating their injured. Most claims of "innocent civilian" injury were made in remote villages where there were no clinics and the U.S. Army medics provided the only medical help, unless there was the option of crossing over to Pakistan to get treated. There was no way the U.S. Army could disprove these claims; there were no marks or tattoos that could be used to identify insurgents.

At the clinic a young Afghan, perhaps eighteen years old, was being treated for a bad leg injury. He was thrashing and screaming. His leg had been blown apart. Nestled in the mass of pulpy red tissue I could see a wink of bone. In Pashtu he screamed that he was in pain, that it was unbearable, it was going to kill him.

Suraya was on duty at the clinic as usual, an assignment she relished. For hours at a time it would be quiet, with no incoming patients. This gave her time to chat up the medics, offer haircuts, gossip, and smoke.

The Afghan screamed until he was past hoarse. The pain! he roared. The pain! Behind his shoulder, out of his line of sight, the medic was prepping a syringe.

Suraya tried to shout over him in Farsi, "The doctors are fixing you."

He didn't care. He didn't seem to understand a word she was saying.

I stood with two other soldiers who were there to report on what had happened. After the boy had been stabilized they would question him and I would interpret. There was nothing for us to do until the boy had been sedated and the bleeding had stopped. I don't know how long the boy moaned and howled. Suraya kept saying that he should not worry, that the doctors would fix his leg, all in Farsi, all lost in translation.

It was an unwritten rule among interpreters that you didn't barge in and correct someone's translation unless you were asked to offer your opinion, but I couldn't stand it another minute. Professional courtesy kept me silent for as long as I could stand the screaming, but finally, in Pashtu I yelled, "The doctors are giving you some medicine. It will take a few seconds, but then the pain will start going away."

Suraya glared at me. The harsh light of the clinic made her appear green, her red lipstick brown. I knew I was making her look bad, and that I would pay for it later.

The boy stopped screaming, took a breath, held up his hand, and nodded. The medic gave him the injection. "Ask him how his pain level is now," he said to Suraya.

"Is gone?" she asked him in her broken Pashtu.

The boy shook his head and groaned. "No!" he cried. "No."

"Yes!" Suraya insisted, "It's better."

"No," said the boy. "No!"

The medic took a few steps back. "What's going on here? What are you two arguing about?"

I told my team that I was going to step in and help. Otherwise, we'd be here all night, and the boy would probably perish simply from being misunderstood. I went and stood at his side, looking into his face and away from his torn leg.

"Brother," I said, "is your pain getting any less, or is it the same as before the doctor gave you the injection?"

"Oh, sister, you speak Pashtu, thank God, thank God. It's a little less, but it's still terrible."

I told the medic, who gave him another injection.

Finally, his pain was under control. The boy lay back on the bed and drifted into a morphine daze. The medic went about making plans to operate. There would be no talking to the boy this morning. Suraya turned her back to me as I left the clinic and trudged back up the hill. It was just barely 6:00 A.M. The sky was whitening in the east; a few birds were chattering.

Haseeba was an early riser. When I returned to our quarters she was sitting outside, drinking her morning coffee from the chow hall. I told her what had happened. "Now I've made an even bigger enemy out of Suraya," I said.

"I bet Suraya has many enemies. Now you've just permanently joined the club," she replied. I could always count on Haseeba to simplify things.

A few days passed. Suraya never mentioned what had happened at the clinic. She sat on her plastic patio chair outside the B-hut and stewed. Then she started spending her time elsewhere. She would get up very early, take her customary hour and a half to do her hair and makeup, and then disappear.

Once, late at night, Haseeba and I had finished watching a movie at the MWR and were walking back up the hill to our hut. The days were hot, but at night we were reminded we were still high in the mountains. The air was cool and pine-scented; the stars seemed close enough to touch. Groups of soldiers sat in front of their B-huts, smoking, talking, and listening to music. Several of them called out "Good night!" to us as we walked to our rooms.

We rounded the corner and heard a giggle. It was Suraya, disengaging herself from the arms of a CAT II we only vaguely recognized. He was tall and lean but otherwise plain. He had worked at a convenience store in Maryland before becoming an interpreter. I only knew this because Haseeba had gone on a mission with him to some governmental meeting.

Haseeba and I went inside. Minutes later Suraya appeared, closing the door sharply behind her.

"I'm sure you're upset," she said to Haseeba, "but Hashruf is mine."

"Hashruf?" said Haseeba.

"Don't pretend you don't know what I'm talking about."

"What are you talking about?" I asked. I assumed Hashruf was the guy she'd just been kissing.

"I know what you're all about," Suraya said to Haseeba. "I know what you're trying to do. You're going after my man and you can't have him."

"Okay," said Haseeba. Suraya stormed to her B-hut and slammed the little wood door, leaving Haseeba and me in the living room, trying not to laugh.

The next day, as luck would have it, I ran into the sergeant major whom I'd met on the day of my arrival, the one who was in charge of the accommodations. He asked how it was going. I told him about Suraya, about the tension and her recent accusation. I stopped short of saying that she was crazy. The sergeant was worried that Haseeba and I were unhappy. If the PRT were to lose the two of us at once, he would be required to replace us, and who knew what he would get from BAF. I asked if perhaps there was another place for us to live on the base.

Within hours, he moved Haseeba and me to a large empty tent across from the chow hall, at the bottom of the hill. Our new home was enormous, already divided into six separate rooms. We only needed two bedrooms, so we removed the partitions and created our own guest space. We washed our comforters, helping the little old local man in charge of the PRT laundry room to spread them out in the sun, since they were too big for the dryer, and then spread them on the floor. We also purchased a machine-made red-and-cream Iranian rug and an old TV at the local bazaar.

One afternoon Paul, one of the PRT officers, poked his head in and we offered to make him some tea. He sat on one of the comforters, and we put out some tea and cookies. He told us how every army installation in the States had a place like this where officers go to relax after hours. "This is just like an OC," he said.

"OC?" I said.

"Officers' Club."

For laughs we started referring to our living room as the Officers' Club. Later we had to adjust our policy, since we also wanted to invite some of our favorite enlisted soldiers to come have tea and watch TV.

We welcomed the chance to display our Pashtun hospitality. We made aromatic green tea, and sometimes we were able to snag some nuts or raisins from the three shops inside the wire. Once a week Haseeba and I hosted a real movie night, when we would make popcorn and serve soda. Over the tinny sound that issued from the TV's speaker you could hear the occasional *kaboom* of a mortar being fired. It didn't even register. The Officers' Club Also Open to Enlisted Soldiers by Special Invitation felt like home, a place where we could relax with good friends after a long day of interpreting. Life was far from perfect, but on a day-to-day basis it was somehow better and more satisfying than the life I had lived in America.

Asadabad also had an empty swimming pool, but its history was benign. The base had been opened by a U.S. governmental agency a few years earlier, and when the PRT took it over, it was decided that the added expense of paying a local pool boy was unnecessary. The pool was drained and converted into—of course—a basketball court.

There was a young blond soldier Haseeba and I liked to watch play basketball. Haseeba had spied him one day leaving the gym, a towel slung around his neck, and told me about him. Haseeba did a little snooping around and found out that his name was Ben, and he was from Georgia. We knew we could find him most afternoons in the middle of an intense pickup game. The cement steps leading down into the pool were our makeshift bleacher seats. When Haseeba and I weren't needed anywhere, we'd wander over and watch him play. I had never done anything as silly as watch a boy play basketball in high school—the Professor forbade it—but in 2007, in the middle of the hottest spot on earth, I did just that; sat on a bench, drinking iced soda, with the sun on my arms, watching the boys show off for us, the girls.

Because it was the dead of summer, and the sun was so hot it could have been classified as a weapon, Ben wore only his regulation army shorts and a T-shirt. When he smiled, his dimples were deep, and his eyes were as bright as the sun.

"There is your rebound man," Haseeba proclaimed. "He's pure eye candy."

"He is probably not even eighteen!" I said. I was thirty-one.

"You better make your move. I think you need him more than I do, but if you don't step up I'm going to steal him from you!" Haseeba teased me. She knew about my broken engagement, about the e-mails I was still receiving regularly from Eric.

Ben was a gunner under John's chain of command, and Haseeba urged me to see if John would make an introduction. I said I had a professional relationship with John and wanted him to see me as a competent interpreter, not some silly girl. I told her to leave it alone. I wasn't ready for another man. It was so much easier not to get into anything.

There was a small bazaar at the bottom of the hill, just inside the wire. One day Haseeba and I hiked down to see if there was anything exciting for sale. I had asked one of the shopowners a few days earlier if he could bring me some fabrics. There was a local tailor at the PRT who worked mending uniforms and sewing on patches. In fifteen minutes I'd purchased enough material for half a dozen outfits.

As I was paying the shopkeeper I heard a voice behind me. "Is it true you're from Portland, Oregon?"

I turned to see Ben, smiling, with his deep dimples and eyes you could lose yourself in. "I'm stationed at Fort Lewis, in Washington. Just a few hours north of you." He ambled alongside Haseeba and me as we walked back up the long hill. He took the bags from me as he talked. He was always a gentleman.

"Yes, I know where that is. The drive is a nightmare," I said.

"It's not that bad," he countered.

"I have a really good friend, Hina, who lives in Seattle, but I hardly ever visit her because of the drive."

"You know you could see her more often now that you know us at Fort Lewis. You could stop there and take a break before continuing on to see her."

It was one of the things that I would grow to love about Ben—this roundabout way of telling me how he felt without making me wary of him.

"Oh, but you see, the great thing about Hina is that she's very understanding, and she loves to drive. So, I see her often, without having to drive for hours," I said. I watched him trying to figure out how he could have been clearer in inviting me to come see him. His reluctance to come out and say it actually endeared him to me more than if he had been aggressive.

After we reached the PRT and Ben excused himself, Haseeba glared at me. "What's wrong with you? Why did you say that stuff?"

"I don't want him to think I'm that easy."

Several days later, at the Officers' Club, we were having a *Sleeper Cell* night. A few years earlier Showtime had produced a miniseries about a Muslim FBI agent who infiltrates a terrorist sleeper cell hatching a plan to bomb Los Angeles. Someone had purchased the DVDs at one of the PRT shops.

Haseeba wanted to invite Ben, but I argued that he was an enlisted soldier. "But we already said it was okay to invite enlisted soldiers, remember?"

"Did we?" Of course I remembered.

She tracked Ben down at the chow hall and issued the invitation. He showed up midway through the episode. It was awkward—John, his boss, and another officer were there. Ben entered our tent, fresh from the shower. My heart knocked a little at the sight of him, but I didn't let my eyes stay on him too long.

Even though Ben and Eric both had southern, more traditional upbringings, their personalities could not have been more different. Ben was expressive. He said whatever sweet thought passed through his head. Once, while I was watching him play basketball and he kept missing his shots, he called time out, then jogged over and said, "I just really wanted you to know that I'm a much better player than this, but you've got me really distracted." When he would come back from a mission, he liked to come to our tent just to smell the air around me. He said that he was too dusty to hug me. "When I'm out there all sweaty and dirty, I think about you and how good you smell." The simplicity of his emotions and the way he expressed them were so unlike anything that I had ever had in my life.

Because John always asked to have me translate on his various missions, Ben and I sometimes ended up in the same convoy. One of the ways I measured how dangerous Afghanistan had become was the number of Humvees in our convoys. When I'd first arrived and had been posted in Farah, Eric and I had tooled around outside the wire in a bulletproofed Land Cruiser. Now no one ventured outside the wire with fewer than ten Humvees.

One day we found ourselves in the same Humvee, which happened to be second in line behind the lead truck. Ben took his position as the turret gunner and I sat in the backseat. Had we been ambushed, my job would have been to hand rounds of ammunition up through to Ben. We set off down the hill. Not twenty minutes after we passed through the friendly village where we'd held our tea party months before, there was an explosion. The Humvee ahead of us had tripped an IED.

The truck commander ordered us out of the Humvee to assess the damage. When we climbed back inside I was trembling. I have been in many convoys that were attacked, and it always unnerved me to think about how close we all were to dying. Why were we spared? What is it that we were still meant to do on earth? Thinking about unfinished personal missions, and my father and Baba and the three people I loved the most being so far away in Portland all got to me that day more than usual. Unexpectedly, I started crying.

"You're going to be fine," said Ben. "It's going to be fine. I promise. Please don't worry. No one will touch you. I'll protect you." He held my hand, there, in front of everyone.

I pulled it away. Before this moment, no one knew anything was going on between us. "Please," I whispered, "you can get in trouble."

"I don't care," he said. "I only care about you. If it makes you feel better to have me hold your hand, then I will do it."

Our flirtation had advanced. Were we now dating? That hardly seemed like the right word. I liked him very much. People had started to realize that if I wasn't out on a mission translating or at the Officers' Club, most likely I was sitting on the bench at the top of the PRT—so if Ben and I wanted to be alone, we went for a walk around the perimeter, just inside the wire. Here people could still observe us, but no one bothered us.

The trail was mountainous. We found a fallen oak that looked as if it had been there for a hundred years. Smaller trees had taken root in its bark. After dinner, and after he had cleaned his weapons for the next day's mission, Ben and I would sit on "our log" and talk. His tour was nearly over, and he'd be returning to the States. He had big plans. Fort Lewis was two hours from Portland, straight down I-5. We could be together every weekend. He talked about our future as if it were already decided.

He held my hand, just as he did after the IED explosion. Once the sun eased behind the mountain it got cold and he put his arms around my shoulders. Ben was an old-fashioned romantic—not only did he not expect that we would sleep together before marriage, he fully expected to wait. He told me that he had watched me for weeks before he approached me because he wanted to make sure I wasn't like those deployed girls who slept around with everyone. He was kind and emotionally honest, and sometimes I felt like there was something wrong with me for not jumping up and down and telling him, yes, let's be together forever, eating peaches in Georgia. He told me that he didn't think he would ever be good enough for me, but he would spend his life doing everything to make me happy.

All of this only served to remind me of Eric, who was now working as a civilian in Hungary, training soldiers. Hadn't he said similar things? And hadn't everything fallen apart the moment we returned to the States and were forced to deal with real-life issues? I hadn't known life in a war zone, and Eric hadn't prepared me for it, for the ever-present fear of death, and the rush that creates, and how that rush fuels fantasies that lead to promises that make perfect sense at the time. Then your tour is over, you leave the wire, and come home, and everything dissolves, like dreams when you wake up.

How could I explain this to Ben, who was on his first tour out of the United States, who really did think that he was going to be with his Pashtun lady until the day he died?

Unlike Eric, Ben was young. He had no baggage, no ex-wife or children, no overpowering demons nourished by twenty years in the military. He said every word in the English language that conveyed his devotion to me, his commitment to our relationship—and his actions followed his words. It made me sad. I just couldn't bear not to be independent. I wondered, as I sat next to Ben listening to him spin tales about our future, whether the pronouncement I'd made years ago about never marrying an Afghan pertained not only to Afghan men but to all men. I felt that familiar sense of dread in the pit of my stomach. I knew then, as I've always known, that it would be easier for me to find happiness alone than worrying constantly that the man I was with was trying to control me and take over my life. That is no way to live, I thought, for me or for any man crazy enough to want to be with me.

TWENTY-SIX

On a frigid day in fall 2007, I opened my in-box to find an e-mail from a Department of Defense company recruiting for a new program. It was called Human Terrain System, and the U.S. Army had already had some success with it in Iraq.

The first Human Terrain Team, or HTT, had been deployed to Iraq in 2003. The program mandate was to map the cultural and social landscape of the country in the same way the armed forces mapped the military landscape. When it came to the wars in Iraq and Afghanistan, it had finally dawned on the coalition forces that we couldn't simply roll into a country with our superior forces and weaponry, perform a little shock and awe, and expect to win the trust and support of the people who lived there. We needed to know about the culture, the way the locals thought, how they operated, what they needed and wanted, and then figure out how we might use all that knowledge to garner local support.

After seeing success in Iraq, the government had deployed the first HTT to Afghanistan, to Camp Salerno in Khost Province. Some of the recruits in this team were finishing their contracts and coming home, and the program was searching for replacements. Would I be interested in joining this first team? I would no longer be an interpreter. My official title would be research manager.

I felt settled in Asadabad. I loved the missions that took me into the surrounding villages, where I was able to chat with the locals. I loved living in the big tent with Haseeba, hosting the Officers' Club, and hanging out with Ben in the evenings.

But during quiet moments when I sat on my bench at the top of the hill, looking out at mountains, at the enormous divots in the earth made by our outgoing mortars and the boulders tumbling into the river, I knew that I was ready for a change. I was growing bored with interpreting and felt conflicted about some of my duties—I was thrilled to be viewed as a Pashtun cultural expert but resentful that my job title as an interpreter didn't reflect this. I felt the itch for change. The desire for a new challenge was always there, percolating just below the surface.

I knew that once I replied to the e-mail, something new would be set in motion. I wrote back, saying that I thought the position sounded very interesting. Before I'd logged off, another e-mail dropped into my box. I realized I was in correspondence with the team leader at FOB Salerno. They wanted me, as soon as possible. E-mails shot back and forth. There were decisions to be made, negotiations to take place. For me to become part of the Human Terrain System I'd have to meet new requirements and undertake new training—six months' worth—back in the States.

Lieutenant Colonel Evan Sanders was the HTT leader at Salerno. He interviewed me over the phone.

"Look," I said. "I want this position. But I have been working with the army for years now. I have been in Afghanistan for almost three years. I am from here. I don't need a course on *Pashtunwali*. I don't need to be taught how to find Kabul on a map. I don't need area studies. And I really don't need to learn how to live in a combat zone."

Evan agreed. He was enthusiastic. He pulled some mighty strings. I asked to be transferred directly. Tiny, mountainous Khost was just southwest of Kunar. The brigade commander could easily have sent a couple of his birds to fetch me. It could have been done in a day—the end of the old contract, the beginning of the new. I could have slid down the southern flank of the country without having to face Mamai, Khalid, and Najiba, who would be deeply unhappy about my new plans.

But for bureaucratic reasons I was still required to return to the United States. I went home to Portland for seven days, before flying to Kansas for training. Evan had succeeded in reducing the six-month training requirement to a few weeks, and then I would head back to Afghanistan. My family and I sat in the big living room in the house my siblings and I had bought for Mamai in Beaverton. It was December, and the afternoon was dark with clouds and rain. Our tea had grown cold. I promised them that this would be the last time. Najiba sat with her arms folded. "You said that the last time," she replied. Khalid added, "I should just lock you in the basement and take away your passport." Mamai wondered for the hundredth time about the unforgivable sins she was paying for.

I told them it was a desk job. I wouldn't even be going outside the wire. Research manager was my new title. Could any position sound more boring? In truth, I had very little information about what was going to be required of me. The job description sounded challenging. I was supposed to identify informational and cultural gaps in the army's knowledge of the region, fill them in with facts about the villages and the local population, and brief commanders and soldiers about the findings. In addition, I was meant to ensure the continuation of said knowledge to incoming units.

My family was unhappy, but they were used to being outraged by my decisions. With Ben, it wasn't so easy. Before I had decided to take the HTT job, Ben's tour of duty had ended and he'd returned to Fort Lewis. I hadn't told him about the job offer because I knew it would upset him. On the days before he rotated out he worried incessantly. His constant questions about how he was going to live without me both touched my heart and made me feel guilty. I loved him but couldn't really imagine us sharing a future—a pattern, it was starting to seem.

Ben was thrilled when I told him I was coming home. I had given him Najiba's cell number, and he had called her every day while I was traveling. He'd assumed I was home for good and that now we could begin making a life together. He drove to Portland from Fort Lewis the day after I'd arrived. When I opened the front door I was struck again by how handsome he was. He was wearing washed jeans with a white T-shirt. I'd never seen him in civilian clothes before.

He took me out to an Italian restaurant downtown. I remember that we went under a large parking structure to get there because I was trying to map out an exit route, a habit I had learned from living too long in a combat zone. The light was low and golden. The waitress brought bread for the table. Ben prided himself on his good southern manners and began ordering for me.

"My lady would like a glass of red wine," he said, as if he'd accomplished a great feat. The girls he'd known before me had been beer drinkers.

"Which one would she like?" the waitress asked as she set the tall wine list between his fork and knife.

"Just the house red is fine," I quickly said to the waitress.

"I think she would like the house red," Ben repeated.

He didn't look at her but reached across the table and placed his hand over mine. His smile was that of an eager young man taking the first steps down a new path. His lady, on the other hand, could not bear another moment of his optimism.

"I'm going to Kansas in seven days," I blurted out.

"Kansas? What are you doing there?"

"Training for a new program."

"Okay . . . Kansas. I can do Kansas." He nodded, thinking, recalibrating our future. His flexibility was a precious trait, one I would need in a mate. He didn't want to be at Fort Lewis forever. There were jobs he could apply for in Kansas, and Kansas was closer to Georgia, where his large family lived, including his twin brother, whom he joked would try to snatch me up the second he laid eyes on me.

"Afghanistan," I said. "The training in Kansas is for a position in Afghanistan."

Since he'd been back in the Northwest his tan had faded. His smile disappeared. The math he'd been doing in his head didn't allow for an equation that included Afghanistan. My house red appeared, with his bottle of beer and a chilled glass. He didn't know how he could get back to Afghanistan. He supposed he could reenlist, but he would have no power to choose where they sent him. But my contract wouldn't be more than a year, would it? He said he would wait for me.

"You can't wait for me."

"I love you. Of course I can wait for you. I can wait as long as you need me to."

"I don't want you to wait for me. You're too young to wait for someone who is at war." I am sure I was referring more to the war within me than the one in my country. "I want you to find someone here you can take care of, a nice girl."

"Now you're being silly. I want to take care of you," he said.

"I might not be coming back, and I wouldn't want you to have to mourn the death of a girlfriend," I said. The words made it true. There was always the chance that I might die. That wasn't new. But I was also tired of flying home between contracts for what had become the usual knockdown argument with my family. What if I loved my new position? I could easily imagine moving to Afghanistan and never returning.

The conversation stuck on his determination to wait for me and my refusal to allow him to. Nothing was decided. We ended the evening by my eating the salmon he'd ordered for me, but not the way I liked it, because he didn't let me tell the waitress to cook it for longer. I remember thinking that I would have to eat raw salmon for the rest of my life if I decided to be with Ben, because I wouldn't ever want to hurt his feelings by correcting him. I tried once again to talk him into breaking up, and not waiting for me. Life was too short to waste on waiting for someone to return from a lost cause, especially when he had so many other options, I argued.

For a while after I arrived at Salerno, he called and e-mailed me every day. In time, our e-mails got less and less regular. In 2009 he sent me his last message, with the news that he was about to get engaged and was giving me one last chance. I pretended I thought he was joking. His new girlfriend, soon to be wife, reminded him so much of me, he wrote. I asked how this could be—was she Afghan? No, he said, but she had long, dark hair and liked to drink red wine.

I PACKED UP my stuff: all my civilian clothes, my shampoo, body lotion, and pounds of Peet's coffee, plus the stuff the army issued me—a gas mask, a mosquito net, and a little steel coffee mug. Twenty pairs of socks. Four uniforms. Knee pads, elbow pads, and random pads for which I never discovered a use. I shipped it all to Afghanistan, all except the military issue. I had to carry that myself.

I spent several days at Fort Leavenworth, undergoing a medical exam and weapons training. In my new role I would be expected to carry a sidearm.

I never imagined I would love shooting. We were required to be certified in the use of one type of weapon, but I was certified in three. Mike was the instructor administering the training. He was retired army and walked with a slight limp. From what I could tell he had a single mood: annoyed. Still, he taught me a lot. Near the end of the training, I think I finally managed to invoke one other expression on his face—surprise.

I'd brought along a pair of beige boots with three-and-a-half-inch heels I'd purchased at Cathy Jean in Portland. I don't know why I packed them. There would never be an occasion to wear them once I returned to Afghanistan. But I loved those boots, so I wore them to the range.

There was old snow on the ground. The sky was a sharp blue. The temperature was so far below freezing it wasn't worth remarking on. There was a waiting room beside the range, with a heater, magazines, and hot water for instant coffee and tea. When my team was called to the range and Mike saw the shoes, he grimaced. "Are you kidding me?"

"What do you mean?"

"How are you going to maintain your balance in those things?"

"I don't know," I said. "I guess we'll find out."

I raised my nine-millimeter and squeezed off a round, easily hitting the center of mass. The targets were man-shaped. I enlarged the first hole with a few more good shots. A pair of young guys training at the target next to mine took notice.

I reloaded my weapon. Mike ordered me to shoot three to the head. The guys cheered as I put three neat holes, all in a row, across the target's forehead. It was impressive, but not *that* impressive. Were they responding to the fact that I was a woman? An Afghan woman? An Afghan woman in three-inch heels? I didn't know, but when the guys, who later turned out to be working for one of the secret U.S. agencies going to Iraq, wanted to turn it into a competition I said sure. It was easy to beat them with the nine-millimeter, a smaller, sleeker weapon that fit my hand. We were shooting for beers. They'd arrived at some complicated equation: The person who wins has to buy everyone else three beers. Or else it was the other way around—the losers had to buy the winner three beers. It didn't matter to me. I didn't drink beer, and I wasn't going drinking with them. I beat them.

Afterward, Mike said, "That teaches me not to assume."

"Especially with an Afghan woman," I said.

"You're Afghan?" he said. We all got to see Mike surprised.

At Fort Leavenworth I met two other HTT members headed for Khost. Audrey was a tiny Texan with a big personality and master's in anthropology from Columbia. She had the dust of the world on her feet; she'd worked in Serbia and had spent time in Kabul trying to educate international NGOs and the International Security Assistance Force (ISAF) on gender issues. I didn't know much more about her than that at the time. I didn't ask her about her personal life, as women tend to do, because I didn't want her to ask me about mine. I didn't want to have to talk about Eric, Ben, or my disapproving family. Audrey didn't seem to mind that I was withholding. We learned that we shared a passion for edamame, and initially, that was enough.

Billy—the second member of the team—and I were staying at the same hotel. We were attending different training sessions, so I rarely saw him. One day he made a beeline for me in the lobby, staring at me intently as I introduced myself. He was tall and too thin, like some long-legged bird, with a head of unruly blond curls and pale eyes. On the bottom of his face was a would-be beard. He was going to be a human terrain analyst, but he didn't have much interest in chatting about what lay ahead of us. He said he used to work for USAID, the United States Agency for International Development, which provides humanitarian assistance around the globe, and told me in great detail how he used to love to ride his bike around Kandahar City.

The day I left I was sent to the infirmary for a physical exam. I also had to be inoculated. The soldiers who received these shots were given them over a course of several weeks. The nurse handed me an information sheet on the injections I was about to receive: inoculations against anthrax, smallpox, cholera, typhoid, yellow fever, hepatitis A and B, and flu. It advised against getting more than one live-virus shot at a time, and I knew there were three in the injections she was preparing for me. When the nurse snapped on her latex gloves I pointed out that anthrax, smallpox, and the flu were all live viruses. "I'm flying out tonight," I said.

"You can't leave the country without these. They won't even manifest you on the flight."

"But what if I get sick?"

"It's up to you. But you can't deploy without them."

I sat on the exam table with my sleeve rolled up, my arm swabbed and ready. The nurse pursed her lips. What was there to do? I could roll down my sleeve, return to my hotel, turn on the TV, and wake up tomorrow to take the months-long training courses.

Instead, I told her to have at it.

Then it was Fort Leavenworth to Atlanta; Atlanta to Shannon, Ireland; and Ireland to Kuwait. Audrey, Billy, and I were on the same flights, but we'd been separated, seated according to our social security numbers. My seat was at the back of the plane, between soldiers I'd never laid eyes on. One listened to his iPod and stared out the window; the other fell instantly asleep, snoring lightly.

Somewhere over the Atlantic all my bones broke at once, every joint snapped, and my skull was squeezed by an invisible vise. My lungs refused to inflate. My body lost its ability to keep itself warm. I struggled to stand up, to see if I could find Audrey. I looked for her long blond hair among a sea of no-color crew cuts. I slipped back into my seat, felt my eyes close for what I was sure was the final time. I was dying, and I was dying alone.

Someone laid a blanket on me. The weight of the rough cloth on my skin made me feel as if I was being crushed. From beneath my closed lids I cried.

Sometime later I found myself lying down across a row of seats. Someone had moved me. A medic was leaning over me. Or maybe he was a doctor. His face was tan, his cheeks creased. His breath smelled like spearmint. The drone of the engine made my jaw ache, my teeth hurt. My temperature was 103 degrees. He told me that I had fainted but that I would live.

"I am not so sure," I said.

"Yes. As long as I'm here, you're not going to die."

He quizzed me about what I had eaten. I told him about the shots, showed him where he could find my yellow ICVP card in the pocket of my backpack.

"What the hell were they thinking?" he asked. "The nurse should have known better."

He gave me an injection, which temporarily solved everything by masking all my pain. I said I was better. I tried to sit up and nearly vomited. "You're not better, you just don't feel anything. That was a little morphine I just gave you."

We landed in Kuwait at night. Outside, it was sultry, humid with recent rain. My eyes kept closing. I felt the crunch of the gravel beneath the doctor's boots. Then I heard my name—*Oh, Saima!*—and there was Audrey, struggling along beside us, lugging one of my duffel bags. A wiry soldier who looked as if he was in middle school had grabbed my other bags. They followed the doctor and me to the large tent that served as the boarding area for other flights.

The doctor settled me in some plastic chairs near the manifest desk. I would need to manifest before I could fly on to BAF, but I couldn't be manifested until my fever went down and I had been cleared by a doctor to travel. I sat with my arms wrapped around myself, teeth chattering. Audrey stood beside the chair, as if she were guarding me. I told her she should fly on to BAF without me. Will had already gone on ahead, and she should too.

"No way," she said. "Don't waste your energy trying to convince me. I am not leaving without you."

"I just need to sleep for a little bit," I said. I knew I still had a fever. My T-shirt and hoodie were drenched with sweat. I was so hot I thought I would explode, then so cold I couldn't talk with my chattering teeth.

"I'm not going anywhere until I take you to the hospital," said Audrey.

We argued a little longer. No one can make me do what I don't want to do. In my veins runs the sort of stubbornness unique to people who've been hunkered down in their mountain villages for millennia. I didn't want to be inside a hospital ever again. Army hospitals are all the same; the portable machines beep and sigh, the overhead vents roar, the air smells of gauze, blood, and disinfectant. They all reminded me of Angelee, the tiny girl who'd been burned in the explosion, whom I'd met during my first weeks at BAF, the little girl for whom I'd done nothing. Why hadn't I tried to find her after her uncle had collected her?

But Audrey was well. She wasn't falling asleep sitting up, woozy from fever. She hauled me up by the arm and steered me out of the boarding terminal and toward the clinic. There a doctor put me into bed. A nurse hooked me up to an IV. Audrey found a place to nap. For three days I lay there. My fever wouldn't break. Several times a day the doctor would inject me with one medicine or another and relief rolled through me. I remember thinking that I liked these injections much better than taking pills—they worked so much faster. I drifted. Audrey sat on the edge of my bed and patted my hand.

On the third day the fever departed. My arms were merely red and swollen. The doctor said the nurse who'd administered the shots should be fired. I defended her. I said I had done what I'd needed to do to get deployed. What I didn't say was that I hadn't wanted to be given a chance to rethink my decision.

ⓣWENTY-SEVEN

Khost City is a big, sprawling metropolis, with rolling green hills and several rivers weaving through it. As the C-130, which already flew pretty low, descended, I was surprised by how green it was, how many fields were filled with corn, wheat, and rice. I spied the famed Khost blue mosque out the tiny window. Almost all big cities in Afghanistan have at least one blue mosque, but the blue mosque in Khost was especially beautiful because it was surrounded by tall green trees, something I had not seen very often in the drought-ridden country of Afghanistan. It must have just rained, leaving everything including the blue mosque shining in the sun. Every color, like the blue of the mosque or the green of the fields, was vibrant and seemed to glow from within. As we flew over Camp Salerno, the contentment I had felt only in Afghanistan settled into me once again, and I knew I had made the right choice by coming back.

With more than five thousand residents, Camp Salerno was a small city within a city. It was built on a dry riverbed, surrounded by olive and almond trees. When I arrived the almond flowers and the orange blossoms were in bloom. The air smelled like expensive perfume.

The camp was not an American creation, unlike the Provincial Reconstruction Teams that seemed to sprout within days in remote regions. Salerno had a brave, well-known local history, as I was later told by a longtime resident, Aziz, the baker on the FOB. When the wind was right, you could smell his famous cinnamon bread from our office. He had quite an operation going. In addition to the bread, he also sold jewelry, trinkets, rugs, and bootleg DVDs of such American shows as *Seinfeld* and *The Simpsons*. One day while sharing warm garlic bread with the slices of cheese I had gotten from the chow hall, he told me the story of Salerno and the three brave young men who with just their AK-47's prevented the Russians from entering Khost. During the time of the invasion, there were rumors that the Russians were going to attack the province. There is a hill inside the wire from the top of which you can see anyone approaching the city from any direction. There were three young men from one of the local tribes who took it upon themselves to prevent the Russians from invading Khost. These young men, with their three AK-47's, went up this hill and decided to guard the whole city, day and night, against the Soviets. The news of this bravery spread through the province within hours, and soon other young men joined them. Within days there was a small army of young Khosti men prepared to die for their motherland. And when the Russians didn't come, it was logical for the locals to claim that it was because they had heard about the bravery of the young men of Khost and were scared off. These young men were instant local heroes, and the hill, because of its strategic location, became a point from which to guard the city from outsiders and has been used for that purpose by the mujahideen and the Taliban and now the United States.

From the start, I found the scale of the American presence in Khost shocking. Up until then, I had worked in small, cozy PRTs where everyone really did know everyone else. For me (and I know this was true for a lot of soldiers as well), the hundred or so soldiers that made up the PRTs became my family, a feeling that made it easier to work in that environment, surrounded by violence and death. Working and living among the U.S. soldiers I knew by name, I had forgotten completely that there were thousands of American soldiers in Afghanistan.

The first few days I lived in a daze, overwhelmed and still weak from my fever, trying to recapture the feeling of living in small PRTs like a big happy family. I was trying to memorize buildings that looked all the same and faces that wore the same expressions. Despite my independent nature, I like belonging to some form of a family, and it doesn't have to be a perfect one. (None of them are!) I knew that being part of the PRT family, and the inherent Afghan desire to belong to a family, had in large part carried me through the deployments thus far.

Although I didn't know why, I sensed that this deployment was different from the ones before. I knew I was starting a new phase in my career, and since my career was so closely tied to my life, this new job was going to have a great impact on me. I had seen the worried-sick look on my siblings' and mother's faces when I told them I was going back, and I didn't want to see that look again. I knew this was my last chance to bond with my forefathers to determine my destiny, and failure was not an option. I constantly fought the panic that resulted from the added pressure of time constraints. When the stress got to be too much, I would hike up the hill where the three young men had kept watch over what they were willing to give their lives for. I would sit there, trying to conjure some of their resolve to strengthen mine. Often I didn't even see the green fields and faraway mud houses surrounding Salerno. Instead I would imagine the lives of the Afghans living there, and wonder if they felt as overwhelmed by their heritage as I so often did by mine.

True to what I had told my family, I had an office and a desk. The office was in a square wooden building. Just inside the door stood a bookcase holding a few volumes on Afghan culture, some of which were old enough to be collector's items. Across from the bookcase there were hooks on the wall, on which we hung our helmets and Interceptor body armor vests. The walls were so flimsy that we had been ordered to put on our gear if the FOB was under Code Red—meaning we had a better than fifty-fifty chance of incoming. Our M-4's were placed in a wood contraption by the door. Although our team was a mix of army and civilians, we were all armed and expected to know how to protect ourselves and one another, if needed.

At first, the ease with which I picked up the weapon and carried it around alarmed me greatly. I had thought that after all the violence and bloodshed of my childhood, their ever-present memory would be enough to make me never want to go near a weapon, much less carry one. Ironically, I think those same memories of hopelessness from my childhood likely contributed to my wanting to train and arm myself as an adult. This was different. I was making sure that if I was ever in the position I had been in as a young girl, I would be able to defend myself and those who depended on me, and I intended to learn and be prepared just in case. I also knew that if my family found out I was armed while working in Afghanistan, this would be the subject of many distressed Sunday meetings, used as another thing I was doing to bring shame to them. They would conveniently forget the huge part weapons and the mastery of guns play in the proud Pashtun culture. They would interpret it as a symbol of my aggression and hatred toward my own people. Not my siblings; I had already told Khalid and Najiba, and both had sent me back teasing e-mails about how glad they were to be physically so far away from me.

SEVERAL LARGE DESKS lined the four walls of the office, which had a huge table with a map of Afghanistan in the middle of the room, and a picture of Hamid Karzai—wearing his famous, colorful long coat and his Persian lamb's wool hat at a jaunty angle—gazing down upon us from one of the walls. Once, an S-2 intelligence analyst who'd been at Salerno for eleven months strolled in to introduce himself. He looked up at Karzai's picture and asked, "Who's that dude?" After that it became a standard question we would ask analysts coming to our office the first time. It was shocking how few knew who he was.

One day not long after we arrived, Billy was going to lunch, and since Audrey was busy, I joined him. We sat at a long table in the chow hall; at the other end four soldiers were eating and talking. I smiled and said hello.

"So," I said, turning to Billy to try to make conversation, "what did you learn about Pashtuns while living in Kandahar?"

"I learned that I really want to marry an Afghan woman." He pulled a piece of pepperoni from his pizza and placed it on his tongue. This was not the first time he had said this—he also mentioned it when I first met him in Kansas, but it was harder for me to take offense while I was in America. But now we were in Afghanistan, and I was very offended.

"You do know that you shouldn't go around saying that."

"What do you mean?"

"It's insulting, you know—inappropriate to say that to a Pashtun female. You do know I'm a Pashtun?"

"Oh. I am sorry," he said. He was amiable and didn't seem to mind my chiding. I thought, but didn't say, How do you pass yourself off as a cultural expert when you know so little about it?

At that moment one of the soldiers at the other end of the table introduced himself and his friends. The fact that we were wearing civilian clothes but were also armed drew a lot of attention, as it continued to do over the following sixteen months. I told them we were part of the Human Terrain Team, and explained what that meant and how it could help them. One of them had been in Iraq. He confessed that he was amazed by how different the cultures were. "I mean, I knew they were different, obviously, but not *this* different!"

We laughed. He might have been eighteen years old. He had a chipped front tooth and dimples. I was happy to suggest to him the basics about treating the locals with respect, asking permission before you take pictures, before you enter a village. The thinking behind the last piece of advice is so that if the women are out getting water or feeding the animals, the men can use the time to get them inside. Of course, one then runs the chance of having insurgents be warned of one's presence, but most of the time the average soldier in Afghanistan is not out looking for insurgents. Billy ate his pizza in sullen silence.

On our way back to our office he complained, "You're all about respect, but those guys weren't respecting the fact that we were having lunch together."

"We're in a combat zone. Not chilling out in a restaurant, having lunch. We're here for the soldiers, and if they have questions, answering them takes priority over eating."

We walked along in silence. Did he think our casual cafeteria lunch was a date? Was him telling me he wanted to marry an Afghan woman his way of "claiming" me? I puzzled over this as we walked back to the office, where Billy went on to his desk and sat there, pouting.

IT DIDN'T TAKE me long to really start stressing.

It became clear almost immediately that the Human Terrain System worked better on a piece of paper sitting on someone's desk in Washington than it did in Afghanistan. We were there because the military had realized, somewhat belatedly, that the wars in Iraq and Afghanistan could benefit from counterinsurgency.

By 2008, the army had started to inject COIN practices into its daily operations, and focus began to shift toward types of reconstruction efforts that would show the locals that the United States was their friend, in Afghanistan at the invitation of their government to lend them a helping hand. This is, of course, oversimplifying a few hundred pages of doctrine into a couple of sentences, but that was the gist of COIN in 2008. In order to bring over the Afghans to the side of the Afghan government, it became crucial to get a real picture of the people's basic needs. In the eyes of the locals, there was nothing worse than wasting resources and lives on projects that they did not need. It showed wastefulness in a country that was still extremely poor, a wastefulness that would and did cause the locals to turn away from their government and Americans in disgust. The only way to build relationships was to understand this complex culture as thoroughly as possible. One cultural mistake could easily undo months of progress in the struggle to win the hearts and minds of Afghans. Even though the buzz phrase on everyone's lips then was "cultural awareness," Afghan culture, and especially the more complex and conservative culture of the Pashtuns, was still an enigma to most Americans, civilians or soldiers, working in Afghanistan.

There are basic informational gaps that make it hard to draw up a knowledgeable and useful overview of the country. If you ask an Afghan what he thinks the population of Afghanistan is, you would get answers from 80,000 to 6 million people, but no one has an accurate number— not the government of Afghanistan, not the United Nations, and certainly not the Americans. Any attempt at census fails as soon as one considers that the majority of the population lives outside of the major cities, Kabul, Kandahar, and Herat. Some might argue that Ghazni is also a major city; others would add Jalalabad to the list. Beyond these the rest of the country is mostly remote villages, where, due to instability and the imminent danger of being seen as working with the central government, census workers are too scared to go. When the U.N. would decide to do a census of the whole country and hire workers in Kabul to collect data all over Afghanistan, they would go only to the main cities. And who could blame them? Apart from the danger, anyone in a village in Paktya who opened the gate would be suspicious of a man with a clipboard asking who lived in the qalat. And even if he gave an answer, it would most likely not reflect reality, since few Pashtuns I know would tell a stranger the number of women living in his house.

Nor do the Americans in Afghanistan know and understand the ethnic tensions in Afghan society. Perhaps it's hard for an American to understand the importance to Afghans of tribal affiliations, but Afghan history is full of ethnic turmoil of one kind or another. The American soldiers and civilians who went to Afghanistan more than a decade ago went there with the mind-set of the American melting pot, a society that had been formed *because* of its differences. However, the reality on the ground in Afghanistan was very different.

It was true that tribal hierarchy as it had existed prior to the Soviet invasion was no longer in place. It was true that Pashtuns were not as united as they had been before the Russian invasion. It was also true that the Pashtuns, Hazaras, Uzbeks, and Tajiks were scattered all over the country, their network fragmented beyond recognition. Maybe it was for all those reasons that no matter where I went there was an inborn distrust of the *other*. I would spend hours in Pashtun villages, listening to the conspiracies against the Pashtuns by the Farsiban. And I am sure that if I had made it to Farsiban or Hazara areas, I would have heard identical theories, with the perpetrators being the Pashtuns. In order to not become part of the ethnic struggle for control, the American soldiers had better learn to take what they are told with more than a grain of salt.

With the introduction of millions of dollars of donations coming in from all over the world, the distrust and competition among these ethnic groups has only worsened. Our enemy, the insurgency, or the Taliban, or Al-Qaeda, whatever we call it, is using this mistrust of the other to incite violence, and where there is violence, there is instability, and where there is instability, there is no governance. According to the COIN doctrine, bringing the masses to governance is the only way to win an insurgency, but how can America win over the masses when the biggest ethnic group in Afghanistan feels slighted by the American actions of the last decade? One of the main reasons why we have regressed in Pashtun areas is because the Pashtuns accuse the Americans of favoring the Farsibans. No matter what the reality, and one can argue it either way, it is important to understand that the Pashtuns' *perception* of this favoritism is just as damaging to the U.S. efforts in Afghanistan as if it were a fact. Let's face it: The Kabul central government has no outreach in these remote villages, but our chances of success might have doubled (or more) had the Pashtun villagers viewed us as friends, not foes.

This is not to say that the Pashtuns are united. I wish they were; it is easier to form an alliance with a united group. The Pashtun tribes are feuding among themselves, too, for the country's limited resources— the land, the trees, even the mountains. These are centuries-old feuds between subtribes, and they will be playing out a long time after the Americans have left the Pashtuns' land. Having said that, it is even more crucial for the Americans in Afghanistan to be conscious of the tribal dramas that make up the environment into which they are sent to live and work.

To make matters even more complicated, our COIN tactics needed to take into consideration the fact that there wasn't simply one insurgency creating the instability. There were many types of "bad guys" contributing to the public's displeasure with Karzai's government. The Division Command at BAF ordered us to collectively call these groups Enemies of Afghanistan (EoA) or Anti-Afghan Forces (AAF). *Taliban* is an incendiary word, a word so heinous that our brigade was commanded never to utter it. I understood but was saddened by that. Once upon a time it was a perfectly good word, a word of respect. *Talib* means "student," specifically a student of the Koran. My Baba was a *Talib,* and a wise and thoughtful man.

The AAF now included the mujahideen, such as Maulavi Jalaluddin Haqqani, who had bravely booted out the Russians with the help of Americans and who had become folk heroes representing the glory of resisting and defeating superpowers. Then came the old Taliban movement of the 1990s, that young and ambitious group of Islamic scholars who took over and established a short-lived government, which was recognized internationally by many countries, including the United States. Their rule was severe, perhaps more strict than I would have liked to live under, but—strangely enough—it worked, in a society that was craving the strict hand of law following the years of lawlessness. These were the good old days when gasoline was 5 rupees a gallon and men could leave their compounds for night prayer without worrying that someone was going to break down their door and rob them or rape their women. The rules were enforced and everyone knew what to expect, which is the biggest deterrent to crime and instability in the absence of a central authority. When Afghans in 2009 expressed their nostalgia for the Taliban, this was generally who they were reminiscing about. And this is also what the AAF promise to restore once they take back Afghanistan from the infidels.

Unfortunately, American soldiers would hear the word *Taliban* and, unless they have an exceptionally talented interpreter, assume that the villagers were talking about the Taliban who were setting up mines and road bombs for killing the soldiers. Unless an interpreter told them otherwise, the soldiers would grow to detest and distrust the Afghans with whom they were sent to build relationships. How could I blame the soldiers for not wanting to get to know the villagers they thought were planting IED in the road? This is where it becomes essential to have interpreters who can not only translate words but also share the history and context behind the conversation. I firmly believe that without that knowledge our soldiers would be better off not talking to any Afghans at all.

Another group of insurgents fighting against the United States is the second wave of Taliban, led by the younger generation, including people like Jalaluddin's son Sirajuddin. One of my first missions at Khost was to visit a village in Paktya that happened to be Sirajuddin's hometown. As is the case in many villages, its people felt completely disconnected from the central government. The elders believed that if Karzai wanted their allegiance, he should involve their respected leaders (such as Jalaluddin Haqqani) in his government. After all, Jalaluddin had fought the Russians bravely with fearlessness and honor, qualities Pashtuns admire and require in their leaders.

In Pashtun culture respect for the father is automatically transferred to the son, but these villagers weren't so sure about Sirajuddin, and the elders were reluctant to transfer their loyalty. Sirajuddin had grown up in Pakistan, was bought by that country's Inter-Services Intelligence (ISI), and—according to the villagers—did not seem to harbor the same love for his people and country that his father did. He was working for the *other*. Regardless of whether he was targeting foreign soldiers or his own people, his methods were considered sadistic. Sirajuddin, they thought, was not like his father, and did not deserve their trust. He fought beneath the cloak of Islam but was after money and power, no better than the infidels he claimed to target.

There is a third type of insurgent, too: foreigners who believe that they are doing jihad by assisting the local insurgents in overthrowing the GIRoA, a puppet regime of the infidels. They might be Uzbeks, Tajiks, Pakistanis, Iranians, or even the rare Westerner who has allied himself with the new Taliban. They might be misguided in their wish to do jihad against the invaders, but they provide the kind of blind faith needed for suicide bombers. In my opinion, this is the hardest group of insurgents to fight; you cannot defeat an enemy who welcomes and desires death during a firefight.

But this isn't all. Add to the mix fighters for hire, who for 100 rupees will, at a determined hour, remotely detonate an IED; boys in the villages whose mothers and sisters are starving, who fight because they don't feel as if they have a choice; opium traffickers with their own henchmen; and garden-variety criminals and smugglers who thrive on the ongoing chaos of the region. After spending five years in Afghanistan, it is my opinion that, when it comes down to it, there are very few hard-core Taliban fighters who want their seventy virgins, and everyone else is in it for other economic or political reasons.

ASIDE FROM FAILING to understand either the lives of the "good guys" or the affiliations and motivations of the "bad guys," there was the same problem I'd noticed the first day my feet hit the ground in BAF: the dire lack of Pashtu-English speakers. There was an army-wide push to gain cultural understanding of the Afghans, but language had been left out of the equation. How could we expect to understand the complex cultural environment without the right linguistic tools? We had several CAT I interpreters who'd been assigned to HTT. Ehsan was from Khost, a twenty-two-year-old father of two who'd studied English in Kabul—but having only one qualified interpreter for a team of six or seven analysts and social scientists was an unreasonable arrangement. Two Farsi speakers were installed in our office who spoke little Pashtu or English, which meant I witnessed firsthand how much was lost in translation when one of them was interpreting for my teammates.

This language barrier and the dearth of knowledge of the region's history, both recent and distant, had created an environment ripe for failure, in which our soldiers were expected to fight for the hearts and minds of villagers. Was it reasonable to expect them to succeed when they weren't armed with the right weapons?

I came to Khost knowing little about the battles that our soldiers were fighting on these linguistic and cultural fronts. As a former CAT II, I knew many other CAT IIs who claimed to have been native Pashtu speakers but couldn't carry on a conversation in Pashtu that was longer than two sentences. My Letter of Authorization, issued by the army, stated my title as research manager, hired to manage a social database, but that was not what I found myself doing. What I knew about Afghanistan had not been taught to me in a class or training course. It would have been impossible for me to tell the soldiers with certainty which tribe to believe, or whose side to take in a centuries-old tribal feud, or any of the other information I knew they needed to complete their mission, but I could try to make them aware enough of the environment they were going to be operating in so they would have a better chance of coming home alive.

The local interpreters had an idea of what was going on outside the wire, but like most Afghans, they were stuck in the middle of it. They too were unsure of whom they could trust, so they kept their mouths shut and let our soldiers make cultural mistakes that, in my view, could have been easily avoided. I came into the program having had no local ties to our Area of Operations (AO) other than the language of my forefathers. I didn't live there, and neither did my family. This gave me the freedom to explain relationship dynamics of a Pashtun tribe without feeling like I was being disloyal to the Pashtuns or feeling like I was taking sides. My loyalties were not as easily manipulated by the tribes around me.

TWENTY-EIGHT

On a clear day in late March, just a few weeks after getting to Salerno, we received word that Colonel Jason McAffee, the incoming brigade commander, wanted to meet the team. Seated around a big table at his TOC were Audrey; Billy; Tom, the research manager whose contract was ending and whom I would be replacing in a few months; Evan, the team leader who'd recruited me; Michael, the HTT's social scientist; and me.

Jason sat at the end of the table. Tall, with salt-and-pepper hair and a narrow face, he looked like he might have been a science teacher in a previous life. I was the last one to introduce myself.

"I'm Saima, from Portland, Oregon, originally from Afghanistan."

"Aha! I've found my Pashtu interpreter."

"I'm the research manager, sir, but I'd be happy to find you a good interpreter."

"So you're from Oregon?"

"Yes."

"My kids love to vacation there. We like to kayak. Do you kayak?"

"I don't even swim, sir."

"No? That's amazing."

"My uncles thought there was no reason to learn, since Afghanistan has no ocean."

He laughed. No one else said anything. The air was charged with their disapproval. I glanced at Evan, who was looking down at his hands folded on the table. We had discussed this already. We'd agreed that while I would have no need for my own interpreter, I wouldn't be anyone else's. But Evan remained silent. Jason was his commanding officer.

"You find me that interpreter," Jason said, "and I'll let you off the hook."

"No problem," I said, thinking, This could be my *Mission: Impossible*.

Later, back at the HTT office, Michael said, "You know that guy is huge, right? He's in charge of six provinces." I knew that Jason led a task force of five thousand American, Czech, and Polish troops serving the International Security Assistance Force (ISAF) in eastern Afghanistan. His area of command extended over six eastern provinces, including Khost.

"I know," I said. "I'm still not going to be his interpreter."

"This is a man who's used to getting what he wants. I'm just concerned that this is going to make the whole team look bad."

I'm headstrong, but I knew Michael had a point. A few days later I went to Jason's office. I stood before his desk and told him that I knew good Pashtu speakers were hard to come by, and that I had meant it when I said I would find him the best one I could. He sat back and smiled. He called in the sergeant first class in charge of the linguists. "Saima is tasked with finding me an interpreter. Help her in any way she needs."

I took my mission seriously. I liked Jason, especially since he'd used the word *tasked* when asking me to find him an interpreter, a verb generally reserved for soldiers—that meant that he thought of me as one of his soldiers. The sergeant first class rounded up every CAT II on the base. There were a handful of Farsibans who spoke not a word of Pashtu. One young punk from Kabul defended himself by saying that everyone in Khost spoke Farsi anyway, so what was the big deal? Once, back in Jalalabad, Judy had said she thought I was the only female in the entire country who was fluent in both Pashtu and English. I was beginning to think maybe I was the *only* interpreter who spoke both Pashtu and

English fluently. My best choice was an older *engineer-saab* from Virginia. His Pashtu was excellent, but he spoke English like a third-grader. Meanwhile, word traveled fast. I was getting a reputation for outing all the faux interpreters, the people who were trying to pass off their Farsi as Pashtu. Unit commanders who were having trouble with their interpreters would come to the office, asking me to vet their CAT I's. The soldiers and the interpreters started calling me the interpreter terminator, or IT for short.

After weeks of searching, I still couldn't find anyone I could recommend with 100 percent confidence. I returned to Jason's office and I told him about the *engineer-saab* but that if there was a meeting he felt was important, I would sit in on it and listen to the interpretation, to confirm that he was getting the whole story.

Not long after this meeting, there was a deeply unfortunate event. A village elder was killed by coalition forces during an Escalation of Force incident. He'd been driving head-on toward the patrol and, despite several warnings, had refused to stop. Our soldiers, following procedure, had fired and killed him and his driver.

At a meeting with other elders of the villiage, Jason said, "My soldiers told him in both Pashtu and English that he needed to stop, and he refused. They fired warning shots, and he refused. My soldiers had no other choice. They followed EOF procedure. They needed to do this for their own safety. How can we help your people understand this? If someone is driving toward us in a car and refuses to stop, how can we tell the difference between this person and an insurgent who wants to harm us?"

The interpreter wrung his hands. "We're sorry," he said to the elders.

"Do the complete translation," I said. "These elders need to have all the information."

"We're so sorry, we're so sorry!" he repeated.

I could tell that he didn't know all the words in either Pashtu or English, but I could also see that he didn't want to disrespect these elders by implying that it was the driver's fault. Regardless of the reasons, as an interpreter he was obligated to translate Jason's speech word for word.

I jumped in and did the translation, which may have caused Engineer-

Saab some shame and embarrassment, but it couldn't be helped. As an American, I wanted to make sure the locals knew our soldiers had not broken any procedure and were not to be blamed for the incident. Like Engineer-Saab, I, too, had my loyalties. It was not easy to admit where they lay.

TWENTY-NINE

Every Human Terrain Team had a social scientist, and Michael Bhatia was ours. Michael was soft-spoken and sophisticated, a Californian of half-Indian decent. He was dark-eyed, wore small, wire-rimmed glasses, and could have easily passed for an Afghan. His credentials were stupendous; he had worked as a social scientist in East Timor and Kosovo, among other places. By the time he came to Khost he'd already edited a book on Afghanistan and had also published a photo-essay. He had been on the HTT for seven months when I arrived.

Our desks were across from each other. We sat together most mornings reading reports, assessing what was known (not much) and not known (a lot) about the people in the province. I liked to listen to my iPod when I read the reports. I tend to have a few favorite songs that I listen to constantly. During my first months at Salerno I listened to a certain upbeat Bollywood tune, sometimes six or seven times in a row.

One day as I was putting on my headphones, Michael started singing the song with made-up lyrics. He had a nice voice.

"You can hear it?"

"I hear that song even in my sleep, thanks to you. You need to expand your horizons. Please let me download something else on your iPod."

"This is Bollywood, Michael. This music is half of your heritage," I teased him.

"That song is *not* my heritage."

"You need to embrace what is in your blood! Trust me, it's much easier to embrace it than to deny it."

He shook his head dramatically. "I'm begging you. Let me give you some Frank Sinatra. Everyone on earth loves Sinatra." In the end, we compromised: I would listen to the song no more than five times a day, and Michael promised not to delete it from my iPod.

Audrey and I, in part because we were female, but also because we were friendly and outgoing, attracted a lot of attention. HTT had an official open-door policy. After 9:00 A.M. a steady stream of soldiers would appear. Word had gotten out that if you had any questions about Afghans or Afghanistan, however ridiculous they might seem, HTT guys were the ones to ask.

They came with all varieties of questions. Why was it disrespectful to ask after a man's wife but okay to talk about his children? How could they avoid talking about religion without seeming rude? Was it acceptable to ask what Afghans did all day? Was it rude to ask the elders how they dyed their beards that brilliant red? Did regular Afghans despise us? Did they have any idea what we were doing here? Was it true that sometimes when we drove through a particularly isolated village on patrol they mistook us for Soviets, the enemy of their worst nightmares? What was the best thing to say to a villager? Who were the movers and the shakers of the community?

I liked the soldiers. I encouraged their questions.

Michael would stand up and place his hands on his hips in mock disapproval. "I've been here for seven months and none of these guys ever asked me anything! I think we need to make some rules around here. For every five guys who show up in here asking questions that they've made up just to visit you, you girls need to buy me a coffee at the Green Beans." Every FOB in Afghanistan had a Green Beans Coffee franchise; ours was over by the PX. The coffee was overpriced and not very good, but it represented an indulgence anyway.

Audrey and I protested, but Michael started making hatch marks on the wall. Whenever another soldier would show up, he'd get out his black Sharpie. "This one doesn't count!" I would exclaim. "He only wants to borrow a book!" Michael would shake his head. "These are the rules. I don't make them, I just follow them." Which, in fact, he did.

We laughed a lot, but it wasn't all fun all the time. Michael and I differed on some fundamental issues, which often resulted in intense bickering. Perhaps it was because we were stuck together in that office for hours on end. We did have meetings at the TOC and went on the occasional mission, but it felt as if we all lived together in that square plywood room.

There was a basic conflict at the heart of our relationship. I knew Michael was working on his Ph.D. while he was there, and I suspected that a lot of the data he was gathering was to support his dissertation. He knew that I was Pashtun and thought that I believed I knew it all. I was at a point in my life where I took everything very personally when it came to Afghanistan, and felt that only those civilians who truly loved and were invested in the development of the country should be allowed to work there. Any other reason, no matter how valid, was not acceptable to me. Our approach to the job couldn't have been more different. Once, I was reading some data he'd gathered during a routine mission to a nearby village.

"You asked them how many doctors they had?" I blurted out while scanning his report.

"It's a standard question."

"You are showing insensitivity here by assuming that there's even a single doctor in the village. After being in Afghanistan for years, we should know that most villages don't have any."

"As it happened, there was a doctor in the village," he said. "I don't see your point."

"The point is that it reveals how little we have learned and retained about these people. Instead of asking how many, it's better to ask where they take the sick to be treated. The Pashtun are impossibly proud. For them to answer 'None' reinforces the fact that they are lacking the ability to provide for the basic needs of their families, and it sets the tone for the rest of the interview."

I rambled on. My cheeks were hot, even though the room was cold and we were sitting in our jackets. These villagers were not required to talk to us at all, and when we conveyed our ignorance, even in something as minor as to how to phrase a question, we risked closing our channels of communication entirely.

Michael sighed heavily. He explained that he had spent two years in Africa, and knew how to conduct a proper interview through an interpreter.

"Whatever you did, wherever you did it, it's not going to work here. We are lucky if we get two hours in a village here, so you're going to have to completely change the way you research and study and think."

"Whoa, take it easy!" said Billy.

Michael and I stopped. We'd forgotten Billy was there.

"Things were a lot chiller in Kandahar," he said.

Sometimes our differences felt insurmountable. Then I would grab Audrey and go to Aziz's bakery.

Aziz was scrawny and milky-eyed, a cagey old Pashtun. His way of saying hello involved blinking one eye shut and wagging his finger at me. Although he was missing a few teeth, his smile was dazzling. Like the rest of the locals, Aziz was puzzled and curious about where I had come from and who my people were in Afghanistan. For the safety of my family still there, I had never disclosed which tribe I belonged to because from there it would be very easy to trace my roots. Everywhere I went, people would try to find out, and I would tell them one tribe or another, sometimes I would even say I was from Pakistan. In all the years I spent in Afghanistan, Aziz was the only one who correctly guessed my tribe. He said it was my accent, the accent I had apparently retained even though I had left my village when I was five. Of course I didn't tell him that he had guessed right.

There was a bench near the bakery. Unlike my bench in Farah, on which I had sat for many hours enjoying the solitude and Eric's company, or the bench in Asadabad at the top of the PRT with the view of the gray-brown mountains and cold blue river below, this bench had nothing going for it aside from being near the bakery and Aziz's mouth-watering bread.

Audrey and I were a team within the team. We shared a B-hut, and only a very thin plywood wall divided our tiny rooms. We could hear everything, every phone call and cough, every sigh of frustration. For the first month we'd shared the building with a female staff sergeant who liked to sing to herself and an older civilian who worked for USAID. They both left when their deployment was over in late March, and so we had the place to ourselves. We liked to stay up late, reading, watching movies, listening to music, and talking.

She was less troubled by what I felt was Michael's cookie-cutter, one-size-fits-all methods. Many afternoons at the bakery she would talk me off the ledge, reminding me that Michael was there for the same reason I was—I loved Afghanistan and cared about its people, and so did he. I couldn't explain to her that Michael made me doubt myself by questioning my qualifications, much like I had been doing myself, and that I wasn't able to face my own doubts voiced by another human being.

This was the first time I had an office in Afghanistan, not to mention the ear of the U.S. Army leadership, so to speak. I was in a position to potentially help my father's people, if I could only figure out how, and be confident enough to advise and affect military operations in the region. Having Michael point out constantly that just being an Afghan didn't make me an expert on Afghans undermined my confidence, and thus my personal goal. I realized that just being an Afghan didn't make me an expert, but being able to speak the common language and having grown up as an Afghan had to at least put me ahead of those who did not speak the language or have the same genes. Those two assets mattered more to Afghans than the academic background—I knew this because they mattered more to *me*.

In the beginning, several days a week we were required to continue our training. One week it was Humvee rollover training. The point was to learn how to unbuckle your seat belt, keep positive control of your weapon, extricate yourself, rescue the injured, and maintain security, in case the Humvee was hit by a roadside bomb and was tossed and rolled. It required a lot of imagination to pretend that the Humvee, which was hooked up to a special device and had been turned over like a chicken on a spit, was imperiled on some lone mountain road.

Our team—Audrey, Billy, Tom, Michael, and I—trained together. During our first simulation I was told to open the door while the Humvee was lying on its side. The door of an armored Humvee weighs hundreds of pounds. Pushing it open while on your side requires bracing yourself and using your hands and feet. My arms were never as strong as they were after a couple of weeks of rollover training.

Medical-emergency training was next. We were schooled in how to stop the kind of bleeding that would kill someone in a minute or two. Soldiers in the simulations were slathered from chin to knees in blood so bright and red it could only have been real.

The medic conducting the course was named Todd. He was small and energetic, and he believed in his mission. When he asked whether we had any questions, I asked about the blood. Where did it come from?

"This is pig's blood, dried into powder, shipped from the States specifically for this training," he replied.

I had already seen my share of blood in the clinics in Farah, Jalalabad, and Asadabad, from the locals with their blown-apart limbs to the suicide bomber bits I'd seen stuck on the sides of a Humvee or splattered all over the road. But I'd never gotten used to it. I wanted to learn how to tie a tourniquet, but I didn't want to be immersed in any blood, particularly pig's blood, which is especially repulsive to Muslims.

I said, "Oh, no. As a Muslim I'm afraid I can't touch pig's blood. I'm going to need to be excused."

Todd frowned; a line appeared between his brows. He put his hands on his hips. "You're right; this is not okay," he said. "This is the stuff I've been using to train the ANA."

He felt bad and worried that he'd been insensitive. But I had pointed it out mostly to avoid getting the blood on myself. "As long as you don't tell them it's pig's blood, they won't go to hell. Don't tell them, but meanwhile, try to get other blood," I suggested.

A couple of weeks later Todd found me at the chow hall, eating a pistachio ice cream cone. Pistachio was my favorite flavor, and it was offered only occasionally. I struggled with the food at Salerno. I couldn't understand why the army put pork in everything. Salads were an option, but the lettuce was sad and wilted, the edges brown. Sometimes I ate Jell-O, like someone recovering from an illness. Todd sat on a chair next to our table and said he'd managed to find a new blood source. "It's not animal blood at all but still looks real. It's already mixed, and they ship it in bags. Now you can take the training."

He stared hard at my ice cream cone. "You do know there's lard in that, don't you?"

"You mean . . ."

"Pig fat. I was surprised too, but I came across it in my research about the blood. There's lard in jelly beans also."

I had no respectable choice but to drop my cone into the trash bin. I had to laugh at how karma got me by making me give up one of my favorite things to eat because I had made Todd feel bad. I sincerely thanked him for his concern for my faith and that of the ANA soldiers. The kindness of Americans could be so touching because it was offered so casually, like it's second nature. Of course, I was not so naïve to think that all Americans possessed this quality.

AROUND THAT TIME I developed chronic migraines. When I opened my eyes in the morning it was the worst—the knife in the eyes, the whirl of nausea. A cup of strong instant coffee allowed me to pull on my clothes and make it to the office. Perhaps it's no surprise that most of my arguments with Michael took place before lunch. By the end of the day the headache would be all but gone, only to reappear in its searing glory the next morning.

The medics at the clinic were mystified. Was it some residual aftereffect of my vaccinations? An allergic reaction? A pinched nerve? I took Advil and did physical therapy. Nothing helped, except the occasional shot of morphine. The relief would be instant, but it was no solution. Plus I worried that I might come out alive from the war but with a drug addiction, a fate of many unlucky soldiers returning from deployments.

Despite its high altitude and relative lack of water, Khost had a lot of mosquitoes, and malaria was a real concern. The soldiers were ordered to take antimalaria pills—to refuse would mean being court-martialed if you wound up contracting the disease—but most civilians were not required to take them (although some did as a matter of course). Because HTS personnel were considered Mission Essential personnel by the army (which basically meant that if one of us got sick, it might endanger the mission), we were also required to take the pills. There were two types available: the daily and the weekly. Both had side effects: The daily gave you diarrhea and headaches; the weekly gave you nightmares.

I was already suffering from nightmares that often jolted me awake, sweating and crying out—particularly a recurring one that featured Taliban invaders sneaking inside the wire. In the nightmare they found my B-hut without problem. They crept into my room while I slept, unlocked the storage locker where I kept my M-4, and then killed me with my own weapon. Not a surprising dream, considering that such a scenario played in my waking mind all day long.

I wasn't keen on the idea of chronic diarrhea, but I was eating so little anyway that I thought it would be the lesser evil. I opted for the daily. I took them in the morning with my vitamins, washing them down with a cup of coffee.

Around the same time that a soldier suggested the daily pill might be the problem, Evan took me aside and said that if my headaches were as bad as they were I should think about returning to the States. In my mind, going back was not an option, not yet. So, without telling anyone, I stopped taking the pills. The headaches disappeared. My usual nightmares roamed my sleeping mind uninterrupted.

THE CHOW HALL had long tables with chairs on either side, like in a high school cafeteria. Most days Audrey and I ate together, sometimes in the company of soldiers. Rarely, we would be there at the same time as Jason and Tim, the command sergeant major (CSM), who would sit with us or invite us to sit with them. I was happy that they felt comfortable enough to do this but also noticed that once they sat down, no soldiers would join us.

With us, Jason and the CSM were able to discuss issues that they couldn't discuss with their subordinates. I wasn't military, and I wasn't in their chain of command. Jason could float ideas, wonder about outcomes, ask hypothetical questions, and afford to look (if even for a moment) like he wasn't sure about something. In a word, he could relax. Not that we could ever have mistaken this for a social lunch; the mission was always a priority and the never-changing topic of discussion.

One day after lunch I wandered back to the office. The day was warm and the air smelled of orange blossoms. Gray clouds piled high in the sky above the brown mountains. The door to the HTT was open, and Evan, Tom, and Michael were sitting around the big table talking. I strolled in, but once they saw me they stopped talking. Their gazes shifted around the room as if they were a trio of strangers waiting at a bus stop. I knew they'd been talking about me.

"Hey," I said. I went to the coffeemaker and started making a new pot.

"When did you talk to Colonel McAffee?" asked Evan. Since the day we'd introduced ourselves to Jason, and I had refused to be his translator, my relationship with Evan had deteriorated. He had a temper. So did I, of course, so it made things that much more difficult.

"I just had lunch with him," I replied. "Why are you asking?"

"Why did you have lunch with him?" Michael asked.

"Because it was lunchtime," I said. "Are there rules against having lunch with the brigade commander?" I turned back to the coffeemaker. I'd brought Peet's coffee all the way from Portland, and we were on our last bag. I ground the beans, keeping us from talking for a bit.

"Were you the one who suggested the mission to Matun?"

There seemed to be a lot of importance attached to my answer.

"Yes," I replied. "Jason thought it would be a good idea, too. It would only be a couple of hours. There's limited space, so if you guys want to go, please go. I didn't suggest it because I wanted to go; I just think that someone from our team should be involved."

"Because he gave me the order to do a mission to Matun, and given the fact that he hasn't been here very long, I wondered how he came up with the idea himself," said Evan. He was bald, and his entire head was turning red.

"Yes, I might have suggested that as a good place to start to get to know his AO."

Evan stood up, then closed and collected a few folders on the table. "If I were you, Saima, I'd be careful. Especially about visiting Colonel McAffee in his office."

"You mean the one with the door wide open in the middle of the TOC?"

"Rumors spread quickly on an army installation." Yet one more thing that Afghanistan and the U.S. Army cultures have in common, I thought.

I looked at Michael, who grimaced a little and shrugged.

I poured myself a cup of coffee, put on my headphones, and went to work. I tried not to fume. It seemed like I was always losing my temper. The sky had been cloudy all day, but suddenly it darkened, much like my mood. The light coming through the door was not enough to read by anymore. Even though it wasn't yet 4:00 P.M. I turned on my desk lamp. The rain came down in sheets, as it tended to do in Afghanistan. Even the weather here was extremist, I thought, wishing I could tell this joke to Michael sitting across from me, but I didn't feel like talking to him yet. Thunder shook the building.

There was a bright flash and a loud crack. I had three computers on my desk. One of them emitted a white flash, and then they all went dark.

"Whoa!" Michael shouted, leaping to his feet. Then Audrey stumbled in, soaking wet from the rain. The hood of her green windbreaker was up.

"We were struck by lightning!" she cried. "It hit one of our antennas, up on the roof!"

Everyone was talking, waiting for the next crash. I started to tremble.

I knew what I looked like, pale and fearful. I folded my hands to stop their trembling.

"I think God must really be upset with you this time." Michael had no idea he had voiced my inner terror by trying to make light of the situation.

"He is," I replied. "He's furious that I'm sitting here with you infidels."

He grinned, and so did I. Humor. That is how you deal with fear and danger in a combat zone.

THIRTY

In early 2008 Khost was still considered a green province. For the most part the villagers got along with the people at Camp Salerno and with one another. The exception was the Sabari district, twenty-five minutes from the base by Humvee. From the highest point of the FOB you could see a mountain, behind which huddled the Zambar, a subtribe of the Sabari, who were furious at the world.

This was the site of one of the longest-lasting land disputes between the two subtribes of the region. Their feud had gone on for many generations, and the situation had gotten so bad that in 2005 the United Nations had been called in to mediate.

The U.N. sent a delegation from Kabul, headed by an Afghan, to try to patch things up. At the suggestion of perhaps a misguided cultural advisor, or maybe a CAT I local interpreter with a bias, the Khost PRT had also become involved in this effort to bring an end to the feud. Using *shura*, the preferred local means of dispute resolution, the U.N. delegation drew up a written agreement, which they claimed was accepted by both subtribes—so a celebration was ordered by the governor of Khost. An immediate cease-fire was announced by the governor on provincial TV, which the U.N. read as problem solved. In reality, this just offered each side a formal reprieve, so they could both regroup, waiting for the foreigners to leave.

The U.N. drew up the terms of the cease-fire, which included one tribe paying off the other for the rights to the trees in dispute. A meeting of the elders from both tribes was called to celebrate. Peace in the Sabari district! It was televised. There was dancing and roasting of lambs. The elders arrived in their snowy turbans and, since they were unable to write their names, pressed their inked thumbs on the dotted line. The U.N. returned to Kabul, feeling satisfied.

Then it was back to the Sabari against the rest of the world. Within days the fighting resumed, as if nothing had happened.

The U.N. was perplexed. What had gone wrong? Allegations flew. One of the negotiators had been bribed by the subtribe that had received the more favorable terms. The other tribe refused to accept them. The first subtribe, which had been accused of bribing the U.N. delegation, went to the governor, asking him to enforce the terms of the treaty. The governor then appealed to the PRT for help. The PRT refused; this was local business and Americans could not look like they were taking sides. This was the correct decision, but it came a little too late, in my opinion, for as soon as we were seen in the *shura,* we became a part of it, and the simple fact of our presence was proof enough that the United States did take sides. As Aziz said of the dispute, "This is life in the heart of Pashtunistan. No one can enforce anything there, not even in a time of peace, much less *now.*"

We at the HTT were fascinated by this dispute. Before we designed the mission to Sabari, we knew none of the history. All we knew was that the district was close to where we lived and worked and there was always trouble brewing. We couldn't figure out why the Sabari were so unhappy and why the two subtribes were constantly at odds.

The cause of the tribal dispute had nothing to do with the insurgency, but the instability and the power vacuum it created was certainly being used by the insurgents to make the insecurity worse. Whenever the government in Kabul failed the people, the insurgency moved in and said, "Karzai's government is a puppet of the foreigners. They're not interested in helping you, but we are. We are fighting to get this country back to you people, if you help us."

The research design of the Sabari mission was simple: We would do an initial mission into the district, just to chat, to see if anyone would tell us anything, and then we would bring the data back and analyze it to come up with an informed overview of the situation. Then we could go back and dig a little deeper. In the process, we'd convey to the tribes of the region our genuine interest and let them know that we would return to build on the relationship.

Of course the army preferred missions that had a clear objective. Although this mission was not that, Jason still liked it, and he ordered the mission.

Not everyone on the team could go. Between the soldiers who had been tasked with patrolling the area and the soldiers pulling security, there wasn't much room for civilians. Tom and Michael were near the end of their contracts, and even though Audrey and I desperately wanted to be included, at the end it wasn't up to me. I made myself feel better by saying that there would be plenty of good missions in the future.

On the morning Michael and Tom left for Sabari, Audrey and I walked them to their Humvee. It would become part of our team tradition. It was early, but you could tell the day was going to be roasting. Tom and Michael were dressed like the rest of the company, in desert fatigues, IBA vests, heavy boots, and helmets. Audrey gave them each a hug. I didn't hug either of them—it's not something the Pashtun in me would allow me to do out in the open where the local Pashtun laborers seemed to be watching my every move.

Besides those laborers, I'd made it a personal rule not to hug soldiers or even touch them, except for the occasional handshake. I didn't think I could lecture them about the rigid brand of respect they were required to show Afghan women and then hug them. It was confusing enough for me to juggle the two different cultures that made me whole; I didn't want to send mixed messages to the soldiers as well. Audrey, who had the softest heart of anyone I knew, gave her hugs warmly and easily, in the American way. I was envious of how free she was to express her emotions. I simply couldn't.

"Did you call your mom?" I asked Michael, in lieu of a hug.

"Ah, no. I didn't want to worry her."

"I think she's probably already worried."

Michael and I had talked before about our mothers, how despite the fact that one was a white American from Southern California and the other a Pashtun from a village in Afghanistan, their worries were identical. All mothers are the same, we agreed.

"How about, I don't want to worry her even more than I already have. She doesn't need to know I'm going on this mission. I'll be back in a week and will call her then."

"True. Still, you never know what's going to happen."

Later, whenever I went on my own missions, I would give Audrey these instructions in case I never came back: My lotions, shampoo, and perfume were to be given to the female soldiers on the FOB. My laptop was to go to our CAT I interpreter. My clothes should be given to any civilian on the FOB who wanted them. Nothing was to be shipped to my mother or my siblings because I didn't want them to suffer the anguish of going through my belongings after I was gone. Plus, I knew my mom would save all my stuff for as long as she lived, and I didn't want Khalid and Najiba to have to see my things in the garage every day.

"I'll give her a call when I get there," Michael said.

We both knew there were no phones or computers where he was going. I shook his hand. He gave a little salute, then winked at his silliness and climbed into the Humvee after Tom.

The mission to Sabari was a week long. I went about my business, reading reports, attending several meetings every day. I went to the gym and walked on the StairMaster in the evenings. I was anxious for the team to return, to see what they had discovered. Before he left I'd given Michael a list of suggested questions to ask the elders, and he had seemed willing to entertain them.

On one side of the bakery Aziz had built a screened porch, where every day he served a simple lunch. Usually it was okra or eggplant and rice. On days when Audrey and I simply couldn't face another bite of overcooked steak or corn bread, we'd have lunch at Aziz's.

We were sitting across from each other on his porch one day, flies buzzing against the screen, when we heard the blast. At this point we'd learned to read the language of explosions. When it was the result of outgoing fire, we'd feel the earth shake, then hear the sound. This time we heard the sound first, then felt a slight tremor. That meant it was not us causing it. It was them.

Audrey and I looked at each other. She was one of the bravest people I knew, but she looked afraid. "That was close."

Later, we confessed that we'd both thought of Tom and Michael at that moment.

Still, we were so used to the sounds of warfare, of whistling rockets and the boom of mortars, that we didn't dwell on it much. We finished our lunch and chatted briefly with Aziz about the difficulty he was having securing good-quality garlic for his garlic bread. We strolled back to the office. The sun was hot on my face, on the part in my hair. The heat plus the good food made me feel sleepy, and I wished I could curl up in a quiet spot and take a nap.

However, a meeting was scheduled at the office. Because the day was so warm the HTT door was open to allow for a breeze. Our purpose in being there was to meet the members of an incoming unit, and Alex, who would be replacing Evan as the team leader.

An hour later, I'd forgotten about the explosion. At war, an explosion was business as usual. I sat facing the open door and saw Tim, the CSM who was Jason's right-hand man, walking slowly toward the office. The sun was on his face. I couldn't see his expression—but I suspected that something bad had happened simply by the way he walked, like he dreaded every step he took closer to what he had to do. He entered the room. Tim had always smiled at me easily. Today his face was gray beneath his tan.

He asked Evan to step outside, and when Evan returned, he wore the same ashen expression.

"Two soldiers and Michael have been killed in an IED in Sabari."

BEFORE MICHAEL'S BODY was flown from Salerno to BAF, there was a hero's flight for him and the soldiers who'd been killed with him. By then I had done three contracts working with the army in Afghanistan, for a total of over three years. I knew many soldiers who had died in that time. As an interpreter, however, I was never aware of what happened to the bodies of these fallen heroes. Interpreters were usually so isolated, but now that I was one of the elite civilians known as the primary staff, working directly for the brigade commander, I got to see the war in a more intimate way, whether I wanted to or not. A hero's flight was one of the rituals I had never known existed, which upset me beyond measure. How much more had I been left out of as an interpreter? I was fuming at myself, at the army, at the contracting companies for excluding me from so much by making me an interpreter all those years. I was furious that I had wasted more than three years playing puppet at meetings between U.S. soldiers and Afghans. In retrospect, I was probably lashing out at anything or anyone just so I could delay facing my feelings.

The hero's flight took place in the middle of the night. The Afghan moon was like a light fixture in the sky. There were nights, like that one, when you could easily read by the moonlight. For safety reasons, planes were no longer flown in the bright moon. They would be too visible to the missiles of the insurgents.

At 11:45 P.M. there was an announcement over the loudspeaker. The bodies had been kept in the hospital until the time came to load them onto the plane. The night was still, no mortars outgoing, no pickup basketball games or heavy metal issuing from the random B-hut. You could hear coyotes in the distance. The sky was splattered with stars. The absence of the wind was not the only cause of silence—there was no sound coming from anywhere. There must have been hundreds of soldiers all around me, and not a sound was made as they stood at ease.

There was no hiding from my guilt in the silence of the night and the light of the moon. I felt guilty for every uncharitable thought I'd ever had about Michael, every harsh word I'd uttered. Audrey and I were there first; we had stayed in our room until the loudspeaker had told us it was time. Evan and the rest of the team came and found us at the front and stood next to us in silence. The thousands of soldiers and few civilians present all stood in silence, alone with their own thoughts. I will never forget the looks on the faces of the soldiers at a fallen hero's flight. The raw emotions were so stark that it took my breath away, and I couldn't look any of them in the eyes. This was one of the rare times when I desperately wanted to not be known as an Afghan. When I wanted to explain my association with *them,* and tell these soldiers that I myself would never forgive the Afghans for each American life lost in that country. Not when I knew firsthand the lives of those soldiers, and had witnessed the goodwill of most of them even when they thought no one but their God was watching.

As part of the tradition, the fallen soldier's team carries the body to the terminal and loads it onto the plane. It could be seven people, ten people. Two people could carry it, but that's not the point. Our team was Audrey, Billy, Evan, and Alex, as well as Farhad and Ehsan, our CAT I interpreters, and I.

We stood in the cold at the entrance to the emergency room, waiting for Michael's body. On a night like this in Khost, you could feel the altitude. My lungs were struggling to draw each breath, and it hurt even more knowing Michael would never breathe again.

Civilians generally don't receive a hero's flight, but the brigade commander had made the decision to treat Michael the same way he would the soldiers. Michael had died in the line of duty and deserved the same honor.

A hospital worker brought Michael's body out in a small truck. It was wrapped tightly in an American flag. We could clearly see its outline. We picked him up. I was by his right leg on the stretcher. As we passed the crowd, soldiers saluted. I knew I wasn't the only one with tears streaming down my face. I swallowed hard to keep myself from making any sound, knowing that once I started I would not be able to stop.

As I carried his body with my team, my hand touched his leg. It was cold through the fabric. I hated that this was how I would remember him. Instead of Michael smiling, laughing, fighting, singing, teasing, it would be this, the feel of a lifeless leg wrapped in the flag. I wished I had broken my own rule about hugging. It had been easy enough to give him heaps of criticism, assuming that he would be around and we could hash out our differences, but I had withheld that final hug.

I felt wretched for his parents, who'd been against his coming to Afghanistan. Michael hadn't listened to them, just as I hadn't listened to my family, but I knew it upset him that he didn't have their support. He had wanted to show them that what he was doing was a great service, one that mattered, and I think his inability to convey the importance of his work to them frustrated him. He had tried to do an outstanding job, not just because he was that kind of person but because on some level he wanted to show them, too. I couldn't imagine how horrible it must have been for his mother to receive the news of his death. For her sake, I hoped that her faith would be strong enough for her to handle the cruel reality that would end her life as she knew it. I longed for her to know that Michael died doing what he loved, and more than that, I wished that God would dull her pain and treat her kindly in the next life, because to go through the death of a child has to be the hardest thing on earth.

My regrets gathered in my heart. I hoped he'd written me off as a nutty Pashtun, and hadn't listened when I'd accused him of using Afghanistan to further his academic career, or of making a thesis out of the Afghan people. I realized, then, that I had criticized Michael for not being more understanding, and yet I had made no effort to understand him.

It took less than five minutes to deliver the body to the waiting C-16. It seemed as if during those minutes I felt more emotions than I had ever imagined humanly possible. It wasn't just that insufferable guilt. I was sad beyond measure because any loss of life is sad, but of course it resonates on a deeper level when it's someone with whom you've shared many hours, someone who has teased you about the guys who might have tried to flirt with you, who has challenged your way of thinking, and who had the potential of being a true friend. There was also the heaviness of relief—which I knew was wrong—the gratitude that it hadn't been me in that Humvee.

I wished I had never known about hero's flight, but at the same time

I knew that there would be many more, and that I would never miss another one. These fallen heroes gave the ultimate sacrifice. The least I could do was to never send one off in the middle of the night all alone.

As we reached the C-16 we passed a row of saluting soldiers with tears running down their faces. The children they'd once been had reemerged. I had lived among soldiers for years, known them to be nothing less than stoic, resolute in carrying out their duty. They could be squirrelly on the base, goofing off in the gym or during their endless pickup games of basketball, but outside the wire they were strong, well trained, and—above all—they had one another's backs. The bond that these soldiers formed was one that no outsider could understand. When a fellow soldier was hit in a firefight and they couldn't save him, they brought back the body, as that bond required. Sadness never slowed them down in the line of fire. But once they loaded their friend onto that plane, briefly their emotions took over. Now they were just young guys who'd lost not just a friend but someone who understood their lives like no other. This was the ugliest part of the war for me, watching these young men sob. I have to imagine that they were also grieving for themselves, knowing that they could be next, and that their families could easily be at the receiving end of a hero's flight. I know I was.

After the hero's flight we walked back to the HTT office. It was close to 1:00 A.M., but none of us wanted to be alone with our thoughts yet. The eastern sky was pale with the dawn when we finally made it to bed.

The next morning we hung Michael's picture next to Karzai's in our office and started working on the next mission.

For those at war, grief is a luxury they can't afford.

THE UPROAR IN the media was immediate and long-lasting. Editorials appeared in newspapers and on websites saying that Michael, a civilian, was outside the wire hunting for bad guys, who then murdered him in retaliation. That this couldn't be further from the truth made no difference. Tom, whose contract was almost up, and who had been riding in the same convoy, escorted Michael's body back to the United States, overnight, and the HTT at Salerno was reduced to Audrey and me. Evan, who was waiting to turn his post officially over to Alex, mostly stayed in his office.

We did not leave the wire for months after Michael's death. To keep from falling into depression, we did all we could to stay busy. On any given day, we had access to hundreds of local laborers on the base, so we decided that if we couldn't leave to engage with the Afghans beyond the wire, we would talk to the ones coming to us inside the wire every day. We designed our own research studies and the questions to ask the laborers. We cleared it with whichever authority was in charge of the group of locals to whom we wanted to talk, and most Afghans were happy to take a break and chat with us.

I spent a week visiting the FOB's main gate, the Entry Control Point. Afterward, at the end of the week, I would brief the commander on my findings and recommendations. Every day more than a thousand locals passed through on their way to work. They worked at the laundry, the chow house, and the MWR. They built buildings and handed out towels at the gym.

The local laborers' biggest complaint was the length of time it took to be processed through the gate every day. I stood at the gate and watched them come in and out for a week to see if there was anything we could do to make the process faster and their experience more positive. This wasn't easy, as security needed to remain the top priority. Any morning a worker might bring a bomb onto the base because an insurgent had kidnapped his son and threatened to kill him if he didn't take the package onto the FOB.

Also, the guards at the gate had never received any sort of cultural briefing, though they had more contact with the locals than anyone else on the base. They'd become lax when they took their breaks; rather than leaving their post, they stood around and smoked, giving the impression that they were still at work and simply ignoring the long line of locals waiting to get in. The locals, of course, felt ignored and disrespected. This problem was easily fixed: The commander erected a break room out of plywood and ordered the soldiers to take their downtime there.

It seemed like a minor adjustment, but I liked the impact made with just this one task, and it made me realize how much more there was outside the wire that I could positively influence. Sitting in the office, talking to the occasional Afghan laborer, who most likely wasn't being completely honest in answering my questions, fearing losing his job if he was, felt like a waste of my position, and I was getting very impatient.

The start of my deployment at Salerno was very rocky, and there were many days during those first couple of months when I almost packed my stuff and said good-bye to the country that was making my life unbearable with the hold it had on me. I didn't understand what it wanted from me, and I yearned for the simplicity of my American life. I climbed up the hill almost daily to figure out my next step, hoping to find some kind of guidance from the spirits of the past. The goal of connecting with people who lived in this isolation offered to them by the majestic and imposing mountains seemed exhausting. Why did I feel the need to do it? Why couldn't I find happiness like millions of other Americans living in America? Those nights of answerless questions were when I would most often dream about Baba. I remember one dream vividly: I was running (I am always running in my dreams), and I knew that someone malevolent was behind me, and gaining. I came across a wall made of mud, and I tried to climb it, but I couldn't get a hold because the mud kept becoming dust that was falling in my eyes and keeping me from looking up. Then Baba leaned over the wall, smiled at me, and reached out his hand. I woke up knowing I was being guided by him, or by my father, or maybe by them together. That feeling of being watched over stayed with me throughout my physically exhausting but emotionally energizing deployment. I never felt invincible—nobody is on that kind of unforgiving terrain—but I did feel blessed knowing that I had a purpose to fulfill, and that I would be given the help from above that I would need to fulfill it.

Over the course of the next fifteen months, I worked with the kind of single-mindedness that drives Mamai and my siblings insane. My personal aim became clear: Talk to Afghans and discover the redeeming qualities of Afghans for which my father gave up his life. But there was a parallel objective as well—to use the knowledge gained in the process to smooth out the discord that was growing—and continues to grow—between my native and adoptive nations. The commander saw the benefit of sending me out into remote villages with a company of soldiers who were tasked to support my research. In the process, I would help the soldiers build lasting relationships with the villagers and encourage them to revisit and see how their relationships could be built upon and passed to incoming units.

Although the process of learning and understanding the human terrain of Afghanistan would always be grueling and frustrating, the job would have been a lot easier in 2005 than it was in 2008 and 2009. In the decadelong fight against terrorism, there were mistakes made—not necessarily by the soldiers on the ground but by the policy makers in Washington, D.C. What *had* really happened from 2004 when I signed the first contract to deploy to Afghanistan to change the cries of the Afghan children running alongside our Humvees from "I love you" to "Fuck you"?

• • •

THE UNIT I was attached to at that time had been on the ground long enough to be curious about the Afghans but hadn't had the time to satisfy their curiosity. One day, when Jason asked me to come to his office, I went in not knowing what he had decided to task me with, but I knew I would potentially have all the resources of the brigade dedicated to it. He would be issuing a fragmentary order, or FRAGO. FRAGOs are how the army leadership issues tasks and orders to its soldiers and officers.

Jason wanted to talk about the Khost-Gardez Pass road, which is the only route in or out of eastern Afghanistan. The road is narrow and winds through the provinces of Khost, Paktya, and Paktika, connecting them to one another, and to the outside world. It took ten years of fighting for the Soviets to pave the K-G Pass road; within weeks after the Russians were gone the local tribes had ripped it up and sold pieces of the road on the other side of the border, just to show spite. By the time I got to Khost, in 2008, USAID dedicated $160 million to open and repave the road but could not maintain security for the crew working on the road. Therefore progress had been excruciatingly slow and a sore topic of conversation with the surrounding villagers. The insurgents had immediately realized the opportunity this road presented. The way to stop a United States–funded project, or any project in Afghanistan, is to plant roadside bombs and IEDs and kill local laborers to intimidate the rest to quit. Jason had decided to make security and stability of the pass his brigade's priority, and I was tasked with what seemed to be yet another mission impossible: to find out why villagers around the road were so "pissed" at the United States, which was only trying to make their area more accessible by finishing this road. Why did they seem to be against the Americans when there was so much to be gained economically by allying with us?

Finally, after all my years in Afghanistan, I found a professional meeting that would also get me closer to my personal objective. I was excited and nervous. I knew the reputation of the Zadran, the tribe that dominated the regions around the K-G Pass, how isolated they were up on their mountain. Even among the willful reputations of all the Pashtun tribes, the Zadran are known as the mountain tribe, immovable like the mountains. They had no industry and they grew their own food. The rest of the world was of no use to them. They were not interested in building any alliances with outsiders. We would drive though a village and not see a single soul, but we knew that people came out once we left. It is an indescribable feeling to go through a town that doesn't want to be seen. It could be a scene from a zombie movie.

For the next fifteen months I flew among Khost, Paktya, and Paktika, the axis of insurgency through which attacks are conducted in all of Afghanistan, on a singular mission: to hold simple, constructive conversations with the Pashtuns to find out why they didn't want to work with the Americans and what had turned them away from us. On the ground we traveled in a convoy of no fewer than ten Humvees and several ANA trucks. I dressed like the soldiers, in camouflage fatigues, body armor, and army-issued boots that became the most comfortable shoes I'd ever worn. I even walked like a soldier, constantly checking my surroundings while moving very fast. I still have to consciously slow down when walking with Najiba or a friend. I wore my nine-millimeter holstered while on the FOB and both the pistol and my M-4 when outside the wire. Once, a friend and commander in the Afghan National Army even lent me his AK-47, so that I could "fit in with all the other armed Pashtuns in the mountains."

Decisions had to be made before I set out on my first mission. Where should we start? That was simple—where we already had an existing U.S. presence in the form of a combat outpost (COP) to support our mission. We decided on a remote COP in Paktya, and the name alone should have prepared me for an experience of a lifetime: Wilderness. Our team consisted of two new social scientists, one CAT I interpreter, and me. We flew to PRT Gardez, in the capital of Paktya, first and were expected to convoy to Wilderness. Once we got there we were briefed that to get to Wilderness we had to go through K-G Pass valleys, most of which had nicknames like Ambush Valley and IED Central. In short, we were promised quite literally a very explosive passage. I contacted Jason in Salerno and updated him on our plans to convoy down the K-G Pass. He got briefed by his soldiers in that valley daily and was well aware of the dangers. After the media frenzy over Michael's death, Jason decided not to take any more chances with civilians, so we air-assaulted to Wilderness.

I had thought that the PRTs were the smallest, coziest U.S. presence on the ground in Afghanistan. I was wrong. COP Wilderness was tiny in comparison, nestled in a sandy valley, with mountains so close that one had to climb them to get a signal for our mobile phones. A civilian contractor had been shot and killed by a sniper just the week before we got there, while trying to get a signal. I didn't use my civilian phone even once the whole time I was there. Although I was not wearing civilian clothes, I still attracted a great deal of attention as the only woman on the COP. There were no bathrooms for women, since a female presence had never been anticipated there. The soldiers were very sweet and respectful, especially when they found out that I was a Pashtun. They would all empty out the bathrooms when they saw me waiting outside. For my part, I drank and ate very little while at Wilderness.

The lieutenant who was in command of the post was twenty-eight but looked a lot older. No doubt Afghanistan had aged him. He briefed my team on what he knew about the people in his AO, which was not much because for some reason not known to him, "these dudes just don't like us." HTT's presence made perfect sense to him, and that made our job easier. Together we planned daily missions for the next five days, which was the duration of this first overall mission. I explained the process to him, and described how we would carry out daily missions, if operational requirements permitted, and would report back to recap and to learn quick lessons for the next one. At the end of the five days, I would go back to my office at Salerno, take a week to analyze the data I had collected, and present a PowerPoint to him and his soldiers via video cam. I would also brief Jason and his primary staff back at Salerno. In the following two to three weeks I would write a detailed analysis, which would be anywhere from fifty to a hundred pages and get distributed to all the soldiers in the area. This product would also become part of an open-access database for all U.S. military and other elements who wanted to read up on the region.

This was the process for the rest of the missions, with the exception that I tried to present in person to the company that had supported me—as the dialogue that followed proved so crucial to the soldiers' understanding. Unfortunately, due to restrictions on movement, I wasn't always able to have these in-person discussions.

Back at Wilderness, we decided which village to go to, which by chance happened to be the one in which the Haqqani family was rumored to reside at the time. It was early evening by the time we made all the mission-related arrangments and decided to start bright and early the next day. The sergeant major offered to give me one of the newly built rooms, but it was a little too isolated for my comfort, so I declined. I wanted to be with my team in case we had incoming or were attacked. So I, the CAT I interpreter, and the two social scientists were all told to sleep on cots in a large room that was being turned into a gym. It didn't have doors or windows, and I remember staring out through the door frame at the mountain peaks, trying to see the sniper who I was sure was hiding up there. The next day Mark, our youngest social scientist, teased me, saying that I had given him the fright of his life when he had woken up and seen that I was sleeping with one eye open, staring out at the mountains.

The next day we left the wire as the sun was just rising from the horizon. As soon as we arrived at our first destination, we were surrounded by eager children. This was a good sign, because the way children treated us was a strong indication of the adults' attitude toward us. The soldiers circled my team, pulling security, with my team members helping out. We had decided that I would lead this mission, since our objective was so broad and we just wanted to gauge the people's thoughts. It would be better if we didn't have to depend on an interpreter. We pulled up to the village in the heart of Haqqani territory. Instantly we were mobbed by bright-eyed, shoeless children. This was again a very good sign. I loved talking to the children. They were always so open and frank, and there was no question that they were offering their real thoughts. I addressed

them in Pashtu, which sent them into a frenzy. One of the little boys
asked what we were doing there.

"You mean here in your village, or here in Afghanistan?"

"No, no, we don't care why you are in Afghanistan. We just want to
know why you are here in our village!" the boy answered, almost rolling
his eyes.

"I know why they are here!" an older boy interjected. "Yes, they are
here looking for Osama," this know-it-all declared, proud of his knowledge. My program's mandate specifically forbade us from looking for
"bad guys," but if the Afghans brought it up, should I pursue the topic,
or change it? I was there to talk to Afghans, so if they wanted to talk
about Osama, I would too.

"What do you know about Osama?" I asked.

The soldiers heard Osama's name, and it had gotten their interest.
The lieutenant in charge asked his own interpreter what was being said.
Interpreters should always translate what's going on, without their unit
having to ask, *What are they saying?* But right then I didn't have time to
lecture him.

"Well, he lives in that house. See that white *qalat* with the green gate?
He lives there. Do you want to talk to him?" A little boy wearing no sandals offered to go get him.

Hmm, my first mission, and I'm going to capture Osama! This was an
unexpected turn of events, but if they wanted to hand Osama over, how
could I say no?

"Yes. Please go tell Osama that Miriam wants to talk to him," I answered with a straight face. The little boy took off, dust flying all around
him, and I watched him go into the *qalat* with the green gate. The soldiers stood with smiles on their faces, eager to see what would unfold. A
couple of them wondered if we should all share the reward on Osama's
head equally, or if I should get more because I was the one talking to the
boys. The other boys were all talking at once, some of them asking me if
I was going to beat up Osama, and I told them that I didn't really want
to but if he forced me, I would. While we were standing there talking,
the shoeless boy returned, but not alone. With him was a six-year-old

boy, who was missing his pants *and* sandals, and who looked like he had just been woken up.

"Here is Osama," the first boy said, pushing the sleepy child toward me.

The rest of the boys, and the soldiers, burst out laughing.

I didn't remember being able to tease adults like that when I was their age. Things must have changed a lot, I thought, but of course, I was laughing, too.

One of the young soldiers, with an easy smile, pretended to grab the little Osama and walk to the nearest Humvee, causing the rest of the boys to scream with panic, "No, no, don't take him! He isn't the real Osama! Really!"

On that first mission, I went into many villages, and after the first couple of villages, they started looking the same. As I was going about collecting data, I was also showing the lieutenant the best way to engage the locals. Upon entering the village, we would look for a group of men; we'd most often find one by the bazaar or right outside the mosque. I would ask the men if we could hang out in their village for a bit and talk to them. Asking permission was not necessary, and most American soldiers forgot to ask, but it showed respect in a culture that values reverence for ownership. The village belonged to the people who lived there, not us; I would tell this to our soldiers a hundred times over the months. Above all, these men were Pashtun, and prided themselves on their famous hospitality. When asked, they were almost always gracious and would most often offer us tea. When I approached the men's gathering I didn't wear my helmet because I wanted them to see that I was female. They may have hated me for that, but they were curious. Before I'd left Portland I had the brilliant idea to put auburn highlights in my black hair. There is so much bleach in the water at the FOB that within days my highlights had turned orange. I carried a notebook and a pen so that I would appear even more harmless. I can't imagine what these men must have thought, seeing me walking toward them without a scarf, armed with two weapons, a pen, and a notebook, with my orange hair blazing in the sun.

The formula of behavior was the same. First I would sit down with the elders. Even though the Zadran are ferocious, they are Pashtun and thus extremely hospitable. We would drink tea in the blazing sun and just talk. They wanted to know if I was married, and sometimes the answer was yes, sometimes no. They would want to know where I was from. Sometimes I would say Kandahar, other times, Jalalabad, but never did I tell the truth.

After a while I would introduce them to some of the soldiers. I urged the soldiers to talk about what they missed about home, what their fears were, what their dreams were for their lives and their children. I advised them to show pictures of their kids, but not of wives. We weren't just there to educate Americans about Afghan culture; learning was a two-way street in Afghanistan. Dehumanizing American soldiers is one of the insurgency's best tricks. So we made it clear that we were people with families we loved, children we adored, homes we missed. And no, back in America, we didn't eat little Muslim children for dinner.

One time an elder wanted to know whether it was true that Americans married their sisters. The troops laughed. "Heck no! But we heard that you guys marry your cousins. We don't even do *that* in America." They razzed one another, but they shared a few laughs and there was a sense of good feelings being established. The hoped-for outcome would be that the elders would spread the word among the village that the American kids weren't so bad. Likewise, the troops would return to their base and tell their fellow soldiers that they'd talked to some cool old Afghan guys that day.

Although most days I felt successful, physically exhausted but emotionally exuberant, some missions just broke my heart. I would come back to the MRAP and just cry, thinking of the suffering of the Afghan people, the hard lives ahead for their children. I remembered how it felt to be running for my life as a child and wanted to protect the sweet, shoeless, often pantless children I saw. At first, the soldiers didn't know what to do when they would see me quietly crying, looking out the window. After a few times, they let me cry in peace, silently offering me water or snacks. Surprisingly I felt no shame doing that in front of them.

Part of the road project involved paving smaller access roads between villages that led to the K-G Pass road. One day we were driving along one of these roads and I saw a bunch of kids between the ages of nine and twelve working on it. It was morning, but it was also summer, and the temperature was scalp-burning hot, and here were these skinny, sweaty little boys breaking up rocks.

I asked Tom, the battalion commander, if we could stop the convoy. I started walking toward the children while the soldiers were still setting security perimeters, which was not protocol, but I was too disturbed. I asked the kids what they were doing, and they said they'd been working on the road since 6:00 A.M. It turned out they were orphans from the surrounding villages. USAID had hired a Farsiban from Kabul to put together a road crew. He'd simply gone to the school and recruited orphans, who viewed it as a chance to make money. The kids were primarily the oldest boys in their family, and this was the only way they could feed their younger brothers and sisters. This was another example of the well-meaning United States thinking we were helping but in reality taking children away from education, as well as creating another opportunity for insurgency recruitment.

The insurgents are masters of psychological manipulation. They know all the Afghan buttons to push. They would track down the elders of the village in which these children lived and say, "Americans claim to care so much about your kids, but look what they're doing. Taking them out of school to work on the roads. And who will benefit from the roads? It is the Americans who are using these roads to get their supplies. You don't even have cars. Why do you need roads?"

ONE DAY AT the gym at Camp Salerno, I was working out when I noticed one of the laborers staring at me as he folded the towels. Being stared at happened a lot. Most likely because I was stressed about one thing or another, that day it really upset me. I was a Pashtun female. He was a Pashtun male. Why was he disrespecting me by staring at me? I knew that I was not acting like a typical Pashtun woman by being in the gym, but still, I felt harassed.

I went up to him and asked him to use the other counter, which was facing a different direction. He moved, but then would turn around every few minutes and even started singing to me at one point. I blew up. I got his supervisor and told him that his laborer was harassing me and I did not feel comfortable in the gym. To make a long story short, as a result, he got fired. Because he was a laborer from around the village, some of the elders came to Salerno to find out why this had happened, as he had told them that it was for no reason. I felt strongly enough about it that I asked the battalion commander if he would let me handle it and talk to the elders. He agreed. On the day of the meeting, we prepared tea, cookies, and juices, in the Pashtun style.

The room was a good fifteen-minute walk from the TOC, so the commander had sent a couple of his soldiers to drive the villagers to the meeting. I greeted them at the front of the meeting room in my jeans and T-shirt, but to show respect and cover my bare arms I wrapped a shawl around my shoulders. Their shock at my addressing them in Pashtu was the usual reaction. They wouldn't have been so surprised had I spoken to them in Farsi because by then there were quite a few Farsiban women working in places like Salerno. After the initial standard questions—Where was I from? Where did I learn English? How long would I be there?—were covered, I brought up the reason they were there. I asked them if the young man had told them what had happened. They answered that he'd told them he was just working and his supervisor, who apparently never liked him, came up and fired him.

The commander had decided to step back and let me handle the situation by myself, and so he wasn't present. I had asked a couple of the Civil Affairs soldiers to sit with me—just so the elders' cultural sensitivities would not be insulted by being alone with me in a closed room—but had asked them not to bring an interpreter. I didn't want the elders to be embarrassed by what I said to them, and I would get away with saying a lot more if the conversation stayed between the Afghans. I had a lot of grievances with the Pashtun men, and as a fellow Pashtun, even as a female, I could criticize them more openly. This is a side of *Pashtunwali* most outsiders don't know about. There is another *Pashtun-wali* rule: You have to protect the pride of any other Pashtuns in front of non-Pashtuns, regardless of how you feel about one another. There is a saying among Pashtuns: "Me against my brother. My brother and I against my cousin. My brother, cousin, and I against the rest of the world."

I addressed them as Baba, because they were my grandfather's age, and because I wanted to remind them that I was one of them. I told them that regardless of how I was dressed in front of them then, regardless of what I was doing for a living, I spoke to them as a native. As a Pashtun female, I had ancient-born rights, and one of them was that I not be harassed by men of my community. This young man had violated my ancient rights, and I was holding them, the elders, responsible for his behavior because, as we all knew, they were supposed to teach young Pashtun men how to treat other Pashtuns.

This is among the complexities of Pashtuns that make it so hard for outsiders to understand their rules of behavior. On the one hand, women are not to be heard from or seen in public, but on the other hand, I, a female of pure Pashtun blood, could stand in front of these men and reprimand them for how they were raising their young men, and how they were losing their customs. I was not breaking any rules because a long, long time ago, when there was peace and stability, women were allowed to call out men in public arenas when they felt threatened or harassed. I was using Pashtun history, which had not been written anywhere, and depended on society's memory for passage to the next generation. How do you explain this to the soldiers sitting with me, as they watched me speak with these men in a language they didn't understand, though they could clearly see the elders' hung heads and read the apologetic tone of their response? This was among the most defining moments in my life, when I felt most Pashtun, and I couldn't even explain the *why* to these soldiers. This was the first time I felt fully accepted as a Pashtun by my father's people, and I became acutely aware of the Pashtun blood running through my veins. It took the two cultures I loved, combined, to give me these feelings of total belonging: The Pashtun in me gave me that nearly genetic knowledge of my people's history, and the American in me gave me the courage to stand up to these elders and claim my hereditary right to protect myself from harrassment.

The elders admitted that it was their responsibility to make sure our traditions were better upheld, and that the young man would be punished and would learn his lesson the hard way. They asked for my forgiveness, which I, of course, gave immediately and freely. I told them it was hard to keep an ancient culture alive and I was trying to hold on to bits and pieces myself, even in America.

I walked the elders to the truck, and the soldiers drove them back to the gate, where they all walked to the village, and I hoped had a *shura*. I knew the young man was going to be hearing from the whole village and didn't envy him that attention. A couple of days later at the gym, a group of the other laborers, also from the same village, came up to my elliptical and stood a little ways back, looking down at their feet. When I removed my headphones, they told me that the elders had sent me a message: The issue had been taken care of and I would never feel harassed by any of the young men in their village. The elders only said men in *their* village. This meant I could still expect harassment from the men in surrounding villages. One village at a time. I thanked the young men and resumed my workout.

Everywhere we went the village elders asked whether I was married. The soldiers were confused. Hadn't I lectured them endlessly about not talking to Afghans about women and wives? Then how did these absolute strangers excuse such rude behavior, poking into my personal life this way? Were they hitting on me? Should the soldiers intervene? If they didn't, would the elders assume they didn't care about my honor? It was so confusing.

I tried to explain that even though the elders spoke to me so freely, I was still a woman in Afghanistan, where the most relevant thing about me was my marital status. I altered my answer depending on whom I was talking to. If I felt the elder respected me, as did the man who reminded me of my Baba, I would tell the truth. No, I was not married. But if we were in a conservative village, I would say that I was married to a nice Afghan man who had given me permission to come back and help our people. In some crowds, I could even joke: "Why would I ever get married? Look at the women in your country. All they do is take care of you men. Why would I want that?" They would protest, "But our women are happy! Go ask them. They have new clothes. They have jewelry." Once in a while, I'd say that my husband had died.

These meetings all took place in the open, beneath the biggest shade trees in the village or wherever people tended to congregate. We had never been invited inside anyone's home.

Then one day we did an assessment at a bazaar on the border of Khost and Paktya. When shopkeepers saw us coming they closed down their stores and hid, even more skittish than usual. I spotted an old man wearing a white turban and carrying a cane, trying to look busy picking up little rocks and placing them on a wall being built for a new store. I approached him from the street, calling out, *"Asalaam alaikum, Baba."* He didn't turn around. Assuming he was hard of hearing, I said it again, louder. By this time, I was standing right next to him. When he turned to me, I will never forget the look of naked fear on his face. I took a step back, realizing he was afraid of *me*.

"Baba, I don't wish you any harm. Please, please don't be alarmed," I tried to reassure him.

"It is not you, daughter, that I am scared of. They are watching from that hill, and when you leave they will be here, beating anyone who was talking to you. Don't you see, talking to you means I am going to be beaten?" he pleaded, looking around with genuine terror.

I stepped away from him, too shocked to even apologize for what I had just done to this poor old man, whose only mistake was that he looked like Baba. Suddenly I missed my Baba terribly. How could I convey the horror I felt for not being aware of this basic tool of intimidation of the insurgents? How could I tell my soldiers to know my people, when I had put this man in grave danger because I didn't understand him, I didn't understand the environment he lived in? At that moment, I wanted to crawl under a rock to hide from my shame, guilt, and deep sense of personal failure.

In all my time in Afghanistan, I had never been more intensely aware of the danger in which our presence put the villagers than I was at that moment. When we single someone out and approach him, we are also picking him to be the one approached, after we leave, by the insurgents, who never forget or forgive.

I walked back to where our guys were pulling security and signaled that we were done and moving on. This failure could easily have caused me to give up and return to Oregon. There was no contractual obligation that I needed to fulfill. But I refused to give up at that point. If anything, my error in understanding served to strengthen my resolve to try even harder to know more about my people. I would never make that mistake again. I might make others, but I would never make the same one twice.

I linked up with Tom, the battalion commander, by the MRAPs and told him I needed a couple of minutes to figure out how to proceed. Thoughts were zipping through my head at the speed of lightning. I would not let the insurgents limit *my* interaction with *my* people. True, they were brutal, and I was restricted by laws of international conduct, but I was a Pashtun and hated the thought that I was being intimidated into giving up on a goal that was so close to my heart. I had to come up with a quick solution because I knew the insurgents were watching, and I imagined them smirking over their victory and their belief that we were about to leave the area. I got it! I would try to talk to a crowd of people from now on and not seek out one-on-one conversations. The insurgents might beat up one old man, but even they couldn't beat up a whole village. Reckless, I know, but my life had already become the story of calculated risk.

I went back to Tom and asked him if he thought we could make an unplanned stop at a village nearby. I wanted to make sure the insurgents were able to see that we did not go back to our COP. We drove around and I noticed a handful of elders sitting outside their small mosque, staring at us as we drove by. We dismounted a few yards from where the elders were sitting. They didn't run off and hide. This was a good sign.

Some kids playing nearby ran up to us, yelling, "Pen, mister! Pen, mister!" I laughed, remembering my first trip outside the wire at Farah several years earlier. At the time I had thought it was evidence of their desire to be educated. Along the way I'd learned that kids ask for pens because they sold reliably well in the local economy.

I looked like an American soldier; the stern-looking Pashtun men didn't realize I was one of them. As I was looking for my recorder and pen the five soldiers around me nudged the kids away a little, in case one of them tried to grab my weapon.

I approached one of the men I assumed was the oldest based on his bright red beard. Pashtun men can be as vain as any other—when their beards go gray, since they don't have Just For Men, they often color them with henna.

"Asalaam alaikum," I said, to which Red Beard replied, *"Wa 'alaikum as-salaam"* (and upon you be peace). He was still wary; a lot of soldiers knew enough to offer the traditional Arabic greeting.

Then I said in Pashtu, "Would you mind if I sit here and enjoy the sun with you guys?" Suddenly, Red Beard and all the men gathered around him started exclaiming to one another, "She speaks Pashtu! The woman speaks Pashtu!"

"Yes, I speak Pashtu. And you don't have to talk about me like I can't understand you. I understand you completely," I replied.

They all asked the standard questions at once. Where was I from? What was my name? How did I know Pashtu? Why had they never heard of me? Why had they never seen me before?

They asked whether I was married, and what my husband thought of what I was doing. I told them I was married, because they would wonder what I'd done to render myself unmarriageable. Did I sleep around? Was I an adulteress? they might wonder.

I told them that I missed my kids. Still, I was happy to meet their children because they were just as bratty as my own brats back home. The elders laughed.

They asked if I was there to find out what they wanted from the Americans. "No. I already know what you want. Clinics. Schools. Food. Clean water. Jobs. You want to feel safe in your community. You want our help, but you also want to be respected."

"You've been talking to a lot of Afghans," said Red Beard.

"I've been talking to a lot of Afghans," I said, "but I am struggling to understand the root of the Pashtun problem. Why are you so unhappy? Why would you rather fight than live in peace?"

"Why do you think?"

"I am the same as you," I said. "As a Pashtun I have a long history, and that history has created an image that I sometimes feel obligated to maintain. The image is of the warrior who fights to the death to protect what is his. If I lived here, I would do that, just as you do. I would fight to the death to protect what is mine. But I am also American, and I see we have a great chance for Afghanistan to do so much better. We have the support of the most powerful country on earth, and also their dollars, to improve our lives and the lives of our children. Instead of seeing opportunity, you are obeying history, choosing to be insulted when these soldiers mean you no harm, but on the contrary are here, risking their lives, to help you."

Red Beard looked at me with ageless wisdom. "We don't have much, but we are going to fight to keep the little bit that we do have. It's important for our kids to go to school, but it's more important, for us elders, to look our children in the eye and tell them we lived correctly, according to our culture."

We spoke about our obligations toward our culture versus our children and a better future for them. We could have talked about this for hours. But I had more pressing questions that had been puzzling me for months.

I didn't know whether I dared ask this one: Earlier in the day I'd been at a meeting at the subgovernor's office where I'd met several elders from this village who'd presented themselves as power brokers, the movers and the shakers of the communities. Were these elders who they claimed to be?

I had first gotten suspicious of such a group of elders in Jalalabad, when I would notice the same token elders representing different villages at different *shura*. Once I started paying attention, I noticed this everywhere I worked in Afghanistan. I started calling them "elders for hire." In my job with HTS, it was more than just a joke for me; I wanted to know why the villagers were sending these men when traditionally they would want to build relationships with us directly.

Red Beard laughed and confessed that these men were simply players. I had long suspected that the elders at all the PRTs were being presented as men of influence when they were only spies—and now my suspicion was confirmed.

This was a breakthrough. I saw with my own eyes. The kind old man I was talking to was the real power broker of this village. He sat in the village center and addressed everyone's problems. He made decisions while I was sitting there, deciding cases, networking, and making sure his people had what they needed from him: cultural knowledge and wisdom that had served as the law of the land for centuries. He was the heart of the village.

I asked him why he was sending others to represent him, and before he could answer, a light went on in my head: Of course, I knew the reason! I remembered the countless accounts of "elders" being killed on their way to meetings with Afghan officials. They were being targeted by the insurgents for working with GIRoA and showing support to the foreign forces—the United States—by coming to these gatherings. This was another form of intimidation that the insurgents were using to subjugate the population of Afghanistan. There was no way Karzai would be able to provide protection for these participants, even as he was calling *shura* after *shura* to convey the participation of Pashtuns in his government. This was causing a lot of resentment toward his government because if he would stop calling these gatherings, the villagers wouldn't have to send elders, and the elders wouldn't be killed on their way there. Just as I had done earlier that day, Karzai had made a cultural blunder, revealing his lack of understanding of how his people lived and died.

This was among the biggest reasons why the villagers were deeply unhappy with the U.S. and ANA presence in their village.

"You have trusted me," I said gratefully. "I have more respect for Pashtun culture than you might imagine. Now I am going to ask you for a favor. If you grant me this favor, I promise I will not violate any laws of *Pashtunwali*." I was really pushing my luck, I knew, but what had happened with the men at the bazaar still stung me pretty bad, and I wanted to recapture a feeling of accomplishment.

"Anything, *looray*," he said, using the Pashtu endearment that means "daughter."

"I don't mean any disrespect to you by mentioning your women in public, but I would love to talk to your daughters, and I would love to talk to your wife, and I would love to go inside the *qalat* and have some tea with them. I will leave my American agenda, as you call it, out here with you. I just want to see some real Pastun women."

He looked doubtful. I kept going, "My mother is a Pashtun woman, and I have not seen her for many months. I miss her so much. I just want to sit and talk with your women for a while."

He sighed. "I told you I would not refuse you anything, daughter. You may go inside, but you must leave your soldiers here. You have to go alone. You have to trust me when I say you will be protected. Here is your test of *Pashtunwali*! You know when I say you will be safe in my house, you can trust me."

It was completely out of the question for me to leave behind all the guys pulling security for me. Tom would not let me go inside unprotected. I might have felt safe knowing that Red Beard had given me his word, but Tom was a military commander and I was his "on loan" from his superior, and no way was he going to risk losing me to *Pashtunwali*. I told the elder that I would have to clear it with my commander.

I took Tom aside and told him what had happened. "I know you're freaking out, but this is a huge opportunity. You'll be able to brag about the fact that under your watch one of your people was granted access to Zadran women. Imagine how happy Jason would be."

"Yes, but what if under my watch I lose a Pashtun woman on HTT? Imagine how upset Jason would be."

He refused to let me go in completely alone. I could take Mark, my teammate. He was twenty-five or twenty-six but looked like one of the many younger boys in the crowd. He was terrified. As we walked over to the old man Mark kept muttering, "They're going to kill me, they're going to kill me."

"Relax," I whispered. "I know these guys. You're going to be fine."

I told Red Beard that I wanted to take him up on his hospitality to meet his women, but I couldn't possibly go in without Mark, who was like my brother.

Even though he was the decision maker of his house, in fact, the whole village, the old man still had to consult the other men, who told him that since he had already promised me anything, he should let me go inside.

As he led Mark and me to his compound, he said, "Daughter, must you be armed?" I told him that these weapons were my responsibility, and he laughed.

"I'm just a little worried," he replied. "A Pashtun woman with American weapons. I hope you don't give my women any ideas!"

As soon as I stepped inside, I felt at home. This *qalat* could have been the *qalat* I spent a year in when I was little, or it could have been the *qalat* that I had spent a week in just a couple of years earlier with my family in Ghazni. There were rooms all around the four walls, a courtyard in the center, colorful rugs spread out on the ground. There were a couple of women sitting there with several children, feeding them. They got up when they saw me, shocked, and probably scared that the Americans had invaded. Before they could panic, Red Beard, who was following a couple of steps behind me, stepped inside the compound and told them that everything was okay. I jumped in quickly, apologizing for scaring them, and talking to them in Pashtu so they could feel safer. Once I was inside, only a few women appeared at first. They wore the most beautiful clothes I'd ever seen, brightly colored tunics woven with gold and silver thread, gold bangles and earrings. Then more and more women arrived. The houses shared common walls, and it looked as if they were literally pouring out of the walls. Sisters, wives, cousins, aunties. Suddenly, I was very homesick.

One by one they came to have a look at the American who spoke their language. They were shocked by everything: my Pashtu, my knowledge of *Pashtunwali*, my M-4, my nine-millimeter, my enormous boots and body armor. Even my bright orange hair, as they each took turns touching it.

I could distinguish them by the way they dressed. The most modest girls, wearing simple clothes with little jewelry, were the single girls, waiting for their arranged marriages. The women in the brightest colors wearing the most opulent jewelry were the newlyweds. The women who wore more subdued colors, smaller earrings, and only a few rings had been married for a while. The woman in charge wore no jewelry at all but had a huge key ring on her belt, with keys to the sugar, the flour, the butter, and the money. She made a jingling noise when she walked. She looked like my own grandmother, just a few hundred miles away.

I paid my respects to her first, and told her that one of my brothers was posted just outside the gate, and to please tell the ladies to stay clear of the gate.

They brought me tea, but I couldn't sit down to drink it—my body armor weighed fifty pounds and my boots were so high I couldn't bend my knees, so I tried to just perch on the edge of a chair they brought out to the courtyard. The women were all sitting on the ground, still staring and talking to me all at once.

If I felt bad for them being shut away from the world, they felt equally bad for me for being in the outside world in my unflattering fatigues, having to deal with the world day in, day out, with nothing but men for company. They worried about my mother—did she know I was wearing these clothes? And doing what I was doing? I said she knew, and she didn't like any of it. They insisted that I should listen to my mother and just go home and be with her. They reminded me of the Muslim wisdom that heaven lies beneath a mother's feet. I said it was too late, I was an American now, and as an American I expected my mother to just simply give me heaven to show me she loves me. They laughed so easily, just like the men outside. It amazed me to realize that in this environment that I found so suffocating, where I would struggle to last a day, they lived and laughed with such ease. I envied them this wonderful ability to find joy when their lives were so harsh and their futures so bleak.

I asked them what they were thinking about, what their concerns were, and they surprised me again. Their issues were the same as those of their men outside: security, employment, education, health care, the well-being of their children, their fear of outsiders causing instability in their community. The difference was that they wanted these issues resolved for their men, so that their men could have jobs and live in a more stable and secure society, so their boys could go to school.

I had thought these locked-away women would be completely out of touch, but apparently their husbands spoke to them (or around them, while the women brought them tea and served them dinner), about the world and what was going on in it. These women, who are clever and well informed, are a lost resource, and Afghanistan—at least as it operates now—is unwilling to benefit from their wisdom and insight. The Afghan men feel so threatened by what is going on in the country—the war, unemployment, insecurity—that they lash out against any efforts that might cause them to lose even more control. Since their women seem to be the only part of their lives they still exert control over, they would rather lock the women up inside the *qalat* than let them join the international development efforts and risk losing control over them.

I was in there for about fifteen minutes. Tom forbade me to stay any longer. I said my good-byes to the ladies, knowing I would most likely not be able to repeat the experience, and savoring the chance to see real-life Pashtun women. They made me promise that I would go home and stop stressing out my mother. The loss of human potential in this house alone broke my heart. I wanted to do so much for the country, and I knew every one of these ladies would have been a perfect partner in my efforts. Leaving with a heavy heart, I walked outside, where both the Afghan and the American men were anxiously waiting.

ℭHIRTY-THREE

One day in the fall of 2009, I was sitting in my office, finishing up a PowerPoint that I had to give to the brigade commander on the last mission I had just completed in Paktya. The day was sunny but awfully cold, which is probably why I was on my fifth cup of hot coffee. I was coming up on my deadline for the presentation and had missed lunch while trying to finish it. Audrey was outside the wire on another mission, and so no one was there to remind me that it was time to eat. I didn't mind. I could always stop by Aziz's for some warm bread and local gossip. As I was thinking about taking a short break, a soldier from the brigade TOC came looking for me. The new commander needed to see me in his office, right away, please.

I sent the soldier back so I could have some alone time while walking from my office to the commander's in the TOC building. In a combat zone, where you work and live in such close quarters, it's hard to get time to yourself, surrounded as you are by obligations, thoughts of work, and other people bustling around. You learn to take every chance you can to step away from it all and savor the isolation, so whenever I would get summoned to the commander's office I would take the longer route from our outside office to his inside the TOC. Unless it was an emergency—and I knew, on that occasion, that it wasn't, or he would have used the phone in the office to reach me. The reflection of the sun off of the gravel was so bright that I had to squint as I walked, but I could still feel the chill in my bones. Appearances were so deceiving in Afghanistan—how was it that the bright sun was so cold? I was in one of my reflective moods, bordering on gloomy. I had talked to Mamai that morning, and as usual she had been crying, worried again that I might not leave Afghanistan alive, and I had to think that maybe she was right. I had been there for well over a year. Was it time for me to take a break, to live a normal life again? I had forgotten what my American life used to be like. When I first got to Afghanistan, I used to think about favorite places in Oregon, and talk about what I would do when I got back home. But lately I had begun to do nothing but talk about Afghanistan, the soldiers, the people; before one mission had even finished I'd be thinking about the next one. Afghanistan had completely consumed my life; I lived Afghanistan and I dreamt Afghanistan. In my dreams I was constantly running away from the insurgents, and for some reason, Najiba and Khalid were there in every one of my dreams, and I was trying to help them escape. U.S. soldiers were conspicuously absent in these dreams. I was all alone, trying to protect myself and my siblings.

Lost in my thoughts, I walked into the commander's office and saw that his political advisor, Kelly, was already there. Kelly was a tiny, petite woman, but God save the fool who thought that her size was indicative of what was inside her! She was beyond knowledgeable in the region, having worked and lived in Pakistan, Turkey, and several of the -stans, among other countries. She vehemently spoke her mind when she felt mistakes were being made, which was the trait that brought the two of us close together in an environment where emotions ran high but no one talked about feelings. Kelly had become something like the older sister I never had and had always tried to be to Najiba. We shared many late-night dinners in the courtyard outside the chow hall, where—because of light restrictions—we had to use our flashlights to see what we were eating.

The brigade commander, Mike, asked me if I would go to the governor's compound with the PRT commander to deal with a situation that was highly political and could easily get out of hand. I had attended the battle update brief (BUB) that morning, so I knew he was talking about the civilian casualties from a night raid in a nearby village. The raid had not been conducted by Mike's soldiers, but because he was the battle-space owner, he was responsible for every action by any soldier, so he wanted to be represented at the meeting. He asked me to be an observer at the meeting and report the villagers' disposition back to him. There were so many things that were not in my job description for which I knew that I was the most qualified person, so there was no question of whether or not I'd go.

We were leaving in half an hour, just enough time for me to tell my team leader that I had to go outside the wire and to prepare. I couldn't find him but sent him a quick e-mail to tell him I would be back in a couple of hours, hopefully; then I met the PRT team, who had come by the brigade TOC to pick me up on the way. The drive to the governor's compound was quick, and for once there were no incidents to slow us down. All the troublemakers were already at the governor's compound, one of the soldiers said through the headset in my ear, which made communicating over the loud noises of the vehicle possible.

The night raids and civilian deaths were just starting to be a political issue in early 2009. Already there was talk that Karzai was upset and wanted an investigation, but this was before he had made a public outcry about U.S. night raids. As I walked in with the rest of the U.S. soldiers, in my military uniform and armed, the villagers glared at us. There were chairs all around the room, and as we walked up to the section where some of the other U.S. elements were already sitting, I heard bits and pieces of conversations, all sounding very intense and upset. The meeting was called to session by one of the villagers getting up to say a quick prayer in Arabic. As soon as he sat down, all hell broke loose. The villagers wanted to know if the Americans were their friends, or invaders of Afghanistan. Not waiting for an answer, they charged ahead with accusations that the Americans had shamed the whole village by going over the walls, inside the compound, in the middle of the night, knowing that there were women, Pashtun women, asleep. Why didn't they just kill the whole tribe? Everyone knew that there was no reason for any of the villagers to live after this kind of shame. I looked to see if the interpreters were doing their job well for the Americans, and what their reaction was. The American faces around me were expressionless, while the Afghan faces were incensed, indignant, full of rage. I tried to make my face blank, too, because in a gathering like this, you do *not* want to stand out in any way. Any emotions on my face would make me the center of attention and thus the target of all those impossible-to-answer questions.

I had heard complaints about night raids all over the provinces but had never been in a room full of villagers who had just been raided. It was a horrendous experience, as I could see the damage that had been done to our relationship with this village as well as the surrounding ones. I didn't know whether it had been worth it. Of course, I knew this was not the place to ask the ones who had authorized the raid, and decided that later I would ask the team who had conducted it. I felt enraged, not just about the cultural offense but also because I realized that Mike's new soldiers, the ones who I was mentoring in building relationships with the community, had just been set back by several years in their efforts. To the villagers, it made no difference which soldiers were looking for bad guys and which ones were building schools. To this village especially, all U.S. soldiers were the same—the ones who had raided their village and insulted the whole tribe.

THE MEETING ENDED when the governor, together with the PRT commander and other parties present, decided to meet again when tempers had cooled down, so they could have a more productive discussion.

As I walked toward the door to follow my group, one of the elders came running toward me, eyes flashing red, screaming, "You took my brother! You came into my house last night and took my brother. Release him now! He is innocent. We have tribal enemies and they gave you the wrong information!"

The elder, not knowing I spoke Pashtu, started looking for a *turjuman,* while trying to block my exit from the room. The two soldiers guarding me started to come between us to push me away from the old man. I told them it was okay, and told the old man calmly, "No, Baba, you are mistaken. I did not come into your house and take your brother, but if your brother is innocent, he will be released."

He looked at me, teary, and said, "*Looray,* you can speak Pashtu; you must know how Pashtun don't like their women to be seen by anyone. How could you come into my house and bring all these men with you?"

I knew what I had been doing the night before, and it was not raiding this man's compound, but there was nothing I could say to convince him that I personally had no part in it. I was held responsible for the Americans' actions, and to this old man, I had been there the previous night, insulting him and his culture. Suddenly, I felt a different kind of responsibility, one that I had been too distracted to see until then. I had been more concerned with arming the soldiers with the cultural knowledge to make their deployment a success, without considering that when they did anything wrong, I could and would be held personally accountable by the Afghans for the actions of all U.S. soldiers.

I WENT BACK into Mike's office in an even more reflective, gloomy mood than I had been in earlier. It was after 9:00 P.M., but you couldn't tell that by looking at all the officers and soldiers still working in their offices. I knew I was going to have a long night finishing my brief, and I needed to talk to Mamai and Najiba again. Sometimes it was therapeutic to hear about their daily lives, their routine American existence, one that I suddenly ached for.

Mike had already gotten an update from his PRT commander, so he knew what had actually happened. He wanted to know what could be done for damage control. He also informed me that Karzai had decided to take a political stance about what had happened, and there were rumors that he would be coming into Khost to meet with the villagers. On the American-leadership side, there was going to be an investigation and recommendations were going to be made to prevent this from happening again. He wanted me to meet with the three-star general who would be coming through Salerno in a few days to conduct an army investigation.

This was Mike's third tour in Afghanistan, all of them in Pashtun areas. He knew the investigation was going to look into what had gone wrong, but he was not interested in that nearly as much as in how it was going to affect our future relations. He wanted recommended courses of action for his soldiers to succeed.

"Saima, no one knows this area, or Pashtuns, like you do. None of the people the general will talk to can give him the background to his investigation that I know you can. I want you to tell him three to five cultural guidelines that those soldiers can follow to show the villagers that we are listening to them, and trying to do things the right way."

I didn't need any persuasion. I was emotionally drained from my encounter with the old man, and felt this chance to try to make things right for both the Afghans and the Americans was a godsend. The burden of my desire to bridge my two cultures, a burden that I had been carrying for years, suddenly felt twice as heavy. I would have done anything to make it lighter or at least more manageable. It was not part of my job description, but again, there was no question in my mind that I would meet with the general.

Over the next week, I met with the general several times, sometimes while grabbing a bite at the chow hall, where we couldn't talk about *why* he was there but could talk about cultures. I wanted to provide him with a cultural background to his investigation so that he could see that the soldiers had done everything right according to their tactical guidelines but had done things completely wrong inside of the bubble of Afghan culture. If he only looked at it as an army mission in isolation, it might be perfectly executed, but if he looked at the raid happening in real time, in a real Afghan village, it was done very wrong. These unofficial "talks" were followed with official meetings at our office in the TOC, where I gave him three recommendations for any future raids. He didn't give me any indications of whether or not he would take my advice or throw the paper he was writing on into the recycling bin to be destroyed with all the other secret documents that were burned by one of the S-2 soldiers when the bin was filled.

The general left and I continued preparing for my brief and the next mission. The highs and the lows of being at war had made me constantly aware of my emotional fragility, as well as that of the soldiers around me.

With that awareness the burden to do my part in the mission became more challenging and consumed even more of my time. It was common knowledge that HTT had office hours to match those of the TOC office hours, meaning we were there until midnight or later. But not everyone was at the office every night. For personal protection, when either Audrey or I was there alone, we would lock the doors and only open them to people we knew or were expecting. On one of those nights, I was alone in the office putting some finishing touches on a product that was being released the next morning. I had *Seinfeld* playing on low volume on one of my computers while I worked on the other one. Watching it instantly took me back to my living room in Oregon, sitting there with Najiba, laughing and drinking tea—those thoughts alone were an incredible stress releaser, something I needed lately more than ever.

I was sitting there typing when suddenly a rock hit the side of the wood structure of the office. I must have jumped up three feet. My heart pumped like I had just run a marathon, and my face felt cold and numb. The first rock was followed by another, and then another, coming in quick succession, not giving me time to move, even if I could have. This went on for a few minutes, but it felt like hours. There was no shortage of rocks—they covered the ground of the whole base. At first I thought it could have been one of the soldiers playing a prank, and I was ready for the knock on the door. The knock never came, and after three or four minutes, there was dead quiet.

The side that the rocks were being hurled from faced the olive orchard (rumored, of course, to be haunted), which was one of the main ways to get to the local interpreters' living section. Was it the ghosts of the past trying to scare me, or was it one of the local interpreters, carrying out an order from outside elders in retaliation for taking the villagers during the raid? For the first time, I didn't feel secure even inside the wire.

I never found out who threw the rocks, if it was one person or ten. That night, I called the guards on duty in the TOC to see if any of them were available to walk me to my room. It was dark and I was shaken to my core. I knew in my gut—and I have always relied on and trusted my gut—that this was like a public stoning for a crime that could have resulted in my death had I been caught outside the protection of the Americans. When I told Audrey what had happened, she made me promise not to stay too late at the office and to make sure that I had my weapon with me at all times. After that, I never went anywhere without my nine-millimeter, not even to the bathroom. I had to prepare myself for the very real possibility that I could be shot and killed by someone I might even know on the base. *Would I be able to shoot another human being to death to protect my own life?* This suddenly became a real question, flooding me with an anxiety and a terror I knew I would feel the effects of for years to come.

LIFE IN SALERNO went on. Half of the team were on missions at any given time. The other half stayed behind finishing up products and briefs, attending brigade meetings and working groups. We took turns going to each, bringing back the highlights to share with the rest of the team. I usually went to the morning battle update brief because it was early, and I could never sleep in no matter how late I went to bed. I would grab my coffee from the office and run to the BUB, where if you were late there was standing room only.

One day, almost a month after the general investigating the night raid had come through Salerno, I went to the BUB early enough to get a seat and was halfway done with my coffee by the time the commander and the command sergeant major walked in with theirs. Everyone stood up, then sat back down once the commander was seated. The BUB began and I was taking short notes to be shared with the rest of the team when a slide came up on the projector that was usually an update from one of the other U.S. elements in the area. The slide presented the commander with information on the missions of the previous day. Once done with that slide, the staff sergeant briefing the commander said, "Sir, we have an update about the investigation as well, followed by a division-wide FRAGO."

I sat up straight. He went into the findings of the investigation, which was classified information, only to be shared on a need-to-know basis. The division-wide FRAGO, an order for all the soldiers in the region, without exceptions, listed my three recommendations to the general. When I had talked to the three-star general, he had asked for recommendations, but FRAGOs were not recommendations. They were orders, not to be questioned but to be followed, word for word.

Seeing my cultural guidelines up on that slide, I was overwhelmed by a feeling of total serenity. Lately, I had been missing my American life a lot. I had been feeling restless, and the effects of my being harassed and symbolically stoned had worn my nerves thin. And, although I felt validated when talking to military personnel about the human terrain of their areas of operations, as they hung on my every word, I did not feel that I had achieved the peak of my professional life. I had stopped being nervous when I was giving advice to Mike or any other commanders in a room full of his officers and soldiers, because I knew I possessed the knowledge they needed to succeed.

But this was different. This was a testament to *who* I had become. I had taken the first significant step toward bridging the two cultures so dear to me, each in its own right. Oh, I knew that I was nowhere near completing my personal mission, but I saw a milestone, and it was up on the projector. My goal truly was a lifelong endeavor, but for the first time, it was not as overwhelming as it had seemed before.

I had come back to my father's country as an interpreter, one who only spoke for others, much like a puppet. Five years later, I was speaking for myself, for my people, to my people, and my words were being turned into orders to be followed long after I was gone.

This was an achievement of personal aspiration for which I would have given up anything, even my life. I had thought that I kept coming back to Afghanistan to better understand the Afghan people, when all along the goal was even more personal. I now knew why my father had chosen death over life as my father, and I forgave him his choice because I finally understood.

ACKNOWLEDGMENTS

I remember when I first learned to speak enough English to tell bits and pieces of my life story to friends. They would say, "Saima, you need to write a book." It took me a long time to write it out for others, and I would not have done so if not for certain people. Their support is what gave me the courage I needed to complete this painful and at times almost unbearable task. Every moment of agony was worth it.

Pashtun men have a bad reputation in today's world, and it saddens me because I know I would be in a completely different place if it weren't for the two most important men in my life, my father and my grandfather, both very proud Pashtun men who possessed pride and courage only found in folklore today. I want to pay homage to them both. It was my father's ultimate sacrifice and my grandfather's unfailing perserverance to keep his promise to a lost son that kept me going when giving up would have been so much easier. I will never forget.

My sister and I differ in so many ways from each other, and although I know she didn't, and doesn't, agree with everything I have done over the years, I know that she always has my back. Knowing she stands with me and behind me is the reason I am able to be who I am. Najiba, you know you are the best little sister I could ever have asked for, and you know that without you I would never have done any of the things worth writing a book about.

I want to thank Mamai, but more than thanking her, I want to apologize for all the suffering I have caused her over the years. I know we started off at opposite ends, but things have worked out as I had envisioned. Today you are exactly the mother I have always wanted, and I hope I am, if not exactly, then at least a tiny bit the daughter you hoped I would be.

I am grateful for my brother, Khalid, for being the best brother in Afghanistan, for not beating me up when all of his friends were beating up their sisters. You might even be the best brother in the whole world for not repressing me, for letting me be who I am, and for standing up for me when I needed you to do so. I am most thankful to you for those times when you didn't necessarily agree with what I was doing but still stood up for me. You not only share our father's love of argyle sweaters but you are also the breathing reminder of him in our small family.

Kabir, you came into my life and took my sister from me. That fact should have been enough to make me dislike you, but you have been the kind of caring and forgiving brother-in-law that makes it impossible to stay mad at you. During the process of writing this book, at times I know I was unbearable. Not being related, I know you could choose to avoid me. You took all of it head-on, and I am thankful to you for being there for me and my family.

I want to say a prayer and acknowledge the ultimate sacrifice that our men and women of the Armed Forces made in the war in Afghanistan. Nothing I say here could accurately convey the debt and gratitude I feel for your sacrifice. May your souls rest in peace and may God give your families the courage to see and remember your heroism in their time of pain.

I want to thank all my friends (and you better know who you are!) for putting up with my PTSD, temper, and just plain difficult personality. I know I have not been the easiest friend to have and I am thankful to each one of you for your support. I hope you realize that you've made me mellower, or maybe you've just gotten better at dealing with my temperament. Either way, I am deeply grateful for our friendship. You have become my extended family that the Afghan in me needs.

Thanks to Karen Karbo for helping me put pen to paper.

And, last but not least, I want to thank my editor, Domenica Alioto. I know I came to you with a mess, and you turned it into a story that I am proud to tell. I could not have done it without your patience and guidance.